Hans G. Nutzinger
Jürgen Backhaus (Eds.)

Codetermination

A Discussion of Different Approaches

Springer-Verlag
Berlin Heidelberg New York
London Paris Tokyo

Prof. Dr. Hans G. Nutzinger
Department of Economics
University of Kassel
Nora-Platiel-Str. 4
D-3500 Kassel, FRG

Prof. Dr. Jürgen Backhaus
Faculty of Economics and
Business Administration
University of Limburg at Maastricht
P.O. Box 616
NL-6200 MD Maastricht, The Netherlands

ISBN 3-540-50648-9 Springer-Verlag Berlin Heidelberg New York
ISBN 0-387-50648-9 Springer-Verlag New York Berlin Heidelberg

Printing: Weihert-Druck GmbH, Darmstadt
Bookbinding: J. Schäffer GmbH u. Co. KG., Grünstadt
2142/7130-543210

PREFACE

When we decided, five years ago, to publish a volume of contributions on the German system of codetermination, we felt a need for a presentation of this complex subject from both the European and the American perspective. Hence we planned this publication as a joint U.S. and European undertaking with one of the editors, Jürgen Backhaus, working at Auburn University (Alabama), and the other editor, Hans G. Nutzinger, teaching at the University of Kassel, West Germany. Most of the technical editorial work was done at the Auburn University Publiction Center, and we wish to thank particularly Mrs. Bess Yellen for her continuing assistance. As one of the editors, Jürgen Backhaus, moved from the United States to the Rijksuniversiteit Limburg at Maastricht (The Netherlands), the final editorial work had to be completed at the University of Kassel. Here we would like to thank especially Mr. Andreas Beschorner for his invaluable text processing work. Also, we would like to thank the following persons from the University of Kassel: Dr. Kornelius Kraft for his valuable assistance in text processing, Mr. Dirk Reh for preparing the index, and Mrs. Kalden for her typing and organizational activities. Naturally, we are indebted to the authors for preparing and revising their contributions to this volume. Last but not least, we wish to thank the Springer Verlag, particularly Dr. Werner A. Müller and Mrs. Bopp, for their assistance and patience during the rather extended production process.

Kassel and Maastricht, September 1988

Hans G. Nutzinger   Jürgen Backhaus

CONTENTS

EDITORS' INTRODUCTION

I

Ours is a time of change in firm structures: the traditional, or "classical", firm as it is modeled in the received economic theory of the firm can scarcely be identified in contemporary industrial reality. What we see instead are numerous attempts at designing organizational forms to accommodate a more complex production process. We can identify factors that necessitate this change, notably the increasing interdependence of world markets, the rapid introduction of products and processes and new, and often broader, skill profiles of the workforce. While we know that changes are on the way, we cannot fathom the precise shape organizational structures will take; in addition, the process of organizational development is quite different in the United States than in Continental Europe. Several Central European countries, in keeping with their legal and political cultures, have experimented with new corporate forms introduced by their legislatures. The process of organizational change in the United States, although dynamic, reveals less clear a pattern and seems generally to be lagging behind. There lies an important advantage for U.S. industries, in so far as lessons can be drawn from the experience abroad.

The process of organizational change is varied and complex. In this workbook we can concentrate on but one important aspect - the role of labor within the emerging corporation. In this respect, five characteristics are especially important. As Eirik G. Furubotn states in his contribution to this volume, the changes that the capitalist firm is currently undergoing will:

1. permit active involvement of labor at all levels of the firm's decision-making process;
2. offer workers substantial job security;
3. protect the firm-specific investments of workers against excessive loss;
4. guarantee workers at least market rates of return on their firm-specific investments; and
5. allow labor a major role in shaping the firm's work rules and production environment.

Codetermination
ed. by H.G. Nutzinger and J. Backhaus
© Springer-Verlag Berlin Heidelberg 1989

The policies of a firm with these characteristics can be said to be jointly determined by labor and capital representatives; hence, we are talking about codetermination.

These changes pose an enormous challenge to practitioners and policy makers alike. But the difficulties of modeling the new codetermined firms are also formidable. In building on earlier work[1] we present herewith a collection of papers. Our purpose is to furnish building blocks for a better economic analysis of complex firm structures. In compiling this volume, we had no intention of presenting a unified theory of the codetermined firm. While such a project would certainly be feasible, it is our conviction that with the knowledge we now possess of what is to be modeled, a clean, uncontroversial theory of the codetermined firm would be premature and invite more problems than it would solve. Such models, once they are accepted by the profession, have a tendency to assume a life of their own, quite independent from industrial reality. Our fellow economists might be led to believe that those models are accurate representations of reality. But what can be said of such efforts? We cannot agree on the best analytical model, the best modeling strategy, or even the features of codetermination to be modeled. Nor is there much empirical knowledge about how codetermination is working in industry. We are presenting this book because we want to advance on all these counts. By emphasizing problems instead of ready- made solutions, we are more likely to invite that advancement. And that is why the present effort is designed as a *workbook*, a point of departure for new research and teaching and a reference for earlier studies. If the editors prevail, this volume should become obsolete once our knowledge of codetermination assumes a more solid shape.

Because we are presenting a workbook and our aim is to stimulate further research, we attempt to explicate differing opinions and research strategies. A glance at the table of contents reveals our purpose. Every paper but the concluding one is followed by a critical discussion that often assumes the proportions of a dissenting opinion. Dissent was anticipated, since we chose discussants who do not always share the methodological persuasions of the author. But even where like methodology prevails, radically different approaches may be worth-while. This is obvious when comparing the papers by Furubotn and Roger A. McCain. Here the intention was to provide basic reference models, but the modeling strategies could not vary more. Thomas Eger and Peter

Weise, quite differently, struggle to fit codetermination and participation within a general equilibrium framework. Whereas these papers emphasize the performance of the codetermined firm, the paper by Jürgen Backhaus focuses on the economics of internal organization. Alfred L. Thimm's assignment   - in line with his previous research[2] - was to introduce the political dimension into the discussion, and Klaus Bartölke and Ekkehard Kappler discuss research strategies from a management research point of view. Considerable confusion remains (and tends to be added) on strictly institutional, historical and empirical issues, which Hans G. Nutzinger hopes to clarify; Kornelius Kraft reviews the state of econometric research on codetermination and maps out a feasible research strategy.

II

A powerful approach to understanding what goes on in a code-termined firm is the economic theory of property rights. But the early property rights views of the codetermined firm universally suffered not only from major misspecifications of what was to be modeled, but also from the overriding notion that codetermination was an instrument of redistribution. Although a viable assessment in some instances, it has been overstated at the expense of allocational issues that lie at the heart of corporate reform. What is more important is the need to accumulate a substantial amount of firm-specific human capital and to develop institutional forms in which this accumulation can take place in the common interest of labor and capital.

The model offered by Furubotn is a break through in terms of incorporating firm-specific human capital accumulation into a joint investment model. Because he is wary of mandating codetermination by legislative octroi, Furubotn introduces a distinction between the joint investment model and a scenario of mandated codetermination. Hans G. Monissen and Ekkehard Wenger's comment on Furubotn's paper reminds us that research on codetermination does not take place in a Coasian world of zero transaction costs. Instead of working out a specific critique of Furubotn's modeling strategy in terms of the institutional development of German codetermination, they chose to dwell on the political *justification* of codetermination and institution and the *legitimacy* of endowing workers with specific rights in exchange for their investment in firm-specific human capital. This reaction to the intellectual challenge posed by Furubotn is by no means atypical of research on codetermination over the last thirty years: instead of taking Coase's seminal paper as an invitation[3] to concentrate on the institutions which imply the transaction costs to contracting and exchanging - costs which, after all, determine the allocational efficiency of economic processes - many researchers find it more fruitful to reflect upon distributional questions in the context of abstract models. More specifically, with respect to German practices, one should keep in mind that, contrary to an impression created in the first paragraph of Monissen and Wenger's paper and also earlier[4], codetermination does not offer labor anything akin to management rights in the firm. Rather, there are certain prerogatives for worker representatives in the supervision of management and (through a completely different line of institutional structures) consultation rights of works councils with management on clearly defined issues.

Roger A. McCain looks at another problem in modeling - participatory firms and systems. He distinguishes between two kinds of workers' influence on enterprise decisions and behavior - codetermination and collective bargaining - whereby the latter is characterized by the existence of certain management prerogatives. Investigating the implications of repeated games he argues that codetermination is efficient in certain ways, but that collective bargaining is not. In his analysis, one deficit usually attributed to codetermination, namely, the foreshortening of the investor's horizon, is actually present under collective bargaining but absent under codetermination; the former is considered a noncooperative game, the latter, a cooperative game. If his modeling of codetermination is applied to the existing institutional arrangement in Germany, at least two problems arise:

(1) Whereas the idea of cooperation is inherent in much of the theory and practice of codetermination, another line of thought and practice, based on the idea of conflict, has been lucidly illustrated by *Muszynski* (1975). By treating codetermination as a cooperative game, McCain looks at only one side of the coin.

(2) McCain overemphasizes the horse trading or, logrolling element, inherent in the system of codetermination. He assumes that investment and wage payouts are decided simultaneously, so that management interests in financial de-

cisions can be traded off against labor interests in wages, and conversely. In practice, the German system of codetermination does not apply to wage negotiations, which are usually left to the traditional collective bargaining system, and the employees' influence on financial and investment decisions is exercised indirectly through their representatives' limited veto power on the Supervisory Board.

So, from an empirical viewpoint, is McCain's modeling an adequate theoretical simplification of the codetermination system? Of course, we could argue that a cooperative game as perceived by McCain should be involved under a reasonable notion of codetermination, but this would leave us without any better understanding of the practice of codetermination. A stronger argument in defence of McCain's perception is that sometimes we find identities between the actors involved in collective bargaining and in codetermination, and logrolling may prevail. But even so, we should not overlook the institutional and legal separation between these two systems that strictly limit the trade-offs McCain has in mind.

McCain's interpretation of codetermination as cooperative repeated games can still be helpful in understanding the dynamics of industrial relations. Ekkehart Schlicht raises more theoretical objections: he submits that McCain's argument in favor of codetermination unduly neglects possible inefficiencies on both the firm and the industry level. Under certain conditions, even traditional collective bargaining might prove superior despite its well-known shortcomings. He looks at transaction costs under alternative arrangements and argues that, in the absence of informational deficiencies and under rational behavior on both sides, the outcomes under codetermination and collective bargaining should be the same; in the absence of transaction costs, even "untrammeled capitalism" should produce the same outcome by giving both sides the opportunity to come to Pareto improving arrangements and contracts. In an imperfect world with transaction costs and informational deficiencies, it cannot be determined a priori whether collective bargaining or codetermination will lead to better results. Schlicht especially criticizes McCain's assumption of the absence of strikes and lockouts under codetermination. The rather low frequency of those forms of industrial conflict in countries such as West Germany and Austria (where collective bargaining and codetermination work side by side) is perhaps not a sufficient justification for assuming that strikes will not occur under codetermination. Another theory problem - which is heavily debated in West German industrial relations - is the extent of shifting the burden from the people employed, who are protected by codetermination, to the unemployed, who have to bear the costs of codetermination in terms of diminished access to job opportunities. In conclusion, we need further information about the specific transaction costs and informational deficiencies in each institutional setting. The issue (which set of assumptions describes the institution of codetermination best) cannot be decided by pure theoretical reasoning; theory must be complemented by empirical research. The essay by Eger and Weise is part of some recent attempts to show in a general equilibrium framework that the predominant form of capitalist work organization is not necessarily efficient, given informational deficiencies and transaction costs. They start with an Arrow-Debreu economy with efficient competitive equilibrium which, however, presupposes the absence of costly information and contracting. Participation, and specifically codetermination, are then seen as a potentially Pareto improving way of coping with real world problems caused by different kinds of transaction costs; the most important problem in this context is workers' relative immobility due to their investment in specific human capital. In his brief comment, Felix R. FitzRoy emphasizes that the central problem involved is the relative (im)mobility of different kinds of factors or factor owners. The exit option underlying the general equilibrium approach is seriously limited because workers' skills are not easily transferable to alternative employment. Although FitzRoy accepts the plausibility of Eger and Weise's theoretical arguments for giving workers extra "rights," such as codetermination, he hints at problems that occur when unions are disassociated from enterprise decision-taking and given a political say instead. That kind of union participation could easily degenerate into more or less redistributive schemes instead of internalizing externalities of entrepreneurial decisions imposed on workers.

As we mentioned earlier, the prevailing view among American economists is that codetermination is a politically motivated restructuring of the corporation that is likely to lead to serious inefficiencies. Despite earnest attempts, nobody has ever been able to find empirical support for this view. Nevertheless, the view prevails, because there is no plausible explanation why codetermination might be an efficient repartitioning of property

rights in the   firm. The paper by Jürgen Backhaus attempts to
tell just such a story. What are the major organizational failures in the large business corporation   which codetermination
helps to overcome? Whether the story is plausible enough has to
be decided by the reader. The comment on the paper shows clearly
that there is room for improvement.

Thimm emphasizes the political dimension of codetermination
by focusing on the steel industry, which (along with the mining
industries) is subject to specific legislation. This sector today
comprises less than thirty corporations which, in turn, employ
less than 3 percent of the West German workforce. Given the difficulties of an overall evaluation of codetermination in the
steel industry, Thimm offers a case study of ARBED-Saarstahl in
which he emphasizes how management and union representatives coa-
lesce in persuading government to support a declining corporation. Thimm's casestudy is impressive, but ARBED-Saarstahl is
hardly typical.Hence Thimm's paper cannot be considered an evaluation of the economic implications of codetermination in general;
rather,the beauty of his approach lies in hinting at the danger
inherent in unions, managers, and politicians using Federal German and European Community law to their own advantage. In this
interplay many factors apart from codetermination are involved.

Accordingly, in his comment Kurt W. Rothschild stresses the
serious limitations of the case study approach, especially in a
declining industry. Rothschild argues for a broader conception of
codetermination: from labor's viewpoint,codetermination is to be
measured not only in terms of efficiency gains but also in terms
of less hierarchic and more humane labor relations. When these
two goals conflict, a normative value judgement is unavoidable,
and that is why codetermination remains such a hotly debated issue.

One of the difficulties in modeling codetermined firms is the
continuous change in the structures to be modeled. The editors
therefore felt it would be important to have a paper which con-
veys the spirit of codetermination and thus gives an indication
of further development. This is nicely done in the paper by
Bartölke and Kappler, who not only outline the development of
codetermination, but also emphasize "alternatives" that should
not be overlooked. Incidentally, the authors also reflect on the
interdependence of scholarly research into codetermination and
the development of codetermination structures. Here, their position is at variance with the optimism shared by the editors and

expressed in the final paper presented. Warren J. Samuels expands on this subject. Among other things, he argues that Bartölke and Kappler fail to recognize two important contributions social scientists make, namely, that they *enlighten* the normative process and *criticize* the status quo.

The final contributions to this volume try to give an overview of both the institutional regulations and the empirical evaluations of codetermination in West Germany. Nutzinger, in a survey of empirical research into German codetermination, describes the most important legal provisions in the field and discusses some basic methodological problems in evaluating the economic consequences of this form of workers' participation - an issue raised in Rothschild's comment. The lack of solid empirical knowledge, however, is attributable not only to these difficulties but also to the lack of reliable empirical research. Apparently, most economists refrain from studying this rather difficult field, leaving the area to other social scientists. Derek C. Jones draws interesting analogies and contrasts between the German system of codetermination and the quite distinct tradition of cooperatives in Britain, Italy, and France. Whereas empirical research in the field of cooperatives is more advanced than in the codetermination area - due in large part to this discussant's efforts - it is not easy to use this experience to improve the methodology for researching codetermination. In the concluding paper on empirical studies in codetermination, Kraft not only surveys selected studies, emphasizing the few econometric attempts in this field, but also outlines an interesting research design for further empirical studies. That design has not been used so far - primarily because of lack of data and financial support. But Kraft's proposal promises that in the not too distant future we will be able to provide more reliable answers to the question. How does codetermination affect efficiency and relative factor prices?

We herewith call upon our fellow economists to join in this research effort.

Jürgen Backhaus   Hans G. Nutzinger

Footnotes:

[1] See Backhaus,Eger, and Nutzinger (1978); Backhaus and Nutzinger
(1982).
[2] See Thimm (1981) as reviewed in Kyklos 4,1982, p. 769f.
[3] Coase (1960).
[4] Monissen (1978).

References:

Backhaus, J., Eger, Th., and Nutzinger, H,G (eds.), *Partizipation in Betrieb und Gesellschaft*. Fünfzehn theoretische und empirische Studien (Participation in the Firm and in Society. Fifteen theoretical and empirical studies). Frankfurt/M. - New York: Campus, 1978.

Backhaus, J. and Nutzinger, H. G (eds.), *Eigentumsrechte und Partizipation*. Property Rights and Participation. Frankfurt/M.: Haag + Herchen, 1982.

Coase, R. "The Problem of Social Costs." *Journal of Law and Economics*, vol. 1 (1960), 1-19.

Monissen, H.G. "The Current Status of Labor Participation in the Management of Business Firms in Germany ". In S. Pejovich (ed.), *The Codetermination Movement in the West. Labor Participation in the Management of Business Firms*. Lexington, Mass.- Toronto:D.C. Heath, 1978, 57-84.

Muszynski, B., *Wirtschaftliche Mitbestimmung zwischen Konflikt- und Harmoniekonzeptionen*. (Economic Codetermination between Notions of Conflict and Harmony). Meisenheim am Glan : Hain, 1975.

Thimm, A. L. The, *False Promise of Codetermination*. Lexington, Mass. - Toronto:D.C Heath, 1981.

PARTICIPATION AND CODETERMINATION
IN A PERFECT AND AN IMPERFECT WORLD
by
T. Eger and P. Weise

1. Introduction

Both empirical and theoretical discussion on participation and
codetermination are marked by a noteworthy vagueness regarding
the concepts and terms used. The terms 'participation' and
'codetermination' are being used, on the one hand, as synonyms
for more humanity and democracy, thus marking general norms and
objectives, and, on the other hand, to put a name to certain legal rules, characterizing herewith a specific organizational
structure of economy. Numerous, colourful aspects and arguments
are involved, but they lack transparency and comparability.

This uneasy situation may be improved by analysing the following two points of view more closely:

a) One might define participation and codetermination so that
   participation refers to the valuation of states and processes
   of economy in terms of humanity and democracy, and codetermination covers the organizational devices implied.
b) One might specify the assumptions the various arguments are
   based on and vary them in such a way that, in one case, participation is achieved without any devices of codetermination
   whatsoever, and, in the other case, participation is only
   attainable provided certain forms of codetermination are in
   existence.

This procedure offers the great advantage that direct recourse
can be made to an already elaborated theory, namely the general
equilibrium theory, and one can subsequently profit from its theoretical conclusions once the underlying assumptions are subject
to change. Moreover, this kind of procedure comprises a further
advantage by permitting that any differences in evaluation of
codetermination become attributable to different model assumptions thus enlarging the transparency of argumentation.

In the first part of this paper, we try to point out that in
the perfect world of general equilibrium theory, no problems concerning participation and codetermination exist. Thus, besides

the market and price mechanism no additional devices of codetermination need to be taken into account when considering individual and collective interests. In the framework of this perfect world, any discussion on participation and codetermination becomes unnecessary. Particularly, it would be wrong to say that, in general, market and price mechanism were neither social nor democratic. Is it therefore correct to say that neither participation nor codetermination cause problems concerning theoretical reasoning and political action?

In the second part of this paper we try to find an answer to this question by qualifying the assumptions of general equilibrium theory, defining the perfect world, in confronting these assumptions with hypotheses on the real world. This comparison leads to the derivation of some necessary conditions for the existence of a participation and a codetermination problem. Then, it remains to be examined if, in this imperfect world, there are devices of codetermination that prove to be more effective than price and market mechanism; that is, does codetermination constitute a sufficient condition for the better functioning of an economic system?

2. Participation without Codetermination

1. First we would like, for our purposes, on a preliminary basis, to define the two terms participation and codetermination. For us, participation simply means the partaking in objectives as well as in results of economic activities; codetermination then means a non-market organizational device enabling individuals to influence objectives and results of economic activities. Whereas the term participation refers to a valuation of states or processes, the term codetermination stands for an organizational device covering activities such as election, negotiation, or other non-market mechanisms.

2. In order to show what kinds of relationships exist between decisions and activities of individuals and the concepts of participation and codetermination, let us consider in the following a contract to be signed between a supplier of labour and a supplier of capital, given the assumptions of the "perfect world" of neoclassical equilibrium theory. The supplier of labour will only agree to the terms of the employment contract provided they are

at least as valuable to him as those of the next best alternative; the same applies to the supplier of capital.

Which alternative options does a supplier of labour have? He
may:

(a) look for employment by another supplier of capital
(b) raise capital to found his own enterprise
(c) act as an individual producer
(d) abandon productive work and consume step by step his initial
    holdings of resources.

ad a) The neoclassical model is characterized by competitive markets for all goods and services, which means for our example that
we not only assume a very fine and precisely structured system of
labour markets differing continuously in the qualifications of
suppliers of labour and in the characteristics of working conditions, but we also assume on every single labour market a large
number of potential and actual suppliers and buyers. Owing to the
competition for cheap labour among the capital holders and the
competition for favourable working conditions among the suppliers
of labour, a competitive wage rate will arise on every one of
those labour markets reflecting the value of marginal productivity of labour as well as the marginal rate of substitution between labour income and leisure. The wage differences that may
arise between the various labour markets stand for implicit competitive prices for labour quality and working conditions. Each
supplier of labour will only join the labour market that enables
him to get his optimal tradeoff between pecuniary and non-pecuniary income. He chooses between given, fully specified employment contracts. It also follows that each employment contract
specifies in detail for all possible states of the world at which
working conditions and wage rates what kind of activities a certain employee has to accomplish from the beginning of employment
to the date of retirement. The individual supplier of labour has
only once in his life to make a decision as to which of the offered employment contracts proves best for him. Accordingly, each
buyer of labour is only interested in joining the labour market
where the bundle of required work quality, working conditions,
and wage rate at a given state of technical knowledge meets his
profit interests to a maximum. A supplier or buyer of labour who
claims for himself terms of trade that are not congruent with the

existing competitive terms will only damage himself by not being able to find an appropriate partner. Under such conditions, the value of the next best option ("looking for another employer") is precisely equal to the value of the chosen option, that is, a costless change toward the next best option becomes possible.

ad b) Furthermore, the supplier of labour has the option to borrow capital himself. Then, he has to pay an interest rate that is equal to the value of marginal productivity of capital with optimal allocation of resources. Thus a producer of goods and services is completely indifferent between the options of financing his production by means of borrowed or owned capital. Owing to perfect futures markets and fully specified contingent contracts, the value of capital employed for a certain use is determined ex ante. For the individuals involved, there are no unforeseen occurrences. This, however, implies as well that a supplier of labour is indifferent toward the options of either being hired by a capital holder or hiring capital himself. Both options have the same value to him. Should he decide to change from one option, namely, looking for a job, to the second option, creating his own job, no costs will occur to him. Furthermore, a holder of capital is unable to compel a supplier of labour with a given set of qualifications to choose a more unfavourable bundle of pecuniary and nonpecuniary elements of income than that the supplier of labour would have chosen for himself.

ad c) If a firm produces under constant returns to scale, the size of the firm is undetermined. No disadvantages will arise to a supplier of labour if he works alone and becomes productive in a one-person enterprise. If there are diminishing returns to scale, a one-person enterprise proves to be the most productive organization. Technological profits would be internalized by the supplier of labour himself. A necessary condition for the working of a one-person enterprise is, however, the investment of a certain amount of capital. If the supplier of labour owns a sufficient amount of capital, alternative (c) will be as valuable to him as alternatives (a) and (b). If he has no funds, he will raise capital on the capital market (see point (b)). Thus, the transition to alternative (a), (b), or (c) causes no utility loss to the supplier of labour.

ad d) This option becomes viable only if the initial holdings of resources are so substantial that the marginal disutility of any working hour becomes larger than the marginal utility of the consumption of additional goods ("Scrooge McDuck-economy").

3. What follows for the terms participation and codetermination if we consider the relationship between interdependent individuals living in a world of scarce resources? In that world, participation of individuals in the outcomes of economic activities is ideal, if the opportunity set of each individual is exclusively determined by the individuals' initial holding of resources being evaluated in terms of equilibrium prices, so that only value equivalences can be exchanged. Concomitantly, participation of individuals in the objectives of economic activities is ideal if each individual satisfies maximally his own needs weighted by the equilibrium value of his initial holding of resources, subject to the restriction of the weighted needs of all other individuals. In the case of ideal participation, then, the societal weight of any individual is exclusively determined by the value of the individual initial endowment with resources for society calculated in a state of optimal allocation of resources.[1] Ideal participation in objectives and outcomes of economic activities comprises not only Pareto efficiency but also absence of power and exploitation in the sense that no single person or group of individuals may take personal advantage by influencing the terms of exchange of goods and services.[2]

General equilibrium theory has shown that, with certain assumptions, each equilibrium relative to a price system is Pareto-optimal and that any Pareto-optimal allocation is an equilibrium relative to a price system for some initial endowment.[3] Moreover, general equilibrium theory has shown that an equilibrium relative to a price system is characterized by the fact that no single individual is in a position to influence the terms of trade, and that a system of equilibrium prices is a means of removing social conflicts.[4] Therefore an equilibrium relative to a price system is characterized by ideal participation. If we conclude that the equilibrium relative to a price system stands for a market equilibrium with perfect competition, then it is proved that ideal participation without codetermination is possible.

Thus it follows that in the perfect world of neoclassical equilibrium theory, no participation problem is involved apart from the ethical problem of initial distribution of resources. No individual is in a position to decide on the desired behaviour of other individuals. Any individual consuming goods and services and thereby causing disutilities to other members of society compensates them by paying a price. The prices are simultaneously determined by the total of all individual decisions separately made. There are only contractual relations between individuals based on a general exit mechanism.[5]

If, in this "perfect" world, any codetermination rights were entitled to suppliers of labour, then the strict separation of individual decision making would be attenuated: inefficiencies and increasing costs of social organization would result. In this context, codetermination as an organizational device would prove harmful and would fail to achieve the intended objective, namely, (ideal) participation. An economist referring to neoclassical equilibrium theory or to some of its folkloristic variants must consider all claims for codetermination as well as for more democracy and humanity as inappropriate, incomprehensible, and above all untheoretical.[6]

3. Problems of Participation in an Imperfect World

1. Until now, we have concentrated on the implications of a pure exit mechanism, namely, the price and market mechanism, which, in a perfect world, leads society to a state of ideal participation. In this world, a pure voice mechanism leads likewise to ideal participation. One can assume, however, that in an imperfect world, both organizational mechanisms lead to different degrees of participation.[7] Let us turn to this supposition by analysing in a first step what kind of participation problems are expected to occur as a consequence of the working of the price and market mechanism.

By qualifying certain assumptions of the neoclassical model,[8] we form a new reference model that enables us to study aspects of efficiency and power as they occur in alternative forms of organization.[9] Our model of a more realistic imperfect world is based on three variations of the neoclassical assumptions:

1) If there are to a certain extent increasing returns to scale, then no individual will usually be in a position to have sufficient holdings of all resources that are necessary to produce a good in an efficient way. Joint production, then, is superior to individual production, that is, several individu-

als may gain if they pool resources in order to produce certain goods and jointly decide upon the use of resources.[10]

2) Since labour power cannot be separated from its owner, problems of information and control arise. Such problems can usually be better solved by local (or other forms of) concentration of labour power.

From 1) and 2) follows:

Concentration of resources and joint production increase productivity, but how can the participants of the joint production processes mutually ensure each other's compatible activities and agree on an imputation and distribution of the joint outcome? As a possible solution of this problem, fully specified and binding contingent contracts could be signed. In a realistic environment, however, this solution becomes unattainable because of a further variation of neoclassical assumptions:

3) Owing to the bounded rationality of man, that is, his limited capacity to receive, store, retrieve, process, and transmit information without error (Simon 1957, 1981; Williamson 1975), fully specified contingent contracts cannot be formulated in a complex world. Thence it follows that the system of futures markets is incomplete.

Under such circumstances, firms in the literal sense arise.[11] Several individuals pool their resources to organize a cooperation through contracts, negotiations, trust, and hierarchy. In an imperfect world not only the three traditional functions of enterprise - supply of goods for consumers, creation of jobs for suppliers of labour, accumulation of profits for capital owners (Drèze 1976) - but also the following three functions must be fullfilled (cf. FitzRoy and Mueller 1984, p. 17 ff):

- function of entrepreneurship, that is, initiating the pooling of resources and continuously readjusting the joint activities to a changing environment
- function of risk-bearing, that is, bearing the consequences of a devaluation of real and human capital in a world of uncertainty
- function of management, that is, internal coordination and control of the current production processes

In such a world, the following conflicts arise:

- conflict between supervisor and subordinate
- conflict between the needs of the worker in the course of the
  working process (" consumptive aspect of work "[12]) and the demands of all other individuals toward the results of the working process
- conflict between maintaining value of real capital and value
  of human capital
- conflict between capital and labour

The resolution of these conflicts depends on how the various
functions are assigned to the cooperating actors, and may take
place in a more or less participatory fashion (i.e. with a relatively low or high degree of inefficiency or exertion of power).

2. In the following we would like to show that the capitalist enterprise is characterized by a systematic restriction of participation of workers in the objectives and results of economic activities: by resolving the above mentioned conflicts to the disadvantage of the subordinates, to the disadvantage of the employees' needs in the course of working process, to the disadvantage
of maintaining the value of human capital, and in general terms
to the disadvantage of labour.[13] First of all, we shall study the
situation of a supplier of labour who has to decide whether to
agree to or reject an employment contract. His consent depends on
how valuable he considers the best of his alternative options. As
in the above mentioned neoclassical case, he has likewise to
choose between four options:

(a) looking for another employer
(b) raising capital and founding his own firm
(c) acting as an individual producer
(d) rejecting productive work completely and consuming his
    initial endowment of resources.

In contrast to the neoclassical case the opportunity set of
the supplier of labour in a more complex environment is characterized by various additional constraints in such a way that he
faces discrete opportunities instead of continuous ones, so that
a higher or lesser degree of utility loss is involved whenever he
changes toward another option. This difference in opportunity

costs is being used by capitalist firms to increase the output of material goods as well as profits and this to the disadvantage of working conditions.

ad a) Owing to the fact that, with bounded rationality of man, employment contracts cannot be fully specified and that labour power cannot be separated from its owner, neither the supplier nor the buyer of labour is in a position to describe and evaluate an employment relation precisely, and this from the first day of employment to the date of retirement. After signing a contract one party will not be entirely informed about the actions of the other, although such actions may strongly influence their own welfare level. Both parties may subsequently face unforeseen occurrences: the supplier of labour as to actual working conditions, the supplier of capital as to actual work quality.

As regards, first of all, the situation of a supplier of labour, there are several arguments that in an ongoing contractual relationship, the value difference between the existing employment contract and the next best alternative employment will increase for the employee as time goes on:

- As far as the employee is acquiring firm-specific qualifications in an ongoing employment relation and he is paid according to the value of his marginal productivity, the value difference between actual employment and the next best employment option will increase.[14]
- Since labour power cannot be separated from its owner, the employment relation also involves social contacts at work. Once an employee decides to leave the firm, he has to give up such contacts and invest in new ones. The difference in opportunity costs will increase all the more if the change in employment accompanies the change of residence.

As to unpleasing, unforeseen working conditions, a supplier of labour will show his acceptance up to the point that the marginal disutility of these conditions is smaller than the marginal disutility of leaving the firm and looking for other employment (or opting for other alternatives, which will be discussed later on). Because labour power cannot be separated from its owner, the supplier of labour is unable to spread his risk by simultaneously engaging parts of his labour power in different jobs.

In contrast, the position of a supplier of capital is usually more favorable.

- It is true that it might be quite costly for an employer to fire an employsee holding a high degree of firm-specific qualifications and to hire sa new employee in his place. However, in large firms an employee with firm-specific qualifications who does not perform may be replaced by regrouping personnel within the firm, thus involving moderate costs.
- The supplier of capital may sell his property share and look elsewhere for appropriate investment options. For corporations at least this insvolves no substantial costs.
- Since capital, in contrast to labour power, is not tied to the person of its owner, a supplier of capital may not only perform his social contacts independently of the location of his capital but also spread his risk by capital diversification.

ad b) Moreover, in a world of imperfectly defined property rights and imperfect futures markets, a supplier of work is faced by additional constraints concerning his opportunity of borrowing capital.[15] If in such an "imperfect" world future factor services have not been sold ex ante and lack insurance against all possible risks by means of contingent contracts, a supplier of capital has to consider a debtor's possible insolvency. The risk of insolvency decreases as the amount of distrainable assets owned by the debtor increases. If an individual owns human capital exclusively, he is therefore disadvantaged in comparison with an individual who owns real capital as well. Since the former the risk of insolvency is higher, he will be obliged to pay a higher interest rate for the higher risk involved, a rate that may be prohibitive. In contrast, the owner of real capital pays a lower interest rate for borrowed capital, gaining a monopoly rent on his proprietary capital. Therefore, a supplier of labour is unable to pass, without involving any costs, to option (b). Owners of proprietary capital have a margin of exploitation.

ad c) If there are increasing returns to scale, the change toward the option, acting as an individual producer, always involves a utility loss for the supplier of labour. This difference in opportunity costs is strengthened in case of insufficient proprietary funds and restricted access to the capital market (see b).

ad d) Here, the same argument as in the neoclassical environment holds. Because labour power is not separable from the owner, this option becomes viable, even for a short transition period, only for owners of real capital. Capability to wait is very different.[16]

It follows that, with the "imperfection" of the real as compared to a neoclassical world, individuals experience additional constraints on their opportunity sets. These constraints imply (a) a communication problem with subsequent inefficiencies and (b) a power problem.[17]

ad a) A communication problem arises insofar as market prices in a real world no longer are sufficient statistics, that is, for the various individuals concerned, market prices no longer contain all the relevant information on marginal rates of substitution and marginal productivity. under such conditions, is all the idiosyncratic information dispersed between a multitude of individuals being transmitted in a complete and unbiased way to those actors who have to rely on it for efficient decision making?

ad b) A power problem arises insofar as not all members of an enterprise are equally mobile or informed. How can those who are relatively mobile and well-informed be prevented from exploiting those who lack mobility and information?

3. Problems of communication and power occur since members of a firm control so-called free variables, that is, variables not specified in the employment contract. Hence, direct interdependencies between the members of the firm arise. More precisely, the problem is how to coordinate the determination of working conditions by managers and the determination of effort by employees in an efficient and powerless way.

Therefore, when we analyse codetermination, two groups of variables are of special interest. Let us name the first group "effort" (or "work quality") relating to all dimensions of labour input, which can be controlled to a certain extent, by employees themselves, such as intensity of work, concentration during work, number and length of recreation breaks, accuracy in production of goods and services, economical use of materials and energy, and careful handling of machinery and tools. Employers may by means of controlling measures deprive the employees of control of these variables to a certain extent.[18] But for positive costs of control, a certain amount of discretionary decision by the employees remains. The determination of such variables influences not only the marginal utility of the employees ("consumption at work"), but also the productivity of the firm. In an initial range, the employees' utility may increase with better work quality. However, it may also be assumed that once work quality exceeds a certain level, the welfare of the employees is decreasing, whereas productivity of the enterprise will increase. From an economic point of view, this range is of special interest.

Let us denominate the second group of variables as "working conditions," which enclose all dimensions of labour input that, on the one hand, lack contractual specification and may, on the other hand, be influenced by the capital owners and their representatives, such as outfit and guarantee of working places, specific requirements of the work effected, flexible work times, extent of hierarchical controls, and supplementary professional training programmes within the firm. Improved working conditions will undoubtedly increase the welfare of the employees. It may be that certain improvements in working conditions likewise raise productivity of the firm. But it is also plausible to assume that, once the improvement of working conditions exceeds a certain level, productivity of the firm will decrease. This range is of special interest from an economic point of view. However, the possibility that a firm's management will raise productivity by allowing working conditions to deteriorate is limited by the possibility that employees will leave the firm.

4. Here, a firm is faced with a problem of strategic interaction.[19] Individually rational behaviour does not necessarily lead to a collectively rational outcome; a latent Prisoner's Dilemma is involved. If a firm's management is not au fait with the individual output of the employee, then compensation is paid according to the average productivity of all employees. Under such circumstances every employee has an inventive to behave as a free rider when determining his own efforts: if a single employee reduces his effort, he may individually profit from such actions (increased consumption at work), whereas resulting costs (loss in income) are borne by all employees.

One might be inclined to assume that a capitalist enterprise solves this Prisoner's Dilemma in the interest of the workers by assigning to capital owners the right to monitor the employee's behaviour at work and to claim the residual (Alchian and Demsetz

1972). When the Prisoner's Dilemma is solved in this way, two additional problems are involved:

1) Provided management is actually in a position of fully controlling employees at an acceptable cost level, they will be exploited by means of steadily increasing work quality combined with deteriorating working conditions, and this to an extent that the individual welfare level, being a function of work quality, working conditions, and income, equals the value of the next best option. The higher the difference in opportunity costs between working within a given firm or working elsewhere, the stronger the exploitation potential becomes.[20] In the era of early industrialization, the next best option meant not working, but starving to death. Effort increased (for instance, by prolonging the working day) and working conditions deteriorated to an extent that the mere reproduction of labour forces was just assured.[21]

Thus, the Alchian/Demsetz view of enterprise management as an external protection of employees against their mutual exploitation is only correct if one of the following prerequisites is fulfilled:

- either no "exit cost" are involved for the employees,
- or the employees may fire management if it does not act in their interests.

The first prerequisite is not fulfilled in the imperfect real world; the second is not fulfilled in a capitalist enterprise lacking codetermination.

2) If the employees control certain dimensions of "work quality" themselves because costs involved by stricter controls exceed yields expected, the capital owners or their mangement face the following problem: Determine the working conditions that maximize productivity and thus profit, taking into consideration two constraints:

- When determining effort, the employees will adapt to the given working conditions and thereby maximize their individual welfare levels.
- A labour supply constraint is given since utility from working

outside the firm in question may not exceed utility from working within the firm. Hereby it is to be considered that the
employees expect the management to determine their "free"
variables in such a way that profit is maximized.

Now it can be proved that, given the usual assumptions concerning production function and utility function of the employees, such a game - employees versus management - will lead to an
inefficient determination of work quality and working conditions
(McCain 1980).[22] That is, the marginal rate of substitution in
consumption between working conditions and work quality differs
from the corresponding marginal rate of substitution in production, and the sum of the individual marginal rates of substitution between working conditions (work quality) and income differs
from the marginal productivity of working conditions (work quality). Working conditions and work quality will be worse than under efficient allocation. This means that both parties could gain
if they exchanged good work quality for good working conditions.

It follows that in an imperfect world, codetermination as a
non-market organizational device must not only avoid the exertion
of power due to asymmetrical information and exit costs, but also
create an incentive for an efficient transmission of information
in order to avoid Prisoner's Dilemma games that arise from incomplete information on mutually beneficial exchange possibilities.

4. Participation by Codetermination

1. Is it possible to solve the above-mentioned participation
problems by means of codetermination without paying the price of
excessive organizational costs? This question is easily raised
but hard to answer. Since, for the time being, we would like to
concentrate on the theoretical foundations of participation and
codetermination, a full and detailed reflexion on this question
lies beyond the scope of this paper. Nonetheless, we wish to outline a reply. Up to now, we have referred to a type of enterprise marked by a largely unlimited, individual freedom of contract that characterizes the capitalist enterprises of the nineteenth century (and later). Unification of the labour force and
collective bargaining as well as governmental intervention initiated a process of organizational learning that resulted in various institutionalized rules, such as promotion ladders, protec-

tion against arbitrary dismissal, limitation of working hours and many other provisions. Accordingly, institutionalized norms were introduced, substituting to a certain extent the pure exit mechanism by means of explicit or implicit voice mechanisms.[23] Hereby power and information asymmetries have been reduced and some causes for inefficiency have been resolved.[24] Such regulations or institutionalized norms stand for nothing else but codetermination: a restructured and renewed definition of property rights preserving non-market forms of organization.

Of special interest is whether the furthermore developed and particularly controversial version of codetermination - namely, codetermination by the employees' representatives on the supervisory board of large coperations[25] - marks an advancement in the organizational learning process of society and subsequently leads to better mastering the power and information problems, or results in inefficiency and excessive organizational costs.

2. In order to justify, from a theoretical point of view, that legally prescribed codetermination entails power reduction, it has to be shown that exploitation of the relatively immobile work force by the relatively mobile capital owners and their representatives can be reduced by codetermination on the enterprise level. Thus the question is who is to obtain the right of decision upon the working conditions?

In the perfect world of neoclassical equilibrium theory there are no positions of power. It is impossible to decide upon the desired behaviour of other people by means of orders and instructions since the others may evade such decisions costlessly; that is, there is no positive price for the right of decision making. In the imperfect world, however, there are positions of power. An individual has the opportunity of controlling the behaviour of others within the range marked by the best and second best option; taking into consideration the anticipated behaviour of others, the individual will make an optimal decision and will, in the extreme, force the others to accept the value of the second best option. Those positions of power, that is, rights of decision making, have therefore a positive price that is determined by the utility gain rendered possible by means of that right.

In perfect markets, this right has a price of zero: it does not enable any individual to gain utility at the expense of others. In a world of imperfect markets, however, everybody has an incentive to acquire decision rights provided the price to be paid is lower than the value of this right. The owner of the right obtains a monopoly rent.

These considerations are important when evaluating the interactions of individuals within a given enterprise. Historically, owners of capital appropriated the right to determine working conditions to the detriment of masters (managers) and workers, owing to their comparatively powerful position. Accordingly, the capital owner acts as an option fixer of working conditions and "presse" the supplier of labour upon the value of his second-best option, hereby gaining rent on his real capital.

Such an enforcement of power could be avoided by legally providing that the relatively immobile employees have the right to determine working conditions. Such a case is to be found in Yugoslavia (Eger and Weise 1978). If capital were fully mobile, such a solution would end in the desired removal of power as well as in an efficient state of the economy. But capital is not fully mobile if, in an imperfect world, such decision rights are entitled to employees. With increasing returns to scale, the capital owner may choose between productive allocation of his capital in cooperation with other factor owners under the restriction of weakly defined rights to appropriate the value of marginal productivity of capital, and less productive allocation of his capital, namely, within the framework of a one-person enterprise, with strongly defined rights to appropriate the value of marginal productivity of capital. Such a choice not only comprises an exploitation of capital owners by employees, but also decreases formation of capital and future consumption; satisfaction of human needs is lower than it could be for a different entitlement of decision rights.

Legally prescribed codetermination merely implies that decisions on working conditions are subject to joint control by capital owners and employees together. On the one hand, capital owners face reduced opportunities of acting as option fixers of working conditions without reversing the inequality of power to the advantage of labour and to the burden of society; on the other hand, codetermination constrains management from injuring workers and capital owners by acquiring a rent due to monopolized information. By having access to a firm's relevant documents, by attending meetings of the supervisory board, and by participating in elections of the managing board, the capital owners and employees can inform themselves in due time and in an undistorted way about the firm's economic situation, the efficiency of various business units and departments, and planned innovations in organization and technology.

3. Let us now turn to the communication problem. To theoretically justify the legal establishment of codetermination, we must explain why the employees and capital owners, or their representatives, do not voluntarily enter into negotiations to provide an efficient exchange of work quality for working conditions. The theoretically "cleanest" solution, namely, conclusion of fully specified and binding employment contracts, remains out of reach, as explained in the preceding chapter. If an efficient exchange is to be effected, alternative organizational devices and incentive systems have to be created and flexibly adjusted toward a changing environment as a result of collective learning processes within the firm.

Such alternative organizational devices could, for instance, be characterized by setting up partly autonomous work groups or by altering the work priorities of middle and upper management insofar as they would no longer direct individual workers' activities but would concentrate on stabilizing the environments of the various departments and of the enterprise as a whole (Emery and Thorsrud 1982).

Such organizational reforms, however, require a state of mutual trust insofar as each party may expect that the other will act cooperatively and reveal correct information as long as cooperative behaviour is reciprocal.[26] In this context, "trust" also implies that everybody considers the risk as minimal that organizational or technical reforms might lead to a reduction in income or status. The purpose of legislated codetermination is precisely this stabilization of trust: trust between capital owners, workers, and management. Trust is established by clearly defining decision rights and by making information about the other parties available. Under these circumstances, they can be expected to successfully search for efficient solutions to the problem of an effective organization of the intra-firm process of production.[27]

It follows that the distribution of decision rights cannot be taken for granted nor can it be seen as a matter of historical fact remaining beyond economic analysis, but that the optimal entitlement of decision rights stands for an economic problem. By means of an appropriate specification or attenuation of decision rights, subsequent actions can be separated and outcomes of actions can be internalized, thus improving exchange of information as well as incentive structures.

4. Codetermination by the employees' representatives on the enterprise level may subsequently help to solve certain problems of participation that are occurring in an imperfect world. One should beware, however, of taking codetermination as an universal remedy for all participation problems.

First, our present argumentation has referred to large corporations in which, to a considerable extent, increasing returns to scale are involved; labour suppliers hold, to a large extent, firm-specific qualifications; and capital owners are only liable for possible enterprise losses by means of their capital contribution. They are furthermore in a position to easily sell at any time their property share on the stock market. Our preceding argumentation regarding codetermination on the enterprise level cannot be applied to small or medium-sized handicraft enterprises, where the "proprietor-entrepreneur" remains personally liable with the total of his property for any possible losses and who has to face considerable costs if he wants to separate from the firm's assets. Also, the employees working in such an enterprise face relatively small exit costs due to their general qualifications. A controlling of the entrepreneurial decisions by the employees according to the codeterminaiton model of large corporations would lead, under such circumstances, to inefficient decisions combined with an inequality of power to the burden of the proprietor-entrepreneur (von Nell-Breuning 1975, p. 10). Should the employees of such enterprises have to face positive exit costs, then their participation should be preserved by means of other forms of codetermination.

Second, representation of the employees within the supervisory board does not automatically lead to better working conditions or to more democracy within an enterprise (Emery and Thorsrud 1982, p. 176). By means of legally prescribed codetermination on the enterprise level in large corporations, however, an organizational device can be set up, making such improvements more probable.

Third, codetermination of the employees' representatives on the enterprise level lacks appropriate representation of the interests of the unemployed, of future generations, and of public concerns such as the integrity of nature. Whereas consumers are relatively mobile [28] the unemployed, future generations, and nature lack such capacity. In an imperfect world, participation of such interests cannot be ensured by either pure exit mechanism or any form of codetermination on the part of the employees. Here, supplementary mechanisms are required.

5. Institutionalized codetermination by the employees' representatives also involves organizational costs, that is, the codetermination mechanism itself leads to a certain consumption of resources (loss in working time, time and trouble spent during the consent finding process, etc.). In an imperfect world, conflicts between labour and capital implying costs of conflict resolution are inevitable. In the era of early capitalism that was marked by weakly defined rights of the employees, such conflicts had been decided to the disadvantage of the workers, owing to the exertion of power; later, because of pressure coming from organized workers, the rights of the employees had been strengthened in the course of conflicts between labour and capital being carried out in cost-intensive labour struggles (Nutzinger 1982, p. 63).

If the costs involved in codetermination are to be investigated, it would thus be deceptive to compare an economy employing codetermination with a conflict-free, optimally working, free-market economy: the advantages of codetermination would be undervalued and the disadvantages overrated. A relevant comparison should be developed on the basis of an imperfectly working market economy where the actual power problems and inefficiencies lead, occasionally, to conflicts and labour struggles. Therefore, it can be assumed that by means of institutionalized codetermination, the costs of overcoming such conflicts may be kept relatively low and that the costs are attributable to those actors who profit from the successful resolution of conflicts.

5. Final Remarks

In environments that come up to the perfect world of neoclassical equilibrium theory economic process should be organized by price and market mechanism. But in environments where alternative options are not fully parametrizable and where differences in opportunity costs prevail, voice mechanisms, rules, and norms as well as modes of partaking in possible profits and losses need to be set up; that is, a codetermination mechanism must be set up to

approach the ideal of a participatory society within the framework of an imperfect world.

Footnotes:

* We would like to thank Viktoria Kleinemeyer, Dorothea Lutticke, Manfred Kraft, and Maja Luksch-Eger for valuable comments on an earlier draft.

[1] Thus ideal participation does not comprise justice, but refers to a statusuo, which means that it is compatible with any given initial distribution of resources.

[2] This statement implies the assumptions of the so-called limit theorem on the core of an economy. See Debreu and Scarf (1963).

[3] See Arrow and Hahn (1971) for a global representation of general equilibrium theory.

[4] "... equilibrium prices appear not merely as a means for attaining economic efficiency in commodity utilization but also as devices for reducing social instability in the acceptance of commodity allocation" (Newman 1965; S. 122).

[5] For a discussion of the organizational mechanisms of "exit" and "voice," see Hirschman (1970).

[6] See, for instance, Pejovich (1978), Furubotn (1978; 1981), Prosi (1978), and Schüller (1983).

[7] See Eger and Weise (1984).

[8] For a similar procedure, see, for instance, Arrow (1974).

[9] Usually, economists analyse organizations in terms of efficiency; sociologists, of power. See the discussion in Francis, Turk, and Willman (1983).

[10] For a comparison of models of exchange and models of pooling of resources in sociology, see, for instance, Coleman (1973; 1974/75) and Vanberg 1982).

[11] "It can, I think, be assumed that the distinguishing mark of the firm is the supersession of the price mechanism" (Coase 1937).

[12] See Enke (1983).

[13] For the point of view of capitalist enterprise as a social institution that systematically restricts the disposition of employees' working time and work method, see, for instance, Marglin (1974) and Edwards (1979).

[14] This point is stressed by FitzRoy and Mueller (1984). See also the literature on segmentation of labour market, for instance, Biehler, Brandes, Buttler, Gerlach, and Liepmann (1981) and Brandes and Weise (1980).

[15] This point, for instance, is stressed by Vogt (1983).

[16] See for such considerations in connection with F. Oppenheimer, Preiser (1948), who stressed the urgency of being employed for the supplier of labour without property. By means of unemployment

insurances and social security systems, an employee may be favoured in his capability to wait.

[17] Elias correctly points out that the concept of "power" involves the "structural particularity of a relationship" (p. 97). "Power" mainly refers to the power differential, the relative weights of power, that is, "who needs whom more? Which functions for the other, whose dependence on the other is larger or smaller? Who is more or less independent from the other?" (p. 82).

[18] The development of capitalist enterprises served, among other points, to strengthen the control of these variables by the capital owners and their representatives.

[19] See Leibenstein (1982) as well as the discussion between De Alessi (1983a; 1983b) and Leibenstein (1983).

[20] Already in 1952 Stützel remarked in an ingenious essay that the "concrete interest for contractual stipulation" ("konkretes Vertragsinteresse") by the supplier of labour is comparatively high. See Stützel (1972).

[21] This is a basic assumption in the model of exploitation by Marx. See Marx (1890).

[22] Emery and Thorsrud describe a possible process leading to such inefficiency as a vicious circle: The smaller the extent of discretion allowed the individual employee by management, the larger is the probability that informal practices prevail and that informal channels of communication are established. This departure from the established rules of the organization will in turn lead to further atempts to narrow the discretionary leeway allowed by management, and further informal departures will follow suit. See Emery and Thorsrud (1982, p. 35-36).

[23] As to the relation of institutionalized norms and exchange activities, see, in particular, Stützel (1972) as well as Schotter (1981) and Axelrod (1984).

[24] As to a representation of this process of development, see Edwards (1979).

[25] This kind of codetermination is named "codetermination on the enterprise level," that is, the management directing an enterprise in the interest of all cooperating factor owners is formed upon mutual vote of all factor owners and is subsequently responsible to them. Codetermination on the enterprise level does not, however, comprise direct participation in the entrepreneurial decision-making process (von Nell-Breuning 1968; 1975). Under the German codetermination law of 1976, codetermination on the enterprise level has been legally institutionalized for joint stock companies and other large corporations holding 2,000 employees or more. The board of management of a codetermined joint stock company, elected by and accountable to a supervisory board, has the exclusive right of entrepreneurial decision making. The codetermined supervisory board, with a (quasi-) equal membership of capital and employees' representatives, elects the members of the board of management and examines the annual balance-sheet and the company report, as well as proposals for profit allocation. In other corporations there is a similar separation between management and control. Legally presented codetermination in Germany only refers to the supervisory board, not to management itself.

For further reform models of codetermined corporations, see von Nell-Breuning (1968); Ott (1977, 189 pp.

[26] As to the difficulty of creating trust, see, for instance, Emery and Thorsrud (1982) and Pöhler (1979).

[27] Improvements in information transfer and reduction of ineffi-ciencies through codetermination on the enterprise level are also assumed by McCain (1980) and Backhaus (1982).

[28] Hereby, an entrepreneur's incentive to make decisions that cause unpleasant consequences for consumers is strongly limited: their behaviour is controlled by exit mechanisms. Nevertheless codetermination already takes place, for instance, through pro-tective legislation on foodstuffs, etc.

References:

Alchian, A.,and Demsetz, H. (1972) "Information, Production Costs and Economic Organization", *American Economic Review* 62: 777-795.

Arrow, K. J.(1974), *The Limits of Organization*, New York: Norton.

Arrow, K., and Hahn, F.(1971), *General Competitive Analysis*, San Francisco: Holden Day.

Axelrod, R. (1984), *The Evolution of Cooperation*, New York: Basic Books.

Backhaus, J. (1982), "Information und Technologie in der mitbestimmten Unternehmung", in: *Eigentumsrechte und Partizipation*, eds. J. Backhaus and H. G. Nutzinger, Frankfurt a. M.: Haag und Herchen, 183-201

Biehler, H., Brandes, W., Buttler, F., Gerlach, K., and Liepmann, P. (1981), *Arbeitsmarktstrukturen und -prozesse. Zur Funktionsweise ausgewählter Arbeitsmärkte.* Tübingen: J.C.B. Mohr.

Brandes, W., and Weise, P.(1980), *Arbeitsmarkt und Arbeitslosigkeit.* Würzburg-Wien: Physica.

Coase, R.H. (1937), The Nature of the Firm. *Economica* 4:386-405.

Coleman, J.(1973), "Loss of Power", *American Sociological Review*, 38,1-15.
---, (1974/75), "Inequality, Sociology, and Moral Philosophy. *American Journal of Sociology* 80,739-764.

De Alessi, L. (1983a),"Property Rights, Transaction Costs, and X-Efficiency: An Essay in Economic Theory", *American Economic Review* 73,64-81.
--- (1983b), "Property Rights and X-Efficiency: Reply", *American Economic Review* 73,843-845.

Debreu, G.,and Scarf, H. (1963), "A Limit Theorem on the Core of an Economy", *International Economic Review*, 4, 235-246.

Drèze, J.H. (1976), "Some Theory of Labor Management and Participation", *Econometrica*, 44, 1125-1139.

Edwards, R. (1979), *Contested Terrain*, New York: Basic Books.

Eger, T., and Weise, P. (1978),"Einzel- und gesamtwirtschaftliche Aspekte des Investitionsverhaltens arbeiterselbstverwalteter Unternehmen", in: *Partizipation in Betrieb und Gesellschaft*, eds. J. Backhaus, T. Eger, H. G. Nutzinger. Frankfurt: Campus.
--- (1984), "Grundlagen einer ökonomischen Theorie der Partizipation",in: *Mitbestimmung: Theorie, Geschichte, Praxis. Konzepte und Formen der Arbeitnehmerpartizipation*, eds. H. Diefenbacher and H. G. Nutzinger, Bd. 1. Heidelberg: Forschungsstätte der Evangelischen Studiengemeinschaft.

Elias, N.(1978), *Was ist Soziologie?* 3.edition. München: Juventa.

Emery,F.,and Thorsrud, E.(1982), *Industrielle Demokratie. Bericht über das norwegische Programm der industriellen Demokratie.* Bern-Stuttgart-Wien: Hans Huber.

Enke, H. (1983), *Konsumtive Arbeit. Ein wirtschaftstheoretischer Beitrag zur Humanisierung der Arbeitswelt,* Freiburg: Rudolf Haufe.

FitzRoy,F., and Mueller, D.C. (1984),"Cooperation and Conflict in Contractual Organizations", in: *Quarterly Review of Economics and Business* (24), 4, Winter 1984.

Francis,A.,Turk,J.,and Willman, P. eds, (1983), *Power Efficiency, and Institutions, A Critical Appraisal of the 'Markets and Hierarchies' Paradigm,* London: Heinemann.

Furubotn, E.G. (1978), "The Economic Consequences of Codetermination on the Rate and Sources of Private Investment ", in: *The Codetermination Movement in the West,* ed. S. Pejovich, Lexington, Mass-Toronto: D.C.Heath. 131-167
---, (1981), "Codetermination and the Efficient Partitioning of Ownership Rights in the Firm." *Zeitschrift für die gesamte Staatswissenschaft,* 137, 702-709.

Hirschman, A. O. (1970), *Exit, Voice and Loyalty.* Cambridge, Mass.-London: Harvard University Press.

Leibenstein, H. (1982), "The Prisoners' Dilemma in the Invisible Hand: An Analysis of Intrafirm Productivity",*American Economic Review,* P and P, 72:92-97.
---,(1983), "Property Rights and X-Efficiency: Comment", *American Economic Review,*73, 831-842.

Marglin, S. (1974)," What Do Bosses Do? The Origins and Functions of Hierarchy in Capitalist Production",*Review of Radical Political Economics,* 6, 60-112.

Marx, K. (1890), *Das Kapital,* Bd. 1, 4. edition, quoted from MEW, Bd. 23, Berlin 1970.

McCain, R. (1980), "A Theory of Codetermination", *Zeitschrift für Nationalökonomie,* 40, 65-90.

Nell-Breuning, O. von (1968), *Streit um Mitbestimmung,* Frankfurt: Europäische Verlagsanstalt.
---,(1975), *Eigentum, Wirtschaftsordnung und wirtschaftliche Mitbestimmung,* Frankfurt: Schriftenreihe der IG Metall.

Newman, P. (1965), *The Theory of Exchange. Englewood Cliffs,* New Jersey: Prentice Hall.

Nutzinger,H.G.(1982),"Die ökonomische Theorie der Eigentumsrechte -Ein neues Paradigma in den Sozialwissenschaften ?"in: *Eigentumsrechte und Partizipation,* eds. J. Backhaus and H.G. Nutzinger, Frankfurt: Haag und Herchen.

Ott, C. (1977), *Recht und Realität der Unternehmenskorporation,* Tübingen: J. C. B. Mohr.

Pejovich,S. (1978),"Codetermination: A New Perspective for the West," in: *The Codetermination Movement in the West,* ed. S. Pejovich, Lexington, Mass.-Toronto: D.C. Heath. 3-21

Pöhler,W.(1979),"Fünf Jahre Humanisierungsprogramm im Bereich des Bundesministers für Forschung und Technologie",in:... *damit die Arbeit menschlicher wird. Fünf Jahre Aktionsprogramm Humanisierung des Arbeitslebens*, eds. *W. Pöhler*, Bonn: Neue Gesellschaft, 9-37

Preiser,E. (1948),"Besitz und Macht in der Distributionstheorie", also published in E. Preiser: *Bildung und Verteilung des Volkseinkommens. Gesammelte Aufsätze zur Wirtschaftstheorie und Wirtschaftspolitik* (Göttingen, Vandenhoeck, Ruprecht), 4. edition, 1970, 227-246.

Prosi, G. (1978), *Volkswirtschaftliche Auswirkungen des Mitbestimmungsgesetzes*, 1976, Köln: Otto A. Friedrich-Kuratorium.

Schotter, A. (1981), *The Economic Theory of Social Institutions*, Cambridge: Cambridge University Press.

Schüller,A. (1983), "Property Rights, Theorie der Firma und wettbewerbliches Marktsystem", in: *Property Rights und ökonomische Theorie*, ed. A. Schüller, München: Vahlen, 145-183

Simon,H.A. (1957), *Administrative Behavior: A Study of Decision-Making Processes in Administrative Organization*, 2nd ed, New York: Macmillan.
---,(1981), "Economic Rationality", in: *The Sciences of the Artificial*, ed. H.A. Simon, Cambridge, Mass: MIT Press,31-61

Stützel,W. (1972), *Preis, Wert und Macht. Analytische Theorie des Verhältnisses der Wirtschaft zum Staat*. reprint of the dissertation of 1952 (Aalen: Scientia).

Vanberg, V.(1982), *Markt und Organisation - Individualistische Sozialtheorie und das Problem korporativen Handelns*, Tübingen: J.B.C. Mohr.

Vogt,W.(1983), "Eine Theorie des kapitalistischen Gleichgewichts, in: *Ökonomie und Gesellschaft. Jahrbuch 1: Die Neoklassik und ihre Herausforderungen*, Frankfurt: Campus, 161-208

PARTICIPATION AND CODETERMINATION IN A PERFECT AND AN IMPERFECT WORLD[*]: Comment

by

Felix R. FitzRoy

Thomas Eger and Peter Weise (hereinafter E-W) have contributed to the small but growing literature that attempts to show that the predominant form of capitalist economic organization under freedom of contract is inefficient owing to informational and contracting costs. More specifically, human capital is disadvantaged because of its lack of appropriability, and legislative correction, for example, in the form of codetermination laws for large firms, can improve welfare - of workers at least.

E-W start with an account of the Arrow-Debreu economy in which competitive equilibrium is efficient, and then explain the irrelevance of this model to the real world with costly information. Strictly speaking, this point is obvious, but of course the ability of 'competition' and 'survival' to generate efficiency without help from central planners or lawmakers is constantly invoked by many economists. Some of them, namely, Hayek and Friedman, even argue the practical benefits of maximum decentralization in the real world and the efficiency of the corporate form. (Williamson)

The formal models of general equilibrium are probably beside the point in this debate.

Unfortunately, E-W do not really enter this debate or meet arguments that observed contractual arrangements are efficient with respect to information and all other costs. Thus, for example, senior employees have relative job security precisely because of their job-specific assets in most capitalist organizations. Tangible and installed capital is often very immobile, so employees have an incentive to expropriate the owners' rights by shirking on the job; hence, ultimate control should rest with owners. Of course, small shareholders are also powerless (Berle and Means), and may therefore demand more 'democratic' powers to restrain managers from expropriating them.

In pure theory it is easy to generate Pareto inferior Nash equilibria with information costs, increasing returns, or other 'imperfections'. In practice there are many inefficient firms and managers in capitalism, and some of them survive for a long time. Cooperative Japanese labour relations with profit sharing but no

Codetermination
ed. by H.G. Nutzinger and J. Backhaus
© Springer-Verlag Berlin Heidelberg 1989

formal codetermination and weak unions are apparently very efficient, but codetermination has not obviously improved the lot of
German workers or made their steel more competitive. Human capital can easily raise venture capital in the United States, but
not so easily in Europe. These are some of the questions that
must be faced in discussing comparative economic organizations.

E-W present a number of theoretical arguments for giving workers extra 'rights,' such as codetermination. While certainly
plausible, their arguments lack attention to what capitalists and
managers really do when workers have fewer (or different) rights.
Potential distributive or allocative benefits from changes in the
legal framework require an understanding of the status quo, and
E-W fail to convey the considerable controversy in the economics
profession about the true goals of the firm, the efficiency of
large corporations, the role of competition, etc. There is much
evidence available to refute the 'non-interventionist' nineteenth
century liberal view of the (best-possible) world, but this evidence needs to be marshalled and integrated with theoretical discussion of codetermination and other organizational change.

E-W have not made a definitive case for codetermination, either on their theoretical plane or from the perspective of those
who are sympathetic with their position. They have, however, focused attention on a number of important points that appear to
support their case, but require further research and integration
of theoretical modeling with a firmer empirical foundation that
is likely to find broader agreement. It is to be hoped that an
increasing number of economists will take up the challenge in
this stimulating area of subtle interaction between conjecture,
fact, and theory.

References:

Williamson, O.E., (1975), *Markets and Hierarchies*, New York: The Free Press.

---,1985. *The Economic Institutions of Capitalism*, New York: The Free Press.

A GENERAL MODEL OF CODETERMINATION

by

Eirik G. Furubotn

1. Introduction

Attempts to compare the so-called "codetermined" firm with the "conventional" capitalist firm tend to run into difficulty quickly because there is, normally, no general agreement on the precise characteristics of the respective organizations being compared. Given the possible variations in the institutional arrangements of codetermination, many different types of codetermined firms are conceivable.[1] Similarly, there are many variant forms of conventional (or non-participatory) firms. And, depending on structure, each separate firm, codetermined or conventional, can be expected to exhibit its own distinctive pattern of behavior. In principle, the new property-rights approach to comparative economics provides a general framework for analyzing the various organizational cases. By examining systematically the effects of different institutional configurations on transaction costs and economic incentives, predictions about the behavior of firms can be made. In this way,then, it is possible to relate variant models of codetermination to each other and to models of the conventional capitalist firm. But the possibility of conducting methodical analysis does not banish all problems. If, as we would anticipate, the behavior of a codetermined firm is quite sensitive to the specific institutional structure established to implement codetermination,[2] the task still remains to define the particular type of codetermined firm we wish to consider. Moreover, if questions of relative efficiency are to be broached,it is also necessary to decide on the type of non-participatory firm that will be used as the basis for behavioral comparisons.

Without endeavoring to set up a very elaborate scheme of classification, it will still be useful to indicate what seem to be the main lines of division among the different forms of capitalist business organization. From a property-rights perspective, an obvious point of departure for any discussion of organizational options is the "classical" capitalist firm. Alchian and Demsetz have focused attention on this basic model and described its special property-rights structure as follows:

Codetermination
ed. by H.G. Nutzinger and J. Backhaus
© Springer-Verlag Berlin Heidelberg 1989

" ...It is this entire bundle of rigths : (a) to be a residual
claimant; (b) to observe input behavior; (c) to be the central
party common to all contracts with inputs; (d) to alter the membership of the team; and (e) to sell these rights, that defines
the ownership (or the employer) of the classical (capitalist,
free enterprise) firm. The coalescing of these rights has arisen,
our analysis asserts, because it resolves the shirking-informa-
tion problem of team production better than does the noncentral-
ized contractual arrangement.[3] "

This set of rights characterizing the " classical" firm represents a sort of benchmark in the sense that the firm organized
consistently with the property arrangements assumed here is closest to the competitive model of neoclassical theory. In particular, labor is not expected to have any role in deciding the policies of the firm or any claim on the firm's residual. Instead,
each worker receives a contractual wage in exchange for his services. No matter what the economic fortunes of the firm, the
worker has the right to receive payment for his commitment of labor time in accordance with the provisions of the contract. Employment is "at will", but since labor is supposed to have virtually costless mobility and to bear no appreciable risk of economic loss, the contractual scheme is regarded as equitable.

Insofar as the firm is interpreted as a coalition of resource
owners bound by contracts, a crucial question that arises is:
What constitutes an efficient set of contracts for the enterprise? Presumably, whenever an improved organizational choice is
attainable, transaction costs will be reduced, new incentives
will be created that induce firm members to become more productive, etc. Moreover, the benefits of restructuring should hold,
ceteris paribus, not only for one period but over time so that
the firm's present value will tend to be enlarged. Historically,
of course, it has become apparent that the rights structure of
the idealized "classical" firm does not always represent the most
efficient structure for capitalist firms operating in the real
world. Thus, variant forms of business organization have developed, and these alternative models show rights assignments that
depart from the classical pattern. From an analytical standpoint,
we can say that the new cases were created as the result of the
partitioning of classical property rights among a wider group of
decision makers. While workers could, in theory, be among the extended group of individuals holding income or control rights in

the firm, there is no reason why such labor participation must always be provided for. And, in the paper, it will be convenient to arrange terminology so that firms excluding labor participation are defined as "conventional" capitalist organizations. Many existing models of the corporation are of this form.

By contrast, "participatory" firms can be defined as those that provide explicitly for the assignment of some property rights in the firm to workers. A continuum of participatory models is conceivable; and, along this continuum, worker rights can range from modest to significant. Presumably, participatory firms emerge either because such reorganization promises objective efficiency or welfare advantages, or because workers simply insist on going beyond traditional wage-labor contracts and securing what they regard as a more appropriate partitioning of ownership rights in the firm. Increasingly, labor seems to have a special agenda for reform. Thus, changes in the capitalist firm are sought that will: (i) permit active involvement of labor at all levels of the firm's decision-making process; (ii) offer workers substantial job security; (iii) protect the firm-specific investments of workers against excessive loss; (iv) guarantee workers at least market rates of return on their firm-specific investments; and (v) allow labor a major role in shaping the firm's work rules and production environment. While other desiderata may exist, the preceding points represent the core of the reform program labor appears to demand. What is interesting to consider, though, is the question of whether the capitalist firm can, in fact, be structured so as to be compatible with these requirements of "industrial democracy" and still be productively efficient.

Codetermined firms represent an important sub-class of participatory firms. They convey considerable power to labor and, generally speaking, are organized in such way as to enable workers to approach the set of objectives (i) - (v) noted above. It must be recognized, however, that codetermined firms fall logically into two distinct groups on the basis of the way they come into existence. That is, codetermination may be adopted voluntarily or the program may be imposed by law. In the voluntary case, movement toward industrial democracy occurs because decision makers believe that reorganization will bring about greater efficiency and lead to a Pareto improvement for the firm. Many different forms of the voluntarily established codetermined firm are possible in principle; but, for each practical application, objective economic calculations consistent with existing market realities must determine the specific property-rights configuration chosen. In short, the structure of the firm emerges from the competitively driven search for superior organization. When codetermination is introduced by legislative fiat, however, the situation changes radically. Although the institutional arrangements specified to implement codetermination can differ widely and produce a variety of (mandatory) codetermined firms, such firms are subject to a basic limitation. Only by chance will the organizational structure established by law match the structure that would be selected freely by efficiency-seeking decision makers. In general, a legally imposed structure must be inconsistent with individual preferences and market requirements; thus, the imposed institutional characteristics take on the nature of arbitrary constraints. Codetermined firms set up in accordance with rigid legislative guidelines must tend to yield second-best results.[4]

From what has been said, it is clear that the "conventional" firm, the "legislated" codetermined firm, and the freely established codetermined firm are all variant types of capitalist structures. Thus, to the extent that we can speak reasonably of a general model here, it must be of a general model of the capitalist firm. Conceptually, the pure organizational problem can be reduced to that of discovering the particular assignment of property rights that leads the firm to maximal economic efficiency. But this formulation implies that the decision makers attempting to range in on an optimal rights system must be free to operate without encountering special constraints. As noted earlier, mandatory prgrams of codtermination do entail certain arbitrary restrictions on structure, and hence models in this category cannot be general. Moreover, a similar difficulty holds with respect to the conventional firm. Since, by definition, the latter rules out the possibility of labor having control rights in the firm, this class of models cannot lay claim to generality either. In effect, then, we are left with the firm that choses codetermination voluntarily as the crucial organization for study. What we observe is, simply, that the standard capitalist framework is flexible enough to embrace codetermination and provide for the legitimate objectives of labor. In the end, there is no need to think of the codetermined firm and the "capitalist" firm as necessarily separate and rival entities.

2. The Economic Environment of the Modern Capitalist Firm

The reasons for the growing interest in programs of industrial democracy are, no doubt, both complex and varied. Some
writers, of course, would assert that nothing more than rent-
seeking behavior is involved and that labor, as a powerful special interest group, is simply using the political system to
bring about wealth transfers from others to itself. But this position seems too one-sided and tends to neglect other significant
factors that must influence the current drive for change in the
organizational structure of the firm. Ultimately, the case for
reform, including governmentally imposed reform, appears to rest
on the conviction that conditions in the modern world differ significantly from the conditions assumed in the standard neoclassical model. In particular, it is now believed by many economists
that lesser reliance must be placed on the use of firm-external
markets as the means for allocating inputs efficiently. It follows that insofar as limitations do exist on the use of external
markets, the firm is forced to operate differently in practice
than basic neoclassical theory suggests. For example, traditional
labor contracts may not be desirable because of the existence of
special conditions that rule out simple wage-labor agreements and
force the utilization of non-market forms of organization.
Bounded rationality, widespread uncertainty, informational asymmetries, opportunistic behavior, and firm-specific investment are
the factors most often emphasized in discussions of contractual
failure. In the case of labor, these factors tend to push the
system in the direction of incompletely specified long-term contracts but, at the same time,impede the formulation of contract
adjustment rules that promote efficient behavior.

Another important theme in the current literature is that,
under the conventional organization of the firm, workers are required to bear a disproportionately large share of the risks and
uncertainties associated with business activity. This result
comes about, in part, because the mobility of labor is much less
than is assumed by neoclassical theory. As a practical matter,
various types of reallocation costs have to be faced by workers;
and the direct and indirect costs that arise when workers move
from one sector to another may be quite substantial.[5] Of particular interest are the losses that workers may suffer because they
have previously made investments in firm-specific human capital.
It is argued that current technological requirements often force

labor to undertake these firm-specific investments and that the latter may be large in value. It follows from this condition that if jobs in certain sectors end and workers have to move, significant capital assets tend to be jeopardized. In other words, workers shifting to new jobs stand to suffer capital losses as well as the loss of current outlays (transaction costs) made in connection with the process of search and movement.

Difficulties can arise, however, even when labor is not forced to leave the firm to seek other employment. This is so because there is always danger that some members of the firm's coalition of resource owners may seize opportunities for predatory behavior. Then, quasi-rents, which should accrue to labor's firm-specific assets, can be expropriated by others.[6] This problem, like the one discussed above, tends to become more severe when labor is denied control rights in the firm and has limited power to anticipate or affect enterprise policies. Nevertheless, labor is not without options. Workers are free to modify their economic behavior within the firm despite existing contracts, and hence the general efficiency of the firm is at stake. If desirable prospective employees are to be induced to join a firm, surrender mobility and expose themselves to risks, they must expect, in return, some long-term stability of employment, and rewards adequate to compensate them for the real hazards they face.

Various managerial strategies are open to provide the necessary assurances to workers. Fundamentally, job rights must be expanded; or, alternately stated, traditional private owner-ship rights in the firm have to be revised. By reassigning property rights, new forms of business organization can be developed; and such action may be taken if the holders of "classical" rights believe that reorganization will produce Pareto improvements for the coalition of resource owners.[7] That is, to be successful, the restructuring must meet labor's requirements with respect to such matters as job security, remuneration, the work environment, etc. And, of course, stock-holders must envision changes that will bring about greater productivity and profits. In any event, it is clear that, quite apart from the fact that rent seekers may attempt to reshape business organization to advance their own narrow interests, there are other motivations for shifting institutional arrangements. There can be sound efficiency reasons for reorganization.

The model of the firm that follows in section 3 is based on a

number of assumptions about the nature of the contemporary capitalist envirnment. Of particular importance to the argument made
in the paper are these propositions:

(i)   In many instances, firm-specific investment must be under-
        taken by the worker who accepts employment in a firm.
        Effectively, this type of investment made by labor repre-
        sents part of the total capital complement required by the
        firm for production and is, therefore, essential to the
        operation of the firm.

(ii)   Although the worker must often undertake (and pay for)
        significant firm-specific investment if he is to be em-
        ployed in a given firm, there still exist other sectors
        in the economy where employment is not tied to worker in-
        vestment,or where necessary investment is positive but tri-
        vial in magnitude.

(iii)   In general, it is possible to separate labor earnings into
        two distinct streams. These are: (a) the returns attrib-
        utable to the specialized investments made by labor in the
        firm; and (b) current wage payments (or pure labor oppor-
        tunity cost) based on the alternatives workers have to be
        employed as " general " inputs in other sectors where no
        firm-specific investment is needed.

3. A Joint-Investment Model of the Firm

To begin the analysis, it will be useful to consider the problems faced by a firm that is about to enter an existing competitive industry. We assume, therefore, that decision makers are
contemplating an investment in the particular type of real capital equipment (K_0) needed for production. At the same time, negotiations are being conducted with the union representing workers
in the industry. The object is to secure a long-term labor force
for the prospective plant. That is, a certain number of workers
(n_0) are to be hired and employed over a specified interval of
time (1, 2, ..., T). The workers chosen are to have job security
in the sense that the firm's intention is to keep the whole group
employed to the planning horizon T. Only if major unforeseen
events imperil the existence of the firm are worker lay offs pos-

sible. For convenience, assume that each individual employed will work a fixed number of hours per period so that, for any given labor force (n_0) selected, there is a definite corresponding number of labor hours (L_0) available for production each period to the horizon.

If they are to be employed, workers of the type required by the new firm will have to make substantial investments in firm-specific capital. Such workers, however, also have the option of obtaining employment as "general" labor inputs in other sectors of the economy. Following Alchian's terminology,[8] workers who do not undertake any firm-specific investment can be regarded as general resource owners. The wage rates attached to the different classes of general labor are determined in competitive markets. And, in the particular case of the workers suitable for the new firm, the wage rates per (general) labor hour that are expected to rule over the time interval 1, 2, ..., T are estimated as: $\hat{w}_1$, $\hat{w}_2, \ldots, \hat{w}_T$. These wage rates represent the projected opportunity costs of labor services (net of any returns to firm-specific investment) and must be met if workers are to be retained. Apparently, then, the workers in question face a basic choice. Since they can find jobs in sectors where they are required to make little or no firm-specific investment, they must consider the advantages of this form of employment relative to the advantages of working and investing in the new firm being organized.

In addition to job security, the workers hired by the new firm will be granted extensive rights to participate in the organization's decision-making process. Significantly, representatives of labor will be assigned seats on the firm's board of directors; and the number of labor seats established will be *in direct proportion to the total investment workers have made in firm-specific capital*.[9] The major function of these labor directors is, of course, to safeguard the interests of workers (n_0) by helping to shape the firm's policies, especially its long-term or strategic policies. Unlike some participatory schemes, the intent here is to treat workers, who make durable investments necessary to the operation of the firm, in precisely the same way as any other investors. Just as the suppliers of specialized physical capital (K_0) have control rights in the firm, so too do workers; and, through their representatives, workers can take action to protect labor-owned resources that are specific to the coalition. Apart from such high-level participation, however, workers have other channels for communicating with management. That is, the firm's organization is assumed to provide for works councils, quality circles, grievance committees, etc. Collectively, code-termination and the other lower-level devices can be expected to lessen the problem of labor alienation.

For simplicity, it will be assumed that each employee of the new firm ($j = 1, 2, ..., n_0$) makes a fixed investment (y_j) in firm-specific assets at period zero (before the organization commences production), and that no further investment takes place over the interval 1, 2, ..., T.[10] Investment for each of the n_0 distinct workers can differ, but it is possible to calculate the average dollar investment per worker for a given employment level and assume that this average holds for any employment level. Then, knowing the fixed relation between the number of workers hired (n_0) and the available labor hours per period (L_0), average investment per labor hour ($\hat{W}_0$) can also be determined. As a practical matter, the average investment per labor hour is likely to be difficult to quantify. This is so because $\hat{W}_0$ depends on the choices of many different individuals and on a variety of cost elements, some of them subjective. At best, then, the magnitude $\hat{W}_0$ must be understood as an estimate only.

The fact that labor is recognized as making a significant investment in the firm, just as conventional stockholders do, is the crucial condition for the model being constructed. Once this position is accepted, workers can be viewed as equity holders.[11] It is the "equity holde" status of workers, of course, that justifies the presence of labor representatives on the firm's board of directors. Alchian has explained the situation concisely as follows:

"...The people who direct and manage a coalition are those own the resources specific to the coalition. Owners of those resources have the most to lose by failure of the coalition. They have a greater incentive to manage or be responsible for the management of the coalition. The so-called stockholders are not less risk averse than (other members); instead owners of the coalition-specific resources want to be the managers more than do owners of the general resources. While it is true that uncertainty and risk are present, stockholders or managers do not bear that risk in order to be motivated. Instead the risk is inevitable, and those who bear it have the greater incentives to control and manage.[12] "

In what follows, then, it will be necessary to take account of the effective (dollar) investment labor makes in the firm, and to indicate how such investment affects the equilibrium solution reached by the firm.

As formulated, the joint-investment model assumes that the new firm being organized is to enter a competitive industry. Thus, the price of the (single) commodity produced is, at each period, a given market parameter. The single-valued estimates for these prices over the planning interval are: $\hat{p}_1$, $\hat{p}_2$, ..., $\hat{p}_T$. Note that the commodity price can vary over time and that the development of prices over the interval 1, 2, ..., T is not necessarily monotonic. It is assumed, however, that the firm expects the market rate of interest (i), and the price of physical capital equipment (Z_0), existing at the moment of calculation (or period zero) to remain unchanged to the planning horizon T. Moreover, only one type of capital good (K_0) exists for equipping the plant and this good has a technically given durability of T periods. Physical depreciation of the capital good used in production is assumed to occur only at the end of the T-th period; but, then, depreciation is total. It follows from this interpretation that the role of maintenance is effectively ruled out. Finally, it should be emphasized that, while important, any capital that labor brings to the firm (i.e., firm-specific human capital, housing, etc.) is distinct from K_0.

The production function is of the "stock-flow" type.[13] An output flow (q_t) appears at the end of each period (1, 2, ...,T) after the durable capital goods (i.e., the capital stock K_0) have been purchased and set up at the end of period zero to cooperate with the labor input (L_0). Investment is of the point-input-multipoint-output type. Thus, at each period, the given capital stock (K_0), operating in conjunction with the uniform labor flow (L_0), produces a certain commodity output in accordance with the technical relations defined by the production function: $q_t = f_t$ (K_0,L_0). This function has conventional properties and, in particular, is globally strictly concave. Capital goods (K_0) are assumed to be malleable ex ante but not ex post. Once the firm has ordered a particular quantity of capital goods, it has tied itself to a certain process of production or type of technical arrangement.[14] This arrangement cannot be changed through later manipulation of the capital stock. In short, neither additions to nor subtractions from the original stock can be made.

By assumption, all of the investment made by labor occurs during the preproduction period (period zero). This investment provides workers with the appropriate skills, housing, etc. so as to ensure the firm of the availability of the labor service flow L_0 at each successive period (1, 2, ..., T) to the horizon. Clearly, labor's investment in firm-specific assets is essential and must be rewarded. But labor's investment does not enter directly into the production function, $q_t = f_t(K_0, L_0)$, as an explicit variable. The situation existing is easily understood; the necessary input flow L_0 would not be available to the firm and production of the commodity (q_t) could not proceed without the special investment by labor ($\hat{w}_0 L_0$). The latter investment proceeds in parallel with that made by the firm on physical equipment but is quite distinct from K_0. Given the job-security objective of the firm, however, workers and their firm-specific investments are tied to the firm. That is, the number of workers (n_0), or labor hours (L_0), contracted for initially must be sustained over the planning inerval.[15]

From the standpoint of the members of the coalition who are organizing the new firm, the key problem is to determine the firm's demand for capital goods (K_0) and labor hours (L_0). Of course, since the average investment per labor hour ($\hat{w}_0$) is known and fixed, a solution for L_0 implies a definite corresponding outlay on the part of workers for the particular types of capital assets that they require. In any event, we can say that magnitudes of K_0 and L_0 are sought so that the yield or net present value (π) of the firm will be maximized over the planning interval 1, 2, ..., T. The capital equipment for the plant has a T period lifetime as noted earlier, but the human capital et al. representing labor's investment does not, in general, have this lifespan. Indeed, it seems reasonable to assume that the average life of the firm-specific assets possessed by workers is greater than T periods. Then, the effective (dollar) investment by labor at the beginning of the planning interval is $\hat{w}_0 L_0$ minus the discounted salvage value of the assets. Specifically, the value of investment is:

$$\left(\hat{w}_0 L_0 - \frac{\hat{v}_T L_0}{(1+i)^T}\right)$$

where $\hat{v}_T$ is the estimated salvage value of assets per labor hour at the end of period T.

The theory of the codetermined firm is said to be fundamentally different and more complex than that of the conventional capitalist firm because the owners of two distinct factors of production, labor and capital, jointly control the codetermined firm but attempt to pursue divergent objectives. Since each party is expected to push its own policies and seek its own interests without much regard for the other, the belief has grown that it is appropriate to analyze codetermination via bargaining-theoretic models.[16] In the case of the present joint-investment model, however, this approach does not seem warranted. Although codetermination exists and labor and capital share decision-making power, no fundamental conflict in goals need occur. Rather, both parties have strong concern with the return realized by capital. Workers are always able to secure wage income based on their opportunity cost ($\hat{w}_1$, $\hat{w}_2$, ..., $\hat{w}_T$) as "general" inputs. But insofar as they also have significant investment in the firm, workers must be interested in the size of the firm's residual. In other words, given sufficient firm-specific investment by workers, there is reason for labor and capital to cooperate in the attempt to maximize the firm's net present value.

If the preceding argument is accepted, the formal problem becomes one of maximizing the following objective function:

$$(1) \qquad \pi = \sum_{t=1}^{T} [\{\hat{p}_t f_t (K_0, L_0) - \hat{w}_t L_0\} (1+i)^{-t}] - z_0 K_0$$
$$- [\hat{W}_0 L_0 - \hat{v}_T L_0 (1+i)^{-T}] ; \qquad t = 1, 2, \ldots, T.$$

This expression takes account of both the revenues generated by production over the planning interval and the initial fixed investments made by capital and labor. The first-order conditions for the maximum are:

$$(2) \qquad \frac{\partial \pi}{\partial K_0} = \sum_{t=1}^{T} [\hat{p}_t \frac{\partial q_t}{\partial K_0} (1+i)^{-t}] - z_0 = 0$$

$$(3) \qquad \frac{\partial P}{\partial L_0} = \sum_{t=1}^{T} [\{\hat{p}_t \frac{\partial \hat{q}_t}{\partial L_0} - \hat{w}_t\} (1+i)^{-t}] - \hat{W}_0 + \hat{v}_T(1+i)^{-T} = 0$$

Strict concavity of the production function ensures satisfaction of the second-order conditions for the maximum, and thus attention can be turned to the interpretation of (2) and (3). Equation (2) says in effect that, at equilibrium, the sum of the discounted VMPs of physical capital (K_0) is just equal to the initial cost of a unit of capital equipment (Z_0). Since Z_0 is taken as a market parameter, the marginal outlay for an additional unit of K (which is highly divisible) is always Z_0. Equation (3) indicates that, at equilibrium, the sum of the net VMPs of labor, appropriately discounted, is just equal to the average investment per labor hour ($\hat{W}_0$) minus the discounted salvage value per labr hour (considered at the end of period T). Note that the return to a marginal outlay by labor (i.e., an incremental investment at period zero or ($\hat{W}_0 - \hat{v}_T (1+i)^{-T}]$) must be calculated on the basis of revenues net of the opportunity cost of (general) labor $\hat{w}_t$. By definition, $\hat{w}_t$ is the cost of a labor hour determined without reference to the return from any firm-specific investment made by workers. Given this procedure, it follows that the hiring of labor by the joint-investment firm proceeds with due regard to the profitability of any labor-financed investment that is undertaken.

The first-order conditions (2) and (3) can be solved simultaneously to give the yield-maximing values of the capital and labor inputs : K_0^*, l_0^* . When these optimal values (K_0^*, L_0^*) are introduced into (1), the maximum value of the yield (π^*) is, of course, found. This magnitude has importance. Clearly, for the firm to be started and investment to take place, it is essential that:

$$(4) \qquad \pi^* \geq 0 .$$

If those organizing the new firm are to be willing to go forward with the specialized investment required, the anticipated yield, or net present value, π^* must be greater than or equal to zero. As usual, $\pi^* = 0$ implies that the proposed investments in the firm (by workers and capitalists) will generate a rate of return just equal to the opportunity cost of capital (i) prevailing in the system. Workers (or the union acting in their behalf) must play a significant role in deciding whether or not to start up

the new firm because they too are making an investment in it -
viz, [$\hat{W}_0 L_0 - \hat{v}_T L_0 (1+i)^{-T}$]. Insofar as $\pi^* \geq 0$, workers will secure their proportional share of the firm's normal or extranormal
profits. Of course, apart from positive returns on firm-specific
investment, workers can always expect to receive $\hat{w}_t L_0$ each period
as long as they are actively employed in the firm.[17] If $\pi^* < 0$,
however, workers would stand to lose on their investment in firm-
specific assets and, presumably, would decide against entering
the coalition of resource owners contemplating the founding of
the firm.

4. Mandatory Codetermination and Behavior of the Firm

The joint-investment model described in section 3 can be said
to be general in the sense that it defines a firm that is not
bound by any special constraints imposed by law or convention.
Given freedom, the firm's stucture of property rights in any way
that promises net advantage. For example, in an effort to reduce
transaction costs , the owner-decision makers may vary property-
rights assignments and, in effect, substitute greater hierarchical organization for market organization. Similary, they can
transfer some income rights to selected factor owners in order to
improve incentives and productivity. How far such manipulation
can go, however, is ultimately an empirical question. Whether the
arrangements specified for the joint-investment firm can, in
fact, be realized depends on the existing conditions of technology, preferences, institutional structure, etc. in the world outside the firm. The type of codetermination system describedc in
section 3 may not be feasible in practice. But if it is not, it
seems important to understand the reasons why this is so. One
possibility, of course, is that, under present circumstance,
codetermination in any form may fail to represent an efficient
choice of business organization. As Jensen and Meckling argue:

" The fact that this system seldom arise out of voluntary arrangements among individuals strongly suggests that codetermination or industrial democracy is less efficient than the alternatives which grow up and survive in a competitive enviroment
(i.e., one where organizational alternatives are on all fours
legally). Of course, it is always possible that the frailty of
industrial democracy is due to some "deficiency" which arises

when individuals are given broader freedom in choosing organizational forms, but it seems reasonable to place the burden of
proof on proponents of codetermination in this exercise.[18] "

   To highlight the properties of the joint-investment model, it
will be useful to contrast it with an alternate model of codetermination that reflects a more orthodox structure. That is, we
wish to consider a firm that is broadly representative of the
type found in legally mandated codetermination programs. Such a
firm will tend to show some arbitrary elements. The reliance on
political intervention to shape institutions suggest that business organization will be chosen, not solely on efficiency
grounds, but on the basis of how organization contributes to the
realization of the social ideals of industrial democracy or to
redistributive goals. For example, parity representation on the
board may be called for even though workers have only modest investment in the firm. Under this type of politically charged system, there can, of course, be no assurance that efficient solutions will be reached.
   The " mandatory " codetermination model is designed to have
characteristics that parallel those of the joint-investment
model. Thus, it is assumed that a group of workers (n_0) is to be
hired en bloc and assured of employment over the time interval
$1,2,\ldots,T$. What is crucial in this case, however, is the bargain
concluded with the union. The terms of the labor contract are
very important because they determine not only the number of
workers to be employed and the duration of employment but the
wage rate That is to be paid at each period to the planning horizon ($\bar{w}_t, t = 1,2,\ldots,T$).[19] Depending on whether the rates agreed
upon are set at relatively low or lesser profits. Forecasts of
future economic conditions play a major role here, and the bargaining problem is particulary acute because job security for
workers implies a requirement on the part of the firm to retain
all workers initially hired (n_0) unless the firm encounters very
serious economic difficulties.
   As before, the firm's objective is to maximize yield or net
present value. But the maximand now takes on a somewhat different
form :

$$(1') \quad \pi = \sum_{t=1}^{T} [\hat{P}_t f_t \, (K_0 L_0) \, (1+i)^{-t}] - Z_0 K_0$$

$$- \sum_{t=1}^{T} (\bar{w}_t L_0) \, (1+i)^{-t} \qquad\qquad t = 1,2,\ldots,T$$

Equation (1') suggests that the firm is undertaking two types of long-term investment - in capital equipment (K_0) and in labor services. More concretely, the contract for workers (or L_0 labor hours per period) can be viewed as a form of investment made by the firm which is committed to use this labor over time interval $1,2,..,T$. From the standpoint of the stockholders, the firm's optimization problem is to find the ideal or yield-maximizing values of K_0, L_0, given the data of the system and the planning horizon T. By assumption, T also represents the lifespan of the durable capital equipment K_0.

$$(2') \quad \frac{\partial \pi}{\partial K_0} = \sum_{t=1}^{T} [\hat{P}_t \, \frac{\partial q_t}{\partial K_0} \, (1+i)^{-t}] - Z_0 = 0$$

$$(3') \quad \frac{\partial \pi}{\partial L_0} = \sum_{t=1}^{T} [\hat{P}_t \, \frac{\partial q_t}{\partial L_0} \, (1+i)^{-t}] - \sum_{t=1}^{T} \bar{w}_t \, (1+i)^{-t} = 0$$

The first-order conditions, equations (2') and (3'), can be solved simultaneously to determine the ideal magnitudes: K_0^*, L_0^*. Note that equation (2') is straightforward and has a completely standart interpretation. But (3') is equally plausible. It says that, at equilibrium, the sum of the discounted VMPs of labor is just equal to the marginal outlay that has to be made to secure another labor hour over the interval $1,2,\ldots,T$. The marginal outlay is given by the sum of the (discounted) wage payments ($\bar{w}_t$ $(1+i)^{-t}$, $t = 1, 2, \ldots, T$) that must go to an additional unit of labor service employed over the planning period. Of course, if investment is to take place and the firm is to begin productive operations, it is required that net present value be greater than or equal to zero.

$$(4') \quad \pi^* \geq 0$$

Ceteris paribus, the magnitude of π^* depends on the contractual wage stream $(\bar{w}_1, \bar{w}_2, \ldots, \bar{w}_T)$ that is established through bargaining with the union.

So far, only the interests of the potential capital suppliers have been analyzed in detail. What is needed next, therefore, is an assessment of the opportunities offered by the firm from the standpoint of the workers who will be involved in production. As befor, assume that workers must make firm-specific investments to be eligible for employment. And total investment by the group of workers supplying L^0 hours of labor servis per period is:

$$\hat{w}_0 L_0 - \hat{v}_T L_0 (1+i)^{-T}.$$

For this group of workers, the objective is to ensure that:

$$(5') \qquad v^* = \sum_{t=1}^{T} [(w_t - \hat{w}_t) L_0 (1+i)^{-t}]$$

$$- [\hat{w}_0 L_0 - \hat{v}_T L_0 (1+i)^{-T}] \geq 0 \quad .$$

We see that the first term to the right in (5′); or the discounted stream of effective returns to investment over the interval $1,2,\ldots,T$, must be greater than or equal to the initial investment made by labor. This condition represents nothing more than the requirement that the net present value of labor's undertaking (v^*) must reach a value (as a result of wage bargaining) such that: $v^* \geq 0$. The presumption here, of course, is that unless the workers secure at least a normal or opportunity return on their anticipated investment in firm-specific assets $(v^* = 0)$, they will not accept the employment contract with the firm. Workers base their calculations on the understanding that the opportunity reward for "general" labor services $(\hat{w}_t, t = 1,2,\ldots,T)$ will be available to them regardless of whether they make any firm-specific investments.

Thus, $(\bar{w}_t - \hat{w}_t) L_0$, $t = 1,2,\ldots,T$ represents the reward stream that will go to labor's capital contribution to the firm; and, ceteris paribus, the greater the contractual wage stream $(\bar{w}_1, \bar{w}_2, \ldots, \bar{w}_T)$, the greater is v^*.

Effectively, the terms of the labor contract decide the division of the firm's residual, given $\hat{p}_t$, i, z_0, etc. For the two parties negotiating the contract, then, there must be limits on the possible solutions that can be reached with respect to wage payments. An acceptable solution for the wage stream $\bar{w}_1, \bar{w}_2, \ldots, \bar{w}_T$ is one that permits:

(6'-a) $\pi^* \geq 0$,

while simultaneously allowing:

(6'-b) $V^* \geq 0$.

In this form of codetermination, the workers secure their monetary rewards via the wage agreement; they do not share in profits directly as legal claimants of the firm's residual. Thus, emphasis is necessarily placed on the bargaining game that goes on between labor and managment. Nevertheless, as long as the condtions noted in (6'-a) and (6'-b) are met, both capital equipment owners and human capital owners are able to make their investments at t = 0 with the expectation of acceptable returns.

At full long-run equilibrium, all investments in a competitive economic system should earn just the normal rate of return (i). But if workers possess some degree of monopoly power through union organization, V^* may remain greater than zero. What the "mandatory" codetermination model suggests, of course, is that workers and capital equipment owners do not share common interests. Workers will attempt to make certain that the wage stream $\bar{w}_1, \bar{w}_2, \ldots, \bar{w}_T$ is large enough to ensure $V^* = 0$; but they have incentive to go beyond this and, perhaps, enforce their demands by causing the industry to shrink. Certainly, if the industry is earning extranormal profits, workers (or the union) can try to set contractual wages rates high enough to capture rents that would otherwise go to firms. Since no definite formula has beeen established to define labor's reward for making firm-specific investments, division of the firm's residual is always subject to opportunistic behavior on the part of both labor and capital. Actually, the problem runs even deeper than this. In practice, legally imposed codetermination may give control rights to workers that are out of proportion to the investment risks borne by labor. Under such circumstance, workers are able to push for major nonpecuniary benefits to supplement their monetary incomes.[20] That is, by securing concessions from the firm with respect to work rules, staffing norms, the work environment, etc., workers can gain, but at the expense of raising costs and reducing profits.

Unless the firm is able to bargain very effectively, the impact of risk and uncertainty will tend to fall in large measure on the firm's residual claimants.[21] This result occurs because the wage rates $\bar{w}_1$, $\bar{w}_2$, ..., $\bar{w}_T$ agreed upon in the labor contract have to be paid regardless of the actual economic outcomes experienced by the firm.[22] What is at issue here is the matter of how risk and uncertainty are to be borne, and by whom. As long as wage payments are fixed by long-term contracts or understandings, the pecuniary rewards to labor need not be tied closely to the actual success of the firm. Although attempts may be made to set contractual wage rates so as to account for possible fluctuations in economic conditions, the system of adjustment cannot, in general, provide full protection against all unforeseen loss or gain because of the operation of primary and secondary uncertainty. Since actuarial calculations do not extend to pure uncertainty, the wage rates paid in a "risky" industry may overcompensate or undercompensate workers relative to the actual experience of the firm. If the firm is obligated to deliver substantial job security and must meet fixed wage bills over a long period, the writing of a contract is very difficult and the accuracy of economic forecasts becomes crucial. Normally, contract adjustment is necessary as new information appears and new circumstances arise. But when such adjustment is impossible, or very hard to arrange, because of union power and extensive labor participation in firm decision making, efficiency tends to suffer. Rewards to labor (and to capital) tend to depart from value productivity levels; and the situation is made even worse if the firm's control over the provision of nonpecuniary benefits is also weakened by participation.

Ultimately, how well or how badly the mandatory codetermination scheme works depends on how responsibly worker representatives act in establishing enterprise policy at the board level, and on how reasonable the union is in setting demands for wages. Yet, without clearly defined contractual guidelines for allocating the firm's residual and for apportioning risk, it is unrealistic to suppose that labor will alway act in a restrained manner. Indeed, given the uncertainties, if labor takes too unassertive a position, workers may be forced to bear excessive risk and fail to receive adequate returns on their firm-specific investments. Of course, if the firm actually finances the investment in human capital and the other firm-specific assets acquired by its employees, the firm will have to take the value of such investment into account when considering subsequent firm policy. There will obviously be reluctance to take actions that will destroy assets of this sort that the firm has paid for. Assuming workers have made the firm-specific investments, however, they clearly lose is they cause the firm to fail before the horizon T is reached. For, then, labor's investments are lost. Nevertheless, workers (and the union) can have relatively short planning horizons so that the firm's existence beyond period T may be imperiled. If labor steers a middle course and allows $\pi^* \geq 0$ as well as ensuring $V^* \geq 0$, the system can function quite reasonably (if not entirely equitably). But the situation is basically unstable, and the potential for major difficulty is always present because labor is always free to move to a more aggressive policy line.

5. Labor Participation and Efficiency: Some Conclusions

The two codetermined firms examined in sections 3 and 4 above are designed to achieve the same fundamental objectives and, thus, show certain broad similarities of structure. Yet there are real differences between the respective models. In particular, the so-called "joint-investment" firm can be said to possess superior properties and to yield superior performance.[23] To understand why this is so, it is necessary to keep in mind that, by assumption, the joint-investment firm develops in an environment devoid of special governmental constraints on structure. Its organization tends to be well adjusted to the technical and market conditions actually confronting the firm. In effect, "classical" ownership rights are partitioned among various members of the firm's coalition of resource owners so that Pareto improvements can be secured and all can benefit. The point is that, ultimately, efficiency is served by institutional arrangements that evolve freely in response to competitive forces. By relying on the self-interest principle, productivity-enhancing incentives can be generated within the firm and transaction costs can be reduced.

A crucial assumption underlying the joint-investment model of codetermination concerns labor's role in production. The notion is that the employees of a firm may often have to pay for and ac-

cumulate various types of firm-specific assets in order to work.
It follows, of course, that employees who make such "reliance investment" are vulnerable; since the value of their assets can be
affected by the actions of other members of the coalition, the
possibility exists that workers may suffer serious economic loss.
The modern theory of the firm now recognizes that this basic
problem is faced by all resource owners holding firm-specific assets, but the full implications of the situation for labor participation in management and in profit sharing are just beginning
to be worked out.[24] In any event, if it is true that workers in
many sectors of the economy are required to make significant
firm-specific investments, and if these investments are essential
to the operation of the firm, the meaning for business organization is clear.[25] Control rights are essential for labor and an
efficiently organized capitalist firm must frequently be a type
of codetermined firm.

As suggested above, the property arrangements of the joint-investment firm promise a number of advantages. What seems of particular importance is that both "capital" and "labor" have a common interest in increasing the profitability of the firm during
its operations to the planning horizon T. Under the structure assumed, workers are primarily investors and only secondarily the
suppliers of labor services. This last assessment may be somewhat
extreme; but as long as workers have a reasonably large invest-
ment in firm-specific assets, $\hat{W}_0 L_0 - \hat{v}_T L_0 (1+i)^{-T}$, they have a
significant stake in the success of the firm because they share
in the firm's profits in proportion to their total investment.
Even if workers are laid off in their capacity as suppliers of
labor services, they still retain their investment interest in
the firm and thus maintain a claim on any profits the firm may
make currently or in the future.[26]

The firm, quite apart frm its pledge to maintain job security
has good reason not to lay off workers unless it becomes absolutely necessary. The reason, of course, is that the employment
of new and different workers later (if subsequent recruiting were
desired) would involve additional investment of the type $W_0 L_0$,
and this investment would have to be compensated out of any profits the firm might make. Such action would necessarily diminish
the profit shares of all of the original participants in the
coalition (both "capital" and "labor" members). Labor turnover,
then, is undesirable from the standpoint of the initial investors
in the firm. But this means that workers who withdraw from the

firm voluntarily before the planning horizon T must be subject to penalty. Presumably, those leaving early would be required to forfeit their claims to returns from any firm-specific invest- ments previously made. Similarly, workers cannot be allowed to sell their claims on the firm's residual to others. This is so because if such claims were traded in the open market, workers would have lesser incentive to avoid shirking and perform dili- gently for the company.[27] The conclusion to be reached here is simple. Under the form of codetermination being discussed, la- bor's rights to transfer residual claims are severely attenu- ated.[28] In contrast to capital suppliers, workers do not have the freedom to diversify their portfolios by selling their "share" in the firm.

Although labor, capital and other owners of firm-specific re- sources have some commonality of interest, this fact does not mean that all problems of motivation are solved in the joint-in- vestment firm. For example, in a large organization with many em- ployees, shirking may still be an issue because any given worker can assume that the cost of his shirking (in terms of foregone profits) is borne largely by others. Moreover, despite peer pres- sure and other influences that tend to restrict shirking, the la- bor effort put forth may be less than ideal because close moni- toring of the work process may be very costly to achieve. It is also true that the placement of the workers' planning horizon (T) can affect the objectives of labor and the behavior of the firm. Common interest among members of the firm's coalition of re- sources owners certainly does not have to hold beyond period T, and may not hold even to T. While the firm may be able to con- tinue its operations indefinitely, through the periodic replace- ment of physical capital, the workers (whose initial contract and claims run only to T) may wish to leave the firm or retire at T. But if this pattern holds, workers may push for policies that yield short-term benefits to T, and oppose other policies (however desirable they may be) that yield major rewards in peri- ods after T. In short, the timing of benefits is crucial and, if workers have relatively short planning horizons, decisions may be taken with respect to investments, technical innovation, product development, etc. that are fundamentally unsound. For example, the firm could be induced to undertake investments that promise good near-term returns and low or negative long-term returns.

The difficulties just alluded to are real and worthy of con- sideration. Nevertheless, the structure of the joint-investment model is such as to give hope that, under more normal conditions, the firm will function quite reasonably. Since all investors, conventional and worker-investors, are granted income and control rights in the firm (allocated in proportion to investment and risk exposure), efficient incentives tend to be generated. This means that, in general, conventional stockholders need not feel particularly threatened by worker participation. In effect, the new codetermination scheme creates an organization paralleling that assumed by the traditional neoclassical model of the firm. Ownership rights and claims to the firm's residual go, ceteris paribus, to those resource owners making specialized investments and assuming risk. Unlike the neoclassical model, however, it is not assumed that all productive factors other than the capital provided by conventional stockholders are "general" inputs having costless mobility in a full-employment economy. Rather, labor is understood to make specialized (firm-specific) investment in the firm on the same terms as any other member of the controlling coalition of resource owners. From this position, it is also clear that profit sharing under the conditions of the joint-investment model is quite distinct from other types of profit-sharing. Rewards go to individuals on the basis of arbitrary rules or conventions.

An important feature of the joint-investment scheme of organization is its provision of basic job security for workers over the time interval $1, 2, \ldots, T$. All workers are assured of a market rate of return $(\hat{w}_1, \hat{w}_2 \ldots, \hat{w}_T)$ on the labor services they supply to the firm over time. The stream of income connected with wage payments, however, represents only one source of labor's reward. Additional income will usually be secured by workers from returns on their firm-specific investments. That is, if the firm is making normal or extranormal profits on its operations, workers will receive their proportionate share of such gains.[29] The arrangement is helpful to firm success because the total outlay made by the firm for labor services at any period t (i.e., $\hat{w}_t L_0$ plus labor's share of profits) varies with the economic conditions faced by the firm at that period. Outlay falls in depressed periods and rises in prosperous periods. This pattern, of course, permits greater stability of employment and contributes to the general resiliency of the firm. Although labor bears the risks associated with firm-specific investment, workers are assured of their appropriate share of any profits made over the planning interval $1, 2, \ldots, T$.

As a practical matter, the most serious problem with the joint-investment approach is likely to be the difficulty of reaching agreement on the magnitude of labor's investment in firm-specific assets. What is required is a clear understanding of the extent to which labor (n_0) intends to finance firm-specific investment. But controversy may well arise between the parties because any figure arrived at is so crucial to remuneration.[30] At best, accurate measurement of the level of labor investment is not easy and, depending on the magnitude actually established, the relative division of the firm's residual will be one thing or another. Nevertheless, the difficulties here need not be insuperable. It is also apparent that if workers make no investment in the firm and are mobile, they are effectively "general" inputs and should have no claim on the firm's profits. To give workers claims on the residual under these circumstances is to take action that, ceteris paribus, diminishes managerial incentives and retards capital formation.

Given labor representation on the firm's board of directors, workers will have access to reliable information on the plans or intentions of the firm with respect to employment, work rules, the production environment, technological shifts, etc. over the planning interval 1, 2, ..., T. Both conventional investors and worker-investors share information on the best estimates of future prices, technology and other relevant data. Thus, labor is able to proceed in any negotiations without the handicap of lesser knowledge than other members of the firm. Efficiency is promoted because the institutional arrangements of the joint-investment model are favorable to the formation of needed firm-specific capital. There are strong inducements for workers to make specialized investments in human capital and other assets because of the protection afforded such investments. Moreover, unique to high-level labor participation is an advantage that appears as a result of the reduction of informational asymmetries. Skepticism about the honesty of management's assessment of the firm's economic situation or its future plans can be allayed, and cooperation between labor and management increased.[31]

Ideally, participation of labor in decision making should tend to bring about not only mutual trust but a general change of attitude on the part of workers. Such changed outlook may lead, in turn, to enhanced productivity. Explanations of why improvements in productivity come about under worker participation are quite varied, but there do seem to be some sound reasons for expecting useful results.[32] For example, insofar as work effort and intra-firm information flows are subject to the discretion of workers, changed business organization can lead to greater work perfor-mance, superior communication and improved overall efficiency. It must be recognized, of course, that productivity effects can be associated with worker participation at levels lower than the firm's board of directors - i.e., works councils, quality cir-cles, grievance committees, etc. In the case of the joint-invest-ment model, however, labor automatically secures lower-level par-ticipation as well as seats on the board. Hence, all of the al-leged productivity advantages of industrial democracy should be present in this form of organization.[33]

According to some writers, participation can be regarded as an important end in itself. That is, less hierarchical organiza-tion is said to diminish workers' alienation and contribute to their overall welfare.[34] Williamson argues that unless problems of alienation and worker "dignity" are considered, the conception of economic organization can be too narrow.[35] Individuals cannot be considered strictly as instruments. Presumably, to understand the organization of work, sensitivity to human needs for self- and social-regard is essential. This judgment may be correct, but it is true that participation can also have counterproductive ef-fects. Workers, for example, may be much more risk averse than normal investors and their desire for security can affect the de-cisions of the firm adversely. Certainly, when a codetermination program is imposed by law, policy distortions tend to appear. There is trouble because, quite apart from wage issues, workers can hold substantially different views than capital suppliers on such matters as technological change, the work environment, plant closure, safety regulations, etc. Under mandatory codetermina-tion, where significant control rights are granted to workers re-gardless of their actual investment in firm-specific assets, la-bor is, of course, able to influence the firm's policy line. But contractual workers are not primarily concerned with the long-term interests of the firm; current employees will not normally maximize their welfare by accepting those policies that maximize the firm's net present value over a long planning interval. Since wage labor was no claim on the firm's residual (even if workers have made firm-specific investments), workers have incentive to gain at the expense of stockholders.[36] Indeed, as long as doubt exists concerning the precise property rights workers hold in the firm's residual, they are likely to use whatever power they have to appropriate as much of the residual as they can and to secure additional non-pecuniary benefits.

From this perspective, efficiency seems to demand a special property-rights structure for the firm. Labor participation can be helpful but it must be linked to a system that makes rewards for both worker-investors and conventional stockholders depend closely on the maximization of the coalition's total wealth. The business organization characterizing the joint-investment model is desirable because it solves certain basic incentive problems and conduces to cooperation among members of the coalition. If labor has undertaken large firm-specific investments, the best strategy for workers is to take actions that increase the net present value of the firm (π). The contractual wage (w_t) received by the firm's workers is dictated by market conditions alone; thus, enlargement of workers' income depends on their increasing the return on firm-specific investment ($\hat{w}_0 L_0 - \hat{v}_T L_0 (1+i)^{-T}$). But to increase such return, policies have to be followed that increase the return to conventional stockholders' invested capital ($Z_0 K_0$). Both parties tend to gain (or lose) together over the horizon T.

The hypothetical joint-investment firm is designed to allocate profits and risk bearing in a systematic way, and thus discourage opportunistic behavior. Ideally, rewards are to be proportionate to the sacrifices made by the respective groups of resource owners in the coalition. In effect, workers who opt for this form of codetermination renounce the possible gains that might otherwise come from bilateral bargaining with the firm in favor of securing a predetermined share of the firm's residual. If workers actually do have large firm-specific investments, as suggested in the literature, they should find the structure of the joint-investment firm relatively beneficial. On the other hand, if labor is closer to being the "general" input described in neoclassical theory, the joint-investment arrangements are likely to be less appealing to workers[37]; With limited investment, the attractions of a share in the residual decline correspondingly, and workers may well believe that their best chance for gain lies more with the use of political power than with freely negotiated contracts determining enterprise organization. Thus, even though it may possess some desirable efficiency properties, there can be no presumption that the joint-investment firm will be widely chosen in practice.

Footnotes:

[1] At the most basic level, it has to be decided whether codetermination is to be voluntary or imposed by law. Another key decision relates to the composition of the firm's supervisory board. Different choices can be made about what groups are to be represented on the board and how votes are to be allocated to the respective groups. Regulations can also vary with respect to the restrictions, if any, that exist concerning the types of issues open to discussion on the board. These examples, of course, merely suggest a few of the institutional dimensions that are subject to manipulation when the codetermined firm is established.

[2] For example, the results produced by a system that denies national union representatives any role in the firm's governance process will tend to be different from the results produced by a system that does allow national-union participation in governance.

[3] Alchian and Demsetz (1972), p. 783.

[4] It is generally accepted that codetermination is not intended to bring about fundamental changes in the distribution of welfare within the economy. Thus, in considering allocative efficiency (which is always defined relative to a particular distribution of welfare), the distribution of welfare that must be used in judging the effects of mandatory codetermination is the distribution that holds before the introduction of the new program. From this standpoint, it seems unlikely that mandatory codetermination will generate Pareto improvements for the system, or even allow the status quo ante to be maintained.

[5] The costs include: (a) the wages lost in the period of job search, (b) the possible loss on the sale of a residence in a declining area, (c) the costs of searching for a new home, (d) actual moving costs, (e) the worker's valuation of forced separation from his original community, (f) lost pensions (when they are not vested) plus other fringe benefits, etc.

[6] Some or all of labor's (possible) monopoly rents may also be expropriated.

[7] See: Furubotn (1985).

[8] See: Alchian (1984).

[9] This firm-specific investment can represent both human capital and physical capital (as in the case of housing).

[10] In practice, it seems likely that the firm-specific investments undertaken by workers will be built up over time. Thus, for purpose of the model, y_j could be interpreted as the present value (as of period zero) of the worker's anticipated investment in firm-specific assets to the horizon T.

[11] Alchian has defined an equity holder as a person holding the rights to the exchange values of resources that are specific to the coalition. Such resources will not be rentable.

[12] Alchian (1983), p. 12.

[13] Strictly speaking, there is a family of production functions based on the different possible patterns of internal organization within the firm. By specifying the particular internal organization (or property-rights structure) that the firm intends to use, it is possible to establish the specific production relation that is relevant to the problem.

[14] While the basic technical arrangement may be fixed once the capital stock is decided, the internal organization of the firm and the work process is still free to change. But, if internal organization changes, transaction costs and incentives can vary and affect the input-output relation.

[15] Under special circumstances, some reduction of the labor force, or some increase in it, may take place. The model developed in this section, however, does not take account of such complications.

[16] See: McCain 1980, Svejnar (1982b).

[17] If necessary, workers can transfer to other firms in other sectors of the economy as general inputs. These alternate jobs will yield workers the same wage payments $(\hat{w}_t L_0$, $t = 1, 2, \ldots,$ T).

[18] Jensen and Meckling (1979), p. 473.

[19] More realistically, the contract might establish a base rate of pay for t = 1 and, then, indicate a per period improvement factor that would apply to the wage rates of subsequent periods $(\bar{w}_2, \bar{w}_3, \ldots, \bar{w}_T)$. Given the length of the contract, some provision for its adjustment over time would, presumably, be made. That is, rules should exist for determining how wage payments can depart from the prescribed pattern if certain stipulated contingencies arise.

[20] It is quite possible, of course, that agreements about nonpecuniary benefits would be included in the basic wage contract. There is reason to believe, however, that more productive bargaining could take place if the discussion of work rules, the production environment, etc. occurred over time as difficulties and problems appeared.

[21] If the firm does not conduct negotiations itself and is bound instead by the outcome of industry-wide bargaining between an employers' association and national trade unions, the firm may find itself in a particularly difficult position. That is, an outcome satisfactry to the "average" firm may not be well adapted to local conditions.

[22] Crisis for the firm may lead to wage reductions and/or productivity concessions. But, then, demands may also be made on government. The object would be to induce the state to aid the ailing firm or industry with subsidies, low-cost loans, tariff protection, etc. Taxpayers/consumers would bear the costs and, in effect, transfer wealth to the unionized workers and to stockholders.

[23] Under special circumstances, however, the two types of firms can yield identical results for given data. What is needed, essentially, is that the contractual wage stream $(\bar{w}_t, t = 1, 2, \ldots,$ T) in the "mandatory" model be set in a particular way.

[24] Oi has pointed out that labor is, characteristically, a quasi-fixed factor of production. The firm tends to incur certain fixed employment costs in hiring a given number of workers, and these costs constitute an investment by the firm in its labor force. Obviously, such investment by the firm in hiring and training activities is quite distinct from the self-financed investments in firm-specific capital made by workers. See: Oi (1962).

[25] If firm-specific investment by labor is zero or very small, the neoclassical contractual model becomes relevant, and the case for labor participation is much less compelling.

[26] Such workers also retain control rights in the firm and continue to be represented on the firm's board of directors.

[27] Since potential buyers would anticipate the consequences of shirking and other counterproductive actions by labor on the profitability of the firm, the claims would tend to sell at a discount.

[28] Workers can, of course, sell firm-specific physical assets, such as housing, if they wish to leave the firm.

[29] Such participation in profits by labor meets the criticism that workers are not rewarded adequately for their acceptance of immobility and risk. See Mueller (1976), p. 424 who notes: "A factor owner, who does not know when he joins a firm the extent of his future immobility, may not secure a contract which allows him to share in both the above and below average revenues of the company, i.e., he is vulnerable to exploitation by the other factor owners. Marx's concept of exploitation rested, in part, on his view that the initial labor contract was asymmetric to the worker's later disadvantage."

[30] It is conceivable that labor's investment in human and other capital assets can be excessive. Then, nonlabor members of the coalition would be reluctant to give workers full credit for such investment in calculating profit shares.

[31] Apart frm creating improved incentives, the organizational structure can also serve to reduce transaction costs. See: Furubotn and Wiggins (1984).

[32] See: Steinherr (1977), Cable and FitzRoy (1980), Svejnar (1982a), Furubotn (1985)

[33] Improvements in productivity may also be achieved through the voluntary partitioning of the coalition's property rights in the firm among some or all of the general input owners.

[34] Steinherr (1977) asserts that: "There is substantial evidence that 'meaningful' participation increases workers' satisfaction per se. Maslow (1954) has developed a hierarchy of human needs which is topped by self-actualization. This requires that the individual be able to express his desires, to participate in shaping his environment and his own destiny. In an empirical study by Blauner (1964) the importance of participation in decision making for diminishing workers' alienation has been strongly confirmed. Further evidence can be found in Blau (1963), ...". See also: Lutz and Lux (1979).

[35] See: Williamson (1984), pp. 200-02.

[36] The dangers of mandatory codetermination have been described as follows: "Of course, everyone in the coalition would like to be on the Board of Directors, if they could, with impunity, divert the specialized asset value to their own welfare. For example, the campaigns for 'worker participation' or 'industrial democracy' or codetermination on boards of directors appear to be an attempt to obtain control of the wealth of stockholders' specialized assets in the coalition - a wealth confiscation scheme. But no firm with that arrangement could profitably obtain new funds for specialized assets. Furthermore, future employees would have to pay incumbent employers for the right to control the specialized assets of stockholders. Control of specialized resources by generalized resource owners is not an economically viable contractual arrangement for creating a voluntary coalition with specialized asset". Alchian (1983), p.27.

[37] A dilemma of sorts exists. If workers have made large firm-specific investments, the joint-investment firm may be seen as an attractive and generally efficient organizaitonal form. But, if the joint-investment structure is chosen, workers necessarily have much of their wealth invested in a single firm. And this means that they suffer because they cannot diversify their portfolios.

References:

Alchian, A.A.(1983),"Specificity, Specialization, and Coalition",
  Working Paper, Department of Economics, University of California - Los Angeles, 1-36.
---,(1984), "Specificity, Specialization, and Coalition ", *Zeitschrift für die gesamte Staatswissenschaft*, 140, 34-49.

Alchian,A.A. and Demsetz,H.(1972),"Production, Information Costs,
  and Economic Organization", *American Economic Review*, 62, 777-
  95.

Cable,J. and FitzRoy, F.(1980), "Productivity, Efficiency, Incentives, and Employee Participation:Some Preliminary Results for
  West Germany", *Kyklos*, 33, 100-121.

Furubotn, E. G.(1985), " Codetermination, Productivity Gains, and
  the Economics of the Firm", *Oxford Economic Papers*, 37, 22-39.

Furubotn, E.G. and Wiggins, S.N.(1984), " Plant Closings, Worker
  Reallocation Costs and Efficiency Gains to Labor Representa-
  tion on Boards of Director " , *Zeitschrift für die gesamte
  Staatswissenschaft*, 140, 176-92.

Jensen, M.C. and Meckling, W. H.(1979)," Rights and Production
  Functions:An Application to Labor-Managed Firms and Codetermination", *Journal of Business*, 52, 469-506.

Lutz,M. and Lux, K.(1979), *The Challenge of Humanistic Economics*,
  Menlo Park, California.

McCain,R.A.(1980),"A Theory of Co-Determination", *Zeitschrift für
  Nationalökonomie*, 40, 65-90.

Mueller,D. C.(1976), " Information, Mobility and Profit ",*Kyklos*,
  29, 419- 48.

Oi,W.Y. (1962),"Labor as a Quasi-Fixed Factor",Journal of Political Economy, 70, 538-55.

Steinherr, A. (1977), "On the Efficiency of Profit Sharing and
  Labor Participation in Management", *Bell Journal of Economics*,
  8, 545-55.

Svejnar,J.(1982a), " Codetermination and Productivity: Empirical
  Evidence from the Federal Republic of Germany";in Jones,D. and
  Svejnar,J. eds.,(1982), *Participatory and Self-Managed Firms*,
  Lexington, Massachusetts.
--- ,(1982b)," On the Theory of a Participatory Firm", *Journal of
  Economic Theory*, 27, 313-30.

Williamson, O.E.(1984),"The Economics of Governance:Framework and
  Implications", *Zeitschrift für die gesamte Staatswissenschaft*,
  140, 195-223.

A GENERAL MODEL OF CODETERMINATION:
Comment

by

Hans G. Monissen, Ekkehard Wenger

1. Introduction

The different legal forms of codetermination or job rights imply specific assignments of decision rights or controlling influence for the workers. There are first individual codetermination
rights for those in the lower ranks of the hierarchy with respect
to the content and the implementation of their labor contract.
But more important are collective decision rights that are exercised by elected workers' representatives. These rights take the
form of representation either in the traditional organs of the
business firm or in separate worker bodies "codetermining" with
management (Monissen 1978). These collective decision rights are
the essence of what is typically referred to as labor's codetermination in the decision-making process of the capitalistic
business firm, a containment also followed up by Furubotn.

Whether this form of codetermination will be justified on efficiency grounds depends, as Furubotn conceives it, on the labor
contract and the competitive structure of the labor market specifying the opportunity costs for the workers already hired. If labor markets were perfectly competitive and complete, workers
would be unaffected by the decisions of management. Consequently,
collective codetermination rights would not be substantiated in
this economic environment. But in reality workers, once hired,
are confronted with imperfections and therefore submitted to adverse (or opportunistic) ex post decisions of the executive authorities because, as Furubotn assumes, they start their careers
undertaking firm-specific human capital investments that they
prefinance. Such investments entail sunk cost elements which once
recognized in the ex ante contracting process, create so-called
quasi-rents. Their existence causes a divergence between labor's
value in use and its market exchange value which specifies its
opportunity costs. According to Furubotn, quasi-rents constitute
"legitimate interest" of the employees that are to be protected
by integrating workers' representatives into the firm's board of
directors.

Codetermination
ed. by H.G. Nutzinger and J. Backhaus
© Springer-Verlag Berlin Heidelberg 1989

The only proper instrument to prevent an unjustified devaluation or destruction of employees' investment in specific human capital is to guarantee and secure a sufficiently high degree of employment stability over the investment cycle. Furubotn claims that the "joint-investment" model he presents will cope with this problem in an optimal way. The property rights structure will develop "in an environment void of special governmental constraints on structure" and, "ultimately, efficiency is served by institutional arrangements that evolve freely in response to competitive force".

It is our conviction that the necessary institutional input for the existence and survival of the "joint-investment" model cannot be provided by either competitive market forces or a benevolent dictator, because the environmental description is inconsistent with a dynamic capitalistic market environment, where firms wax and wane and their financial structure reflects imperfections, risk, and uncertainty. Nevertheless, Furubotn deals with an important economic problem; namely, how quasi-rents can be protected by specific contractual arrangements and how the efficient creation and use of specific human capital in a competitive capitalistic environment can be ensured without governmentally imposed restrictions. In our paper, we develop a completely different interpretation of and an alternative solution to the problem posed by Furubotn. Both economic theory and market-derived institutional arrangements lend strong support to our concept as a relevant alternative. The protection of specific human capital is thereby related to the notion of an "exploitation-free" wage path that is not imposed by law but that may evolve under extended freedom of contract.

2.The Coase Theorem as a Useful Starting Point

According to the Coase Theorem (Coase 1960; Monissen 1976, 1983), it is not evident that specific human capital has to be protected by collective codetermination rights. If the theorem applies, then the creation, efficient use, and destruction of human capital are independent of collective codetermination rights. In addition, the optimal time schedule and the number of dismissals are completely separated from the issue of which contracting party prepaid the investment outlays. Under a Coasian perspective, codetermination rights have no ex post allocative consequences but only affect the distribution of remaining rents if the business venture should prove unprofitable. If workers' representatives have the right to block dismissals under a guaranteed labor contract, efficient adjustment of the number of employees will be combined with severance payments.

Thus, in a Coasian world, the ex post effects of codetermination rights are concentrated entirely on the distribution of rents without distorting the efficient use of human and nonhuman productive resources per se. The ex ante or, more exactly, precontractual environment may only involve allocative effects if there is a change in the allocation of risk among the contracting parties, as would be the case with positive transactions costs. This environment invalidates the application of the theorem.

Because it seems economically desirable to release workers from the employment risk associated with individual wage contracts vis-à-vis the stockholders, who are in a much *better position* to diversify risk, it appears that codetermination rights increase allocative efficiency. Economic theory, however, reminds us that the prevailing wage rate will be lower than that existing under the alternative arrangement without collective codetermination rights. This comparison by itself, however, is biased, because there is no economic basis for Furubotn's argument that the only efficient way to allocate risk is by establishing collective rights instead of relying on individual contracts that restrict the employer's right to dismiss if no severance payment is guaranteed.

Only if such restrictions are insufficient to induce Pareto-efficient contracting are there special reasons for analyzing problems related to the distribution of decision-making rights. The content and extent of codetermination rights are thereby conceptually determined by a dynamic process based on both ex ante contracted restrictions and decision rights that will be operative in the implementation phase. In a Coasian world decision rights are redundant because the actions of the members in a productive coalition will be fully specified, including contingent specification in an uncertain environment. With the conclusion of the employment contract the actions of its parties are limited to execution of the optimal labor contract.

Since in a Coasian world there is no need for post-contractual decision rights, we may conclude that a prerequisite for effectively dealing with codetermination issues is to analyze how the underlying assumptions have to be modified and what empirical conclusions can be derived when we proceed to a non-Coasian environment.

3. Decision Rights, Contractual Restrictions, and Codetermination Rights

In general, labor contracts are characterized by the fact that at the time they are drawn not all contingencies (and thereby the optimal actions of the coalition members) can be anticipated. What constitutes the implementation in concrete instances will be determined by decisions taken according to the decision rights agreed upon initially. This later implementation necessarily carries distributive risks or even the danger of open distributional struggle but has been accepted as a flexible tool for coping with unanticipated changes in environmental conditions.

The traditional labor contract is characterized by the - reciprocal right of short-term cancellation and the clear-cut authority of the employer. The employer's authority would be neutralized if the signing of labor contracts did not presuppose sunk costs and therefore require a longer pay-off period. Otherwise, labor services would be contracted in infinitesimal quantities on spot markets involving no transactions costs or need for the employer's discretionary authority. Thus, Coase's "nature of the firm" (1937) would remain unsubstantiated. But because sunk costs arise at the beginning of the employment contract and usually during the initial contract period as well, it is mutually advantageous for both contracting parties to continue employment during an implicitly stated minimum length of time. Nevertheless, the parties insist on the right of short-term termination and forgo the stipulation of a minimum contract period, a provision that reflects the difficulties of anticipating conditions under which a future continuation of the labor contract would be disadvantageous for either party. Free negotiation in the absence of transactions costs implies that the employment contract will be terminated only if both parties explicitly consent. unilateral termination will not occur as long as the other party is prepared to make sufficient concessions to avert realizing less advantageous alternatives outside the firm. Under these circumstances all decisions to terminate employment will be Pareto-efficient and will never occur against the will of the dismissed party.

Only if renegotiation of the contract is characterized by high information and transactions costs or legally imposed restraints efficiency aspects relating to the initial distribution of the rights to terminate the employment relation become significant. In all instances, the contractual right to terminate employment will have distributive consequences, because a unilateral right delimits the set of distributions under which the continuation of the employment relation is to be reconsidered.

If spot markets for fully specified, infinitesimal quantities of labor services existed, the set of relevant distributional alternatives would either contain only a single element or would be empty, which means that either a contract with a determinate distribution would be drawn or one of the parties would not enter into a contractual agreement. If markets are imperfect, the majority of existing employment relations leave room for redistributive activities, because under normal conditions both contracting parties are better off than they would be with pre- or post-contractual alternatives. Workers' decision rights and other rights affecting the employment relation are no longer void of importance, because they determine the distributional position of the workers. That by itself is not a sufficient justification for granting collective codetermination rights to counterbalance the employer's authority. The unilateral right to terminate the contract suggests that the employee is always able to secure at least the distributional position offered by the next best alternative. Without sunk costs, workers would have sufficient incentives to engage in team production yielding cooperative rents, even though there would certainly be no guarantee preventing the extreme case in which all rents are appropriated by the stockholders. With sunk costs to be borne by the workers, however, a mutually advantageous labor contract has to offer a wage differential over the next best post-contractual employment alternative. This quasi-rent is the financial source for the amortization of their proportionate sunk cost components. Here, the right to terminate the contract is inadequate protection for the employee, and therefore the contractual arrangement should prevent the employer from exercising his bargaining power to appropriate the employee's surplus over the next best alternative by extorting wage concessions or by excessive use of discretionary power. under unrestricted entrepreneurial power to redistribute cooperative rents at the expense of incumbent employees, the latter could not be induced to take over sunk costs. Consequently, rents

from team production that might be created under a superior contractual arrangement must be foregone.

Under the traditional labor contract, workers' quasi-rents are
partly protected by restricting the employer's discretionary authority with respect to content and powers of decision. More important, the contracted wage level is agreed upon for a minimum
contract duration with the further implicit or explicit stipulation that the wages are fixed from below and general wage reductions are only permissible if the firm faces "extraordinarily"
poor business conditions. Though the employer's right to terminate the contract remains unaffected, it proves an ineffective
means on redistribution as long as wage reductions are ruled out.
But precisely because wage cuts must be made conditional upon
credible signs of the employer's financial difficulties, it may
happen that with high transactions and information costs Pareto-
optimality will be suspended: wage reductions will now be made
dependent on dismissals which, in retrospect, occur against the
will of the employees. The inefficient destruction or the inefficient use of specific human capital could become an inevitable
consequence (Hart 1983, pp. 3ff).

The terms of the traditional labor contract, therefore, do not
exclude the possibility that under certain, not necessarily unlikely, circumstances the quasi-rents of employees will be annihilated by the inefficient allocation of specific human capital
following ex post involuntary dismissals. This may occur in particular when the quasi-rents of the employer become negative as a
consequence of unfavorable market conditions, and the workers are
still receiving positive rents under the initial provisions of
the contract. Then one might expect that wage concessions could
be negotiated to stabilize employment, provided reliable information is available about both the total amount and the distribution of rents. Without this informational proviso, the employees
are reluctant to accept wage cuts because these might be too
large or unjustified.

The danger of annihilating quasi-rents is not restricted to
extraordinarily poor business conditions. Given entrepreneurial
authority, management might consider labor-saving investment projects (so-called rationalization investments). Apologists of industrial democracy are generally critical of such projects because the investment calculus, they argue, only yields a positive
net present value by ignoring the existence of incumbent workers'
rents.[1] These investments are labeled "socially undesirable," and

pressures arise in favor of legal restrictions. Codetermination
is allegedly the appropriate social and economic instrument to
block this type of investment. The true diagnosis, of course, is
that specific human capital will be less productive under the
changed market conditions: it is not the profit greed of capitalists but the false scarcity prices under the existing legal environment which leads to an inefficient destruction of human capital. The capitalistic investment calculus places the correct economic values on all scarce resources, but contractual restrictions prevent an adjustment to market clearing prices. The real
economic problem is only to exclude "unjustified" wage reductions
by ex post opportunistic behavior under the classical labor contract.

To protect workers' quasi-rents from appropriation, one might
consider a solution à la Furubotn. An alternative would allow for
severance payments binding the employer more directly to the legitimate interests of the employees without affecting his decision-making rights. Moreover, the employer could be obliged to
inform employees about major changes in business policy to allow
for early adjustment and due consideration of their interests. An
issue of particular importance is the removal of informational
barriers that may lead to dismissals even when employees are
willing to concede sufficiently large wage reductions (Furubotn
and Wiggins 1984).

Both the existing literature on codetermination and the process of legislation in countries that have enacted codetermination laws are characterized by the close linkage of rights to intervene, obligations to severance payments, and informational duties.[2] The importance of these provisions for the protection of
workers' rights calls for careful analysis, the basic elements of
which can only be outlined.

4. Quasi-Rents and Codetermination
4.1. Codetermination and Corporate Planning

Participation of workers' representatives in the planning and
decision-making process is advocated because a capitalistic management does not pay heed to the quasi-rents of the workers. The
popular argument is that labor-saving investment projects yield
seemingly efficient results because the net present value "does
not include" the discounted stream of quasi-rents annihilated by

dismissals of employees. Price theory reveals that "capital orientation" of management is at most a necessary condition. Additional conditions have to prevail preventing a correct social evaluation of these investments based on changed scarcity values of embodied specific human capital. In the event of these additional conditions, it is correct to argue that a capitalistic management will indeed "disregard" the prior formation of specific human capital. A major problem in determining the magnitude and distribution of employees' quasi-rents lies in the high costs of continuously assessing employment alternatives outside the firm. Even more important is the interest of employees to understate the surplus over the next best alternative before the notice of a pending dismissal. Obviously, if employees were to continuously reveal their true estimates to the employer, labor's distributive share would be endangered. There is, however, a willingness to reveal if a labor-saving investment is up for decision, but the resulting flow of information will generally be too late if the decision has already required a longer gestation period. Costly pre-commitments prevent a reconsideration of the investment decision even if the adjusted wage rate is now part of a revised calculus.

In general, contractual imperfections and information costs impede the adequate protection and conservation of quasi-rents and the proper assessment of the private and social values of specific human capital. Apparent efficiency considerations once more suggest employees' representation in the decision-making process of the firm, provided that workers' representatives have exactly the information at their disposal which a capitalistic management is not allowed to have because its misuse could adversely affect labor's share in the total distribution. But the proposal only works if it is possible to bind the representatives effectively to the interests of their clientele. Moreover, capitalists have strong incentives to redirect the decision-making authority of labor's representatives by granting pecuniary or nonpecuniary allotments at the cost of the represented employees. Even disregarding this opportunistic behavior, labor's influence in the planning process does not generally lead to economically desirable results. By "protecting" the quasi-rents of the employees in one specific firm, the quasi-rents in related firms are completely ignored. The correct social evaluation of all costs and benefits will only come about under profit maximization using the proper scarcity values for specific human capital. If the lump sum costs of specific human capital are generally protected by blocking labor-saving investments, it is in the first instance to the disadvantage of the related investment industry if the latter is characterized by a high degree of specific human and nonhuman capital. As specificity seems likely in investment industries, the protection of quasi-rents in customer firms would prevent the creation of quasi-rents in this industry. The argument in favor of protecting quasi-rents by collective codetermination rights automatically raises a dilemma: should all quasi-rents be protected by granting decision rights or can an economically justified criterion be presented in order to discriminate against quasi-rents of minor social importance which do not substantiate decision rights?

Protecting all quasi-rents over and above scarcity values by decision rights will finally endanger an economic system based on decentralized decision making. Within a net of interrelated economic activities the result would be tantamount to the paradoxical situation where everyone decides on everything. The social costs of such an arrangement are certainly higher than the annihilation of quasi-rents by labor-saving investment projects.

Let us now take up the criterion problem of how to evaluate quasi-rents according to their social importance. Even if the "narrow" economic efficiency calculus of optimal allocation is ignored and income shares are emphasized, collective codetermination rights to protect particular rents seem at variance with distributive justice. If we relied, for example, on the popular criterion of ranking the degree of direct material disadvantage, we should draw attention to the fact that the annihilation of firm-specific human capital with the ensuing income losses is very often less important than the general economic consequences of a fall in local real estate values or the collapse or decline of smaller local business firms. Perhaps when a major factory shuts-down, the terms of agreement should be negotiated not with workers' representatives but with authorities of the county or community affected. Efficiency considerations, however, are not fully reflected in such arrangements because optimal contracting and allocation require negotiation of the terms of these contingencies before a major firm settles down. Consequently, it is economically desirable not to rely on codetermination rights but to enforce competition among municipal or communal authorities in order to achieve an optimal spatial distribution of firms.

The workers' right to block labor-saving investments in order to preserve specific rents is questionable for another reason: it also distorts the allocative efficiency of newly founded firms. The protective measures only restrict entrepreneurial decision-making authority within the organization. Where market competition prevails, everybody has the right to appropriate or annihilate rents or to affect relative prices by marketing new products or introducing new means of production. In general, the legal systems in the Western world have very wisely refrained from protecting the market value of positions endangered by the intruding competitor; the Western world has resisted instituting a general property rule (Buchanan and Faith 1982).

It is difficult to understand why the entrepreneur should do without these innovative rights, especially if the renunciation is of questionable usefulness for the workers. It is very likely, for example, that the company would lose its staff of technical and managerial experts who develop and introduce technical innovations with the consequence of lower profitability even to the risk of going bankrupt. The bankruptcy risk would be further increased by high debt-equity ratios, which are advantageous to financiers if workers' claims on protected quasi-rents can be invalidated by relying on secured debt instead of equity capital. Hence, protective effects of rights to block labor-saving technological change depend heavily on "me-first-rule" favoring workers in cases of bankruptcy and on restraint of competition clauses to which the firm's technological experts may be submitted.

Needless to say, the protection of workers' interests will not be perfect either regarding the ever-present restriction by the value of marketable assets in the event of bankruptcy. Despite this restriction and even without the institutional provisions considered above, there remains at least some protective effect of codetermination rights. It is not costless, however, to drive a firm into bankruptcy by transferring human capital and debt-financed assets into a newly founded company; consequently, old companies with proaected employees will frequently survive.

Whatever the degree of protection by codetermination rights, the anticipation of their future consequences is reflected by market conditions and the wage rate of newly hired employees. The more effectively quasi-rents are protected, the lower will be the initial market-determined starting wage rate. As regards the life cycle of a representative worker, codetermination rights result in a steadier wage path because lower wages in the initial employment period will reduce the probability of wage cuts at a later stage of the employment cycle.

The steadier wage path may not necessarily be undesirable, but other consequences of codetermination rights are extremely detrimental. There is no reason to expect that codetermination rights will only be exercised to maintain the status quo. It is indeed very likely that any potential increase in the market value of the company dependent on decisions subject to codetermination will be, in part at least, appropriated by the workers. The ultimate consequence will be that any change in business policy not initially anticipated has to be paid for by sufficiently large concessions to the workers. This cost will be reflected in a further reduction of initial wages, which will, of course, grow over time with seniority as long as market conditions prove favorable. Any wage level once attained will be protected unless the firm goes bankrupt, and hence the overall probability of wage cuts is reduced in comparison with a system without protective rights. But human capital risk calculated over the potential employment cycle of a representative worker will certainly increase. The worker who happens to decide for a company experiencing unanticipated favorable results will enjoy steadily increasing wage levels. In contrast, a worker starting his employment career with a firm that goes bankrupt after some time will lose a substantial part of the expected value of his life-time income. Thus, the eventual lowering of the "risk" of wage reductions in consequence of protective codetermination rights has to be traded off for a sizable increase in the risk of human capital during a worker's life-cycle. The intensified exposure to firm-specific (unsystematic) risk brought about by collective codetermination rights is certainly not in the interest of a representative worker.

The pressure to take unsystematic risks will be increased by the fact that the continual forcing of concessions from the company owners creates contract-specific risks that reduce the incentives for stockholders to finance firm-specific investments. Because their quasi-rents are permanently endangered by exploitation, the only protective device is to charge labor with the burden of financing specific investments in order to strengthen their bargaining position. The workers' loss risk has to be sufficiently large to prevent blackmailing blockades intended to extract rent from the stockholders. To sum up, the notion of a complete or partial safeguard of a wage level once attained is only compatible with extremely low initial wages and blocked mobility both temporally and intertemporally over the life-cycle.

Admittedly, ex ante contracted sharing rules may reduce the increased distributive risk brought about by codetermination rights. The Furubotn proposal institutes a proportionate claim to the residual profits which will be added to the market wage rate as determined by alternative uses in competitive markets. This residual claim is proportionally related to the amount of investment in specific human capital. Certainly, the proposal brings about a high degree of common interest and reduces the latent incentives for reciprocal exploitation. Furubotn himself, however, indicates that his proposal is burdened with several difficulties that render his sharing rule a rather doubtful instrument for mitigating distributive conflicts.

The problem of the time horizon underlying the profit streams, differences in individual risk preferences, and heterogeneous expectations - as well as measurement problems related to the investment components of the workers - are sufficiently strong impediments to prevent implementation of his proposal. In addition, it is nearly impossible to determine labor's opportunity costs because generally there is no spot market where scarcity values can be observed over time. As an alternative, labor's opportunity costs could be based on pre-contractual forecasting; but under such an arrangement unanticipated developments command revision of the contracted sharing rule, and conflict mitigation is counteracted. Moreover, a profit sharing rule does not eliminate conflicts resulting from the workers' preference for an improved work environment. Because workers are the sole beneficiaries but bear the costs only in proportion to their profit claims, codetermination rights as regards the quality of the workplace are a source of permanent distributional conflict.

A crucial yet unresolved point in the Furubotn proposal is how to treat newly engaged workers. His model brushes this question aside by starting an allocation ab ovo. If a new worker shares in the distribution of the already created residual claims, efficiency requires that his entrance to the firm be connected with an admission fee. Otherwise, it is reasonable to expect that the incumbent workers will change the maximization calculus by redirecting interest to the maximization of rents per capita. As a result, the capitalistic environment would be transformed to a social arrangement illustrated by the workings of the Yugoslavia firm to which Furubotn explained. If admission fees are arranged, however, companies not quoted on the stock exchange face a serious problem: the value of the whole business firm must be reassessed whenever a new worker with firm-specific capital is hired. It may be that stock exchange quotation obviates this assessment. But the problem remains that a potentially qualified worker will only be available if his risk preference and expectations of the future course of the business venture do not significantly deviate from the corresponding parameters of the incumbent workers. This is implicitly assumed in the Furubotn model. The advocated sharing rule is therefore a problematic proposal. On the one hand, the distributive risks cannot be sufficiently reduced by instituting collective codetermination rights and, on the other hand, the opportunities to enter into new labor contracts are severely restrained.

4.2. Workers' Codetermination Rights and Severance Payments

The preceding considerations suggest that to safeguard workers' quasi-rents by instituting collective codetermination rights is an extremely hazardous venture. Generally, a business firm restricted by such provisions would be at a grave disadvantage when operating in a competitive environment with free labor contracting. If collective rights are imposed by law, the inevitable consequences are, among others, risk avoiding business policies, bureaucratic investment decisions and implementations, payment depending on seniority, proportionate increases in quasi-rents, extreme immobility of labor, and reduced adaptability to changing market conditions. It remains an open question whether the West German legislators, who were pioneers in mandatory codetermination in the Western world, were aware of these inherent difficulties. One might speculate that only their conservative attitude toward radical socioeconomic experiments prevented them from granting workers' representatives any direct influence in corporate planning. According to German law, codetermination on the corporate level is limited to the supervisory board (Aufsichtsrat),[3] which enjoys no executive power [4] even though it appoints the members of the executive board (Vorstand). Appointments to the executive board, however, can be made against the unanimous vote of labor's representatives on the supervisory board, providing there is unanimity among stockholders' representatives. Thereby, workers' codetermination on the corporate level can be overridden.[5] There remains, of course, workers' codetermination on the plant level, although the ensuing rights are mainly defensive.[6] Legislators' intention to grant workers influence on plant-level decisions notwithstanding, the rights of the works council are largely limited to the initiation of a complicated legal procedure, by which mangement can be forced to compensate those workers who are adversely affected by certain plant-level changes which are specified by law (Betriebsänderungen).[7] In practice, therefore, codetermination mainly materializes in negotiations over indemnification payments. The laws governing these procedures may reflect a hope that due consideration will be given to the consequences that arise for employees from the closing of plants or from the dissolution or restructuring of corporations under bankruptcy proceedings (Gessner and Plett 1982, p. 127). In economic language, we may interpret these protections as pressure on employers to incorporate the quasi-rents of incumbent employees into the investment calculus.

In general, however, the efficiency of employment decisions will not be improved by correct anticipation of severance payments; particularly if we consider firms in shrinking industries, where decisions are not related to conditions of further profitable employment but to the optimal timing of dismissals. Contractual impediments to the lowering of wages will result in dismissals prior to the economically efficient point in time. The employer will initiate employment adjustments if steadily decreasing revenues will reduce his own quasi-rents to zero. But protected wages still yield positive surplus values. Thus, informational and institutional impediments cause inefficient early dismissals, because temporarily postponed dismissals would still create cooperation rents for all the parties involved.

Should the employer be faced with the usual severance pay obligations, dismissals will not be delayed, as would be desirable, but brought forward. Indemnities acknowledged by the courts usually depend on the monthly pay and the time served in the company. If the increase of potential severance payments over time exceeds the interest costs, the increased payment obligation will lead to earlier dismissals. As severance payments are frequently calculated on the basis of half a month's pay for each year's service [8] and the monthly pay itself is raised by several percent each year as a result of collective bargaining agreements, the time of dismissal is very likely to be advanced.

Consequently, if prohibitive transactions costs exclude ex post agreements on wage reductions, the usual severance pay scheme is Pareto-inferior to a dismissal policy based on unrestricted employer's power to hire and fire. Improved efficiency can only be achieved for workers close to retirement, so that dismissal can be postponed until the age limit is reached and a severance payment becomes unnecessary. This holds true not only for workers in dying branches but also for those who are dismissed as a result of labor-saving technological changes. The parties are, of course, quite at liberty to negotiate an ex post agreement to reduce wages. But why should severance pay obligations remove or even lower the barriers to such an agreement?

Some explanation of the link between codetermination and severance pay obligations is warranted. One might hope that workers' ex post employment alternatives could be more effectively allowed for in codetermined indemnification schemes than with ex ante restrictions written into labor contracts. This hope echoes the argument so often encountered in recent literature that codetermination would improve the flow of information between employer and employee, thus facilitating wage reductions to prevent an inefficient allocation of specific human capital (Furubotn and Wiggins 1984).

The practice of codetermination in West Germany offers no grounds for such expectations. As a result of plant level-codetermination, schematic severance obligation patterns have emerged which disregard individual cases. Indemnification to be paid is determined by formulae in which the most important variables are the worker's current wage, length of service, and age (Vogt 1981, pp. 150-167). This schematic treatment induces even members of the legal profession to complain that no consideration is given to differences in income between the current and next best employment (Beuthien 1982, pp. 184-185; Grub 1983, pp. 873-875). There are two possible explanations for the observed phenomenon. On the one hand, gathering information that is vital for Pareto-efficient dismissal and severance strategies may be so costly that, even with codetermination rights, it is not worth the effort. On the other hand, codetermination rights are exercised by elected representatives who have little interest in following Pareto-efficient strategies (Downs 1957).

Neither economic theory nor empirical evidence seems to indicate, therefore, that the severance pay obligations emerging from codetermination rights are a suitable instrument for preserving quasi-rents. A Pareto-efficient postponement of dismissals would be possible if severance payments were to be lowered over the employment time. Obviously, this would be consistent with Furubotn's model in which newly hired employees finance firm-specific human capital. In practice, exactly the opposite can be observed.

The increase of severance payments with age can be explained in large part by the fact that, due to institutional barriers against lowering wages, the quasi-rents of aging workers tend to rise as their performance falls, and it is this group of workers that experience particularly high wage losses through dismissals. Until it proves possible to divert the attention of the public from these visible losses to a comparison of workers' life-cycle income streams (see next section of this paper), severance obligations will distort dismissal decisions in such a way that quasi-rents are annihilated rather than preserved. It remains an open question whether this undesired effect has to be weighed against risk considerations relevant at the time the contract is drawn. By means of severance obligations part of the human capital risk could be shifted to the employer, which may be desirable from the standpoint of efficient risk diversification. However, if we indeed observe a reduction of the employees' risk, this leads to a conclusion diametrically opposed to the linkage between codetermination and severance pay obligations as intended by current legislation.

The employer is only prepared to bear a proportionate increase in risk if codetermination rights are denied to those employees protected by claims to severance pay. Otherwise, protected workers may exercise their rights by adopting expropriation strategies should he wish to adjust his business policies. Under such prospects, employers will react by reducing starting wages, thereby reversing the intended shift in investment risk. The reduction in starting wages implies that employees would prefinance their own severance payments, even though they might in fact never receive such a payment. The human capital risk may materialize not in a dismissal but in an inability to extort higher wages from a stable employment relation.

4.3. Codetermination, Information Rights, and Wage Setting

As noted, advocates of codetermination, by granting decision rights to the workers, expect a better flow of information that would prevent the inefficient use of human capital and the endangerment of rents (Furubotn and Wiggins 1984; Schneider 1983). Early consultation with workers' representatives, they argue, allows careful long-term planning of employment adjustments by disclosing efficient employment alternatives both within and outside the enterprise. Employees should be given the time and the opportunity to weigh outside prospects against continued employment at a lower wage compatible with the company's ability to pay. Reducing information costs may also help to overcome workers' distrust of the financial statements submitted by management as evidence of the company's performance. A supplementary suggestion would be to link wages to the company's financial results. Such an agreement is proposed by Furubotn for that part of the remuneration which could be earmarked as amortization of prefinanced investment in specific human capital. The quasi-rents of employees and stockholders would then be more closely correlated than would a regime with fixed wages. The high cost of renegotiations in order to avoid the breakdown of mutually advantageous employment relations could be reduced.

First, it should be emphasized that the contended close relationship between codetermination rights and the provision of information on the company's financial results is superficial and misleading. It would suffice if workers' representatives were granted access to files and the right to attend relevant meetings and to raise issues. Second, an improved flow of information by itself is insufficient if wages are to depend upon the company's financial success. Obviously, such an arrangement cannot suspend the question of how business profits are calculated if they are to be incorporated into wage formulae. For companies quoted on the stock exchange, this question might be evaded if workers could receive a certain number of shares in addition to a modest fixed wage. Share values are, however, dependent not only on the company's performance, but also on its dividend payments. Accordingly, complicated rules would be needed to prevent any undue influence of dividend policy. Even though such problems could be solved in principle, the solutions would exceed the intellectual power of the typical worker involved. The fact, however, remains that unsystematic risk will be imposed on the workers if the arrangement does not allow them to sell their shares. That adverse effect alone is important enough to question sharing rules as an improvement relative to the alternative regime with higher fixed wages and increased risk of dismissal. For the typical employee who is forced to bear unsystematic investment risks, whether such risks materialize through reductions in income due to dismissal or through a fall in the value of his company's shares is immaterial.

The concept of "share-wage" raises an additional problem because the price of a share, especially in a highly diversified company, often bears no relation to the value of the human capital the worker would realize upon leaving the company. As a result labor's mobility incentives associated with income risk are adversely affected. This undesired effect can only be eliminated if the variable element in a worker's remuneration can be geared to his economic performance in a department or even at the individual workplace. A precondition for such a form of wage-setting would, however, be to eliminate any discretionary assessment in the cost accounting system. Elementary economic reasoning illustrates the absurdity of this suggestion and renders a closer examination superfluous.

In the absence of a reliable measure of economic performance, an efficient distribution of rents between workers and stockholders presupposes that contractual agreements can be renegotiated. In such an environment an improved flow of information bears considerable distributive risk. The employee's unrestricted access to available information clears the way for expropriation strategies at the expense of stockholders. Hence, the latter must insist upon shifting a substantial part of the investment risk onto the employees.

The ever-present distributional conflicts within the business firm can be mitigated by removing wage negotiations from the individual firm onto a branch level, as in the Federal Republic of Germany. It would, however, be presumptuous to believe that this will completely eliminate intra-firm wage conflicts. Not even the explicit declaration of firm wages above contractual wages is excluded by industry-wide collective bargaining in West Germany.[9] Moreover, an abundance of pecuniary and non-pecuniary devices are used to improve the distributional position of the worker without open declaration of compensations exceeding the union level. These range from promotion to a higher wage bracket to a more leisurely work-pace and reductions in working time to company sports facilities.

Linking codetermination to informational requirements could conceivably be of mutual advantage if it were restricted to extremely unfavorable business conditions, that is, when direct expropriation of rents is suspended and the common interest is to facilitate wage reductions in order to stabilize employment. The available empirical evidence for West Germany bearing on this issue is inconclusive. Relevant episodes pertain to large companies on the brink of bankruptcy, where wage reductions amount to cosmetic concessions signalling only mutual concern (Wenger 1984, pp. 211-212). This evidence, however, may be biased since employees had reason to expect that government would intervene to subsidize the further payment of wages or to finance a generous severance arrangement. Experience in the United States indicates that wage reductions intended to ward off bankruptcy often coincide with workers' representation on the board of directors (Furubotn and Wiggins 1984). There are instances where union contracts have been renegotiated, even before expire, in exchange for labor's influence in corporate planning; but, as the case of the U.S. airlines illustrates, it does not appear that these firms thereby gain a superior position for coping with competitive market pressures. Eastern Airlines, the largest carrier with workers' representatives on the board of directors, recently accepted a friendly takeover bid by a well-known union buster.

It is also doubtful whether information rights related to codetermination, which materialize in the timely involvement of employees in the process of personnel planning, improve the overall efficiency of dismissals. It cannot be denied that in a situation where dismissals are unavoidable, it is a great help for those concerned if they are informed in advance.[10] Frequently, however, workers' performance under pending dismissals is difficult to police. If the prospect of not being dismissed is the main incentive for satisfactory long-term performance, a worker served notice will reduce his efforts.[11] Prenotification merely of the number of workers to be dismissed will lead to inefficient rivalry among workers competing for continued employment. This effect could be policed to a certain extent by reducing the wages of those potentially retained in order to finance the severance pay made to those dismissed. Uncertainty concerning the persons who are to be dismissed, however, will induce a costly search for potential jobs outside the firm even by those who eventually re-

tain their current employment. Whether these costs are offset by
the benefit of the more informed choices made by those eventually
dismissed must remain open. The inclination of codetermination
bodies for schematic solutions that has already emerged in the
instance of severance pay certainly reinforces the already existing tendency toward allocative inefficiency.

5. Quasi-Rents and Collective Action

Collective action by unions or elected codetermination bodies
creates and reinforces just those conditions under which an individual employee needs collective protection. If the labor market
could be organized as a spot market, unions and codetermination
would be superfluous. The same would hold if the worker could be
relieved of any investment risk. The latter may be achieved by
instituting an "exploitation-free" wage path, which can be maintained in alternative uses because it does not render the next
employer's retraining investment unprofitable (Wenger 1986). Under the reasonable assumption that the present value of the
worker's future stream of marginal value products is reduced by
leaving an employment relationship with an "unfair" employer, the
exploitation-free wage path differs radically from the actual
practice of long-term labor contracting. After exceeding the instantaneous marginal value product in an initial stage of the employment relationship, it drops below the instantaneous marginal
value product during later years. If such a wage path could be
realized, at least approximately, the worker's quasi-rents would
be negligible, and the sunk costs of labor-financed investment in
human capital would be insignificant. Consequently, the risk of
labor income related to the worker's life-cycle would be considerably reduced and the need for protection would be met by the
worker's option to leave his job. Specialized investment would be
financed almost completely by stockholders, who are in a favorable position to diversify the risks associated with specialized
investment. Hence employees' quasi-rents could be ignored in management decision making and the widespread but dubious claim to
include workers' interest in corporate goals would lose both purpose and justification.

The solution suggested, however, cannot be achieved or even
approached in an environment dominated by organized labor's collective action. If stockholders bear the whole risk of special-

ized investment, they are able to commit themselves credibly to a strategy of not accepting the demands of individual employees for higher wages unless another employer offers higher remuneration. As specialized workers in general do not gain from job-hopping and isolated shifts are not a major problem for a firm, the quasi-rents of stockholders are relatively well protected against the expropriation efforts of individual employees. But organized workers with a right to strike are a credible threat for the appropriability of returns on specialized investments financed by stockholders. For organized workers, a strike threat is nearly riskless if no labor-financed capital is at stake; stockholders, however, bear an all-out loss of their investment in specific human capital and additional losses resulting from temporarily unused nonhuman capital if collective bargaining does not lead to a resumption of work. Given the assumed financing arrangements, the bargaining position of stockholders is so weak that they are unable to protect their quasi-rents. The by now familiar consequence will be that they have to insist upon workers bearing a wellbalanced share of sunk costs of specialized capital (Alchian 1984, pp. 13-15). To the individual employee, the necessity of earning quasi-rents in order to recover his share in sunk costs creates a need for protection by unions and/or codetermination bodies. Unions, for evident reasons, systematically engage in intensifying protective needs by enlarging the worker's share of investment and extending its pay-off-period. Interest symbiosis between labor's representatives and "job-owner" explains why bargaining on behalf of workers with high seniority is of utmost importance on the strategic agenda of unions and codetermination bodies whether workers' interests are organized on the plant, company, or industry level.

Empirical studies in the United States, where collective bargaining usually takes place at the plant or firm level, show significant correlations between unionization and seniority rights and fringe benefits (Blau and Kahn 1983; Freeman 1981); fringe benefits typically depend on years of seniority or even on the worker's remaining with the firm until retirement. Recently, there has been a growing tendency toward two-tier wage contracts providing for large wage differentials between newly hired and senior workers with the same jobs.[12] Collective bargaining in Germany, usually organized on an industry level, likewise redistributes rents in favor of older workers. Protection against the consequences of technological change and even explicitly guaranteed wages for less productive workers with high seniority are afforded by numerous union contracts.[13] These tendencies seem to be enforced by codetermination rules. The obligation to compensate workers adversely affected by certain changes at plant-level, which is now imposed on all firms with more than 20 workers by the plant constitution law, follows the lines of widespread voluntary agreements between firms and unions in the German mining and steel industries,[14] where the boards of corporations were subject to particularly far-reaching codetermination rules (Monissen 1978, pp. 68-69).

Quasi-rents of employees with high seniority are consequently very large precisely because workers organize themselves collectively. In general, therefore, voluntary exit is associated with substantial financial losses. Thus, the individual is heavily exposed to and needs protection against the exercise of power. As a consequence, many undesired effects are to be expected. Reduced exit options increase the susceptibility of the organization to corruption. Workers' representatives will try to profit from their rights to influence the distribution of quasi-rents among workers, management, and stockholders. The frequency of legal action increases, and stockholders are ready to invest large amounts in the relevant decision makers.[15] Moreover, the monitoring of management becomes more and more complicated. The higher the workers' quasi-rents, the stronger the argument in favor of relieving managers of their function as stockholders' agents and converting them into mediators between capital and labor or even advocates of the commonwealth.[16] How far managers are meeting such a demand can hardly be monitored because such monitoring presupposes not only the availability of financial information but also knowledge of many far less accessible efficiency indicators. Incumbent managers, therefore, can expect reduced monitoring, if they are promoted to advocates of the commonwealth. This provides a reasonable explanation as to why numerous directors of large German business firms are very open minded with respect to the abandonment of the capitalistic enterprise (Reuter 1981).

If all these undesired effects were to be weighed against the prospect of collective protection of quasi-rents significantly reducing the workers' risk-exposure, would the lowering of risk be worth the price? The protection of quasi-rents, however, fails if the employer goes bankrupt; moreover, with increasing pressure on the wages of newly hired workers and higher participation in the firm's financial success, the worker's risk of losing his quasi-rent through an unfair wage reduction is transformed into the risk of his wages increasing too slowly or not at all. Collectively organized protection of quasi-rents would do little against this kind of risk, even if the unions were to negotiate agreements securing future growth of wages; the limited liability of corporations would render such contracts void. Of course liability rules are open to change, too. The abolition of limited liability, however, would certainly not improve the position of workers, but would drastically reduce wages and the private demand for labor.

The reduction of workers' income risk by collectively organized protection of quasi-rents essentially amounts to reducing the size and probability of wage cuts and improving severance pay if dismissals are allowed. This view, however, rests on a misleading concept of "risk." A better way is to define risk in terms of life-cycle, that is in terms of the total value of labor income. This risk which is increased by the collectively organized protection of quasi-rents undermines the prospect of better risk allocation, because workers have to finance more and more specialized, risky investments in human capital. Consequently, the workers' position would be improved not by conceiving workable codetermination arrangements but by just the opposite. Instead of implementing an institutional device that aggravates imperfections in the labor market and therefore intensifies workers' need for protection, one should investigate how the undisputed imperfections of today's labor markets can be reduced. Such an investigation could start from the concept of an "exploitation-free" labor contract, characterized by workers' opportunity to change employment without reducing the present value of their future labor income. Because of decreasing retraining abilities, such a labor contract implies a wage path above the instantaneous marginal value product during the initial stage of the working life and the reverse relation during the subsequent and final stages. Consequently, the employer has to prefinance a much larger part of specialized capital than today. His willingness to do so, however, presupposes that workers can be prevented from appropriating the return on such investments. As to firm-specific investments, it is sufficient to exclude workers' right to a collectively organized strike by contractual arrangements. This will enable stockholders to protect their quasi-rents, whereas the guideline for the firm's wage-policy is to pay just enough to dissuade profitable workers from using their exit option.

Industry-specific investments in human capital need not be financed by stockholders, if workers are to be protected only by the exit option; such investments do not lose their value if the worker chooses another job within the same industry. Industry-specific investment, however, though not linked to an individual firm, is exposed to non-systematic risk. Hence it may also be desirable to shift the financing and risk to stockholders. Their willingness to take such risks depends on measures to prevent uncompensated job changes within the same industry.

If both firm- and industry-specific human capital is financed by the employer, an individual worker essentially bears the risk of a devaluation of his general earning abilities but is relatively well protected against the risks of division of labor. The result is a considerably reduced risk in terms of lifetime income. Running counter to conventional thinking, this reduction in risk is brought about by transforming the "risk" of declining labor income into a sure prospect.

In comparison with a codetermination arrangement, the labor market reform outlined above seems to be so superior that inevitably one wonders which deficiencies have been overlooked. We offer a preliminary conjecture rather than an answer: possible deficiencies do not outweigh the advantages. If that is true, why doesn't the labor market produce the suggested solution by itself? The strong tendency of workers to organize indicates that the ideal presented is incompatible with the interests of the parties involved. That, however, is true only from the viewpoint of an already employed "job owner." An economic perspective is different. Though it has to be conceded that a "job-owner" will not renounce his right to unionize and strike if his employer is already exposed to that right, the economist's question is whether a worker who is not yet employed will be willing to sell his rights to organize and strike in exchange for a higher initial wage.

A similar problem is to prevent workers from going over to competing firms after the employer has financed industry-specific human capital. After the employer's investment the worker will not renounce his right to leave or to enforce a higher wage by threatening to leave; before the investment, however, he may be willing to accept a restraint of competition clause.

If one again takes up the question of why labor markets do not produce the suggested reform by themselves, two reasons are obvious. Both are related to restrictions of the freedom of contract imposed by law. Workers cannot sell their right to organize and strike at the time they are hired.[17] A promise not to organize and strike is void, because it cannot be enforced in court. The same holds with respect to clauses restraining competition. In many cases, they are invalidated by judicial decision. If they are to be acknowledged, the employer usually has to pay compensation, which in Germany amounts to one half of the last salary for the time to which the clause applies.[18] Consequently, an employer willing to invest in industry-specific human capital cannot rely on restraint of competition clauses. In theory, he could instead secure a claim to be refunded by the employee if the latter leaves the firm too early after employer-financed training; in practice, the amounts to be refunded and the periods of commitment acknowledged by German courts are so small that a rational employer is restricted to financing minor investments in workers unless the investment is firm-specific or his employees are locked in by high quasi-rents.

Obviously, the workability of the suggested reorganization of the labor market can be easily tested by observing the consequences of suspending imposed institutional and legal restrictions. Whether codetermination will survive in a world of extended freedom of labor contracts is doubtful because the current status of codetermination is mainly the result of far-reaching government intervention. Isolated experiments with voluntary codetermination, as spectacular as they may seem to the public, are weak evidence for Furubotn's conjecture that codetermination rules materialize as elements of efficient organization structures.

Footnotes:

The authors acknowledge helpful comments by Louis De Alessi.

[1] This line of reasoning is familiar from early German socialist ideas (e.g., Bauer 1931, p. 863 et passim).

[2] In Germany this is evident from §§ 111-113 of the Plant Constitution Act. The same issues have been raised in the campaign for plant-closing laws in the United States (cf. Millspaugh 1982, pp. 297-303).

[3] An exception applies to corporations submitted to § 13 of the Montan Codetermination Act, where a labor director (Arbeitsdirektor), as an employee representative becomes a member of the executive board. Montan-type codetermination, however, is rapidly dying out (cf. Spieker 1981 pp. 86-87). Within a decade there may no longer be any independent corporation to which the Montan Act applies.

[4] This is explicitly stipulated in § 111 Abs. 4 of the Corporation Law (Aktiengesetz). The by-laws of a corporation, however, may require the consent of the supervisory board in specific instances. More than one-third of the corporations regulated by the Codetermination Act of 1973, however, have no consent requirements. In the remaining firms, consent requirements are severely restricted in order to keep workers out of corporate planning (Steinmann and Gerum 1980). Pending legislation of the European Community is expected to change the situation. According to Act 12 I of the revised draft of the 5th EC-Guideline, a minimum list of consent requirements will be mandatory.

[5] There remains a problem with management incentives related to internal promotion to the executive board, because the spirit of the codetermination law is based on mutual understanding, not on conflict of interests. This works in favor of candidates "acceptable" to workers' representatives on the supervisory board.

[6] As to the distinction between offensive and defensive codetermination, cf. Wenger 1984, pp. 208-214.

[7] Cf. §§ 111-113 of the Plant Constitution Act (Betriebsverfassungsgesetz). Recently, however, the courts have tended to acknowledge the right of the works council to interfere with entrepreneurial decisions through injunction. The hazardous consequences of such extended codetermination rights are not yet fully recognized by economists, as they have so far only been discussed within the law profession (Eich 1983).

[8] This is common practice accepted by German courts (Vogt 1981, p. 117). In many European states similar rules are effective (Gessner and Plett 1982, sp. 125). In the United States a law requiring one week's pay for each year of service is operative in Maine (Maine Severance Pay Law, Tit. 26, § 625-A, pp. 83-85).

[9] According to the annual report of 1983, BMW pays 14% more than stipulated by the industry-wide wage contract.

[10] Note that such prenotification requirements have been a major issue in the campaign for plant closing laws in the United States (Millspaugh 1982, pp. 297 and 300-301).

[11] This may be illustrated by the fact that management consultants assume that, as a rule of thumb, the value of an employee is reduced by 10-20 percent when he is served notice (Streim 1982, p. 139).

[12] This is especially true for the airlines. Major carriers such as American Airlines have wage differentials of 20-50 per cent.

[13] For a comprehensive survey of union contrasts cf. Weise 1983.

[14] It has to be noted that compensation schemes in these industries did not always emerge from voluntary agreements: severance payments were frequently subsidized by the government (Görg 1979, pp. 11-19).

[15] The relevant practices are mostly illegal and therefore kept secret, but sometimes emerge in the courts. Recently, a court invalidated an election of the members of a workers' council, because a large automobile manufacturer had financed and otherwise supported the election campaign of "friendly" candidates (Cf. Wenger 1986). A good example of the high costs involved in the decision process is the requirement of mandatory arbitration in codetermination affairs. Here, judges of labor courts are appointed as chairmen of arbitration commissions. The resulting discretionary power forces employers to tolerate high arbitration fees. For a day's work as chairman of an arbitration commission a judge frequently receives more than his monthly earnings as a civil servant (Schlochauer, 1983).

[16] The related paternalistic attitude on the basis of a collectivist-functional interpretation of the workings of society is codified in the so-called Davoser Manifest of leading European managers (European Management Forum 1973).

[17] In Germany, the right to organize and strike follows directly from the Constitution (Art. 9 Abs. 3 Grundgesetz) and cannot be disposed of by individual contracts. In the United States, it is an unfair labor practice under Section 8 (a)3 of the National Labor Relations Act to discourage membership in any labor organization by discrimination in regard to hire or any condition of employment. Many countries have enacted similar restrictions on freedom of contract. It is interesting to note that the expansion of organized labor in the United States is significantly related to the prohibition of the "yellow dog contract," that is, a contract not to organize. The first major wave of unionization took place during the last decade of the nineteenth century when newly enacted State laws prohibited the yellow dog contract. At the end of the decade, these laws were held unconstitutional. The growth in union membership was considerably reduced or even reversed after 1904, when employers took the offensive against unions. During World War I, a National War Labor Board had to settle labor-management differences and recommended that the right to organize should not be denied or abridged by employers. Union membership grew rapidly through 1920 and then fell back sharply until 1933. The enactment of the National Industrial Recovery Act in June 1933 was the beginning of the most extensive organization drive in the history of the American Labor Movement. According to the law, no one seeking employment was to be compelled to refrain from joining a labor union. In the following twelve years, union

membership rose from 2.9 to 14.8 million (Taft 1964, pp. 162, 164, 212-229, 317, 319, 414, 417-419; Reynolds 1978, p. 339).

[18] The maximum time is two years and many other restrictions must be observed as laid down in §§ 74-82a of the commercial law code (Handelsgesetzbuch).

References:

Alchian, A. A. (1984),"Comments on Furubotn's Rights to Jobs."
    Paper presented at the Liberty Fund Conference on Government
    Regulation of Entrepreneurial Decisions, Washington D.C.,May.
--- ,and Demsetz, H. (1972),"Production, Information Costs, and
    Economic Organization",*American Economic Review*,62,777-795.

Bauer, O.(1931),*Kapitalismus und Sozialismus nach dem Weltkrieg*.
    Bd. 1 Rationalisierung - Fehlrationalisierung, Berlin.

Blau, F.D, and Kahn, L.M. (1983), "Unionism, Seniority, and Turn-
    over." *Industrial Relations* 22,362-373.

Beuthien, V. (1982), " Der Sozialauftrag des Sozialplans - Ar-
    beitsplatzabfindung und arbeitsvertragliche Risikoverteilung,"
    Zeitschrift für Arbeitsrecht,13(2),181- 205.

Buchanan, J.M.,and Faith, R.L. (1981), " Entrepreneurship and the
    Internalization of Externalities", *Journal of Law and Economics*
    24,95-111.

Coase, R. (1937),"The Nature of the Firm",*Economica*,4,386-405.
--- ,(1960), " The Problem of Social Cost. " *Journal of Law and
    Economics*, 3,1- 44.

Downs, A. (1957), *An Economic Theory of Democracy*, New York.

Eich, R.A.(1983),"Einstweilige Verfügung auf Unterlassung der Be-
    triebsänderung", *Der Betrieb*, 36(12),657-662.

European Management Forum, ed.,(1973), *Third European Management
    Symposium, Summary of Plenary Sessions, A Final Report*, Davos.

Freeman, R.B. (1981),"The Effect of Unionism on Fringe Benefits."
    Industrial and Labor Relations Review, 34,489- 509.

Furubotn, E.G. "A General Model of Codetermination." This volume.
--- ,and Wiggins, S.N.(1984)," Plant Closing, Worker Reallocation
    Costs and Efficiency Gains to Labor Representation on Boards
    of Directors",*Zeitschrift für die gesamte Staatswissenschaft*,
    140,176-192.

Gessner, V., and Plett, K.(1982), *Der Sozialplan im Konkursunter-
    nehmen:Die Praxis eines autonomen Regelungsmodells im Schnitt-
    punkt von Arbeits- und Konkursrecht*, Köln: Bundesanzeiger.

Görg, A. (1979), *Entschädigung bei unverschuldetem Verlust des
    Arbeitssplatzes*, Königstein.

Grub,V. (1983),"SozialplanwillkÜr? Thesen aus der Sicht des Prak-
    tikers", *Zeitschrift fur Insolvenzpraxis*, 4(7),873-875.

Hart,O.D.(1983),"Optimal Labour Contracts under Asymmetric Infor-
    mation: An Introduction",*Review of Economic Studies*, 504(1),3-
    35.

Millspaugh, P.E. (1982), "The Campaign for Plant Closing Laws in
    the United States :An Assessment", *The Corporation Law Review*,
    5,291-307.

Monissen, H.G. (1976), "Haftungsregeln und Allokation: Einige einfache analytische Zusammenhänge", *Jahrbuch für Sozialwissenschaft*, 27(3),391-412.

---,(1978),"The Current Status of Labor Participation in the Management of Business Firms in Germany", in: *The Codetermination Movement in the West*, ed. S. Pejovich, pp.57-84. Lexington.

---,(1983),"Externalitäten und Wirtschaftspolitik: Anmerkungen zu einigen Neuinterpretationen",*In Aktuelle Wege der Wirtschaftspolitik*, ed. A. Woll, Schriften des Vereins für Socialpolitik, Neue Folge, 130, Berlin, 51-78

Reuter, E.(1981), " Wir verschenken kostbarste Zeit." Manager *Magazin*, 11(10),88-91.

Reynolds, L.G.(1978), *Labor Economics and Labor Relations*. Englewood Cliffs.

Schlochauer, U.(1983)," Die betriebliche Einigungsstelle: Ein zunehmendes Ärgernis", in: *Das Betriebsverfassungsgesetz auf dem Prüfstand*, eds. B.Ruthers and W. Hacker, Stuttgart, 99-103

Schneider,H.(1983),"Mitbestimmung, unvollständige Information und Leistungsanreize:Überlegungen zu einer funktionsfähigen Unternehmensverfassung", *Schweizerische Zeitschrift für Volkswirtschaft und Statistik*,119,337-354.

Spieker, W.(1981), " Montan-Mitbestimmung in den 80er Jahren - Sicherung oder Tod auf Raten ? ", *Das Mitbestimmungsgespräch*, 27(3),79-87.

Steinmann, H. and Gerum,E.(1980),"Unternehmenspolitik in der mitbestimmten Unternehmung", *Das Mitbestimmungsgespräch*,26(2),40-48.

Streim, H.(1982),"Fluktuationskosten und ihre Ermittlung." *Zeitschrift für betriebswirtschaftliche Forschung*,34,128-146.

Taft, P.(1964),*Organized Labor in American History*, New York.

Vogt, A.(1981), *Sozialpläne in der betrieblichen Praxis*, 2d. ed. Köln, 1964.

Weise,P. (1983), " Zur arbeitsmarktpolitischen Problematik von Kündigungs- und Besitzstandsregelungen für ältere Arbeitnehmer",*Zeitschrift für Wirtschafts- und Sozialwissenschaften*, 103,255-281.

Wenger, E.(1984),"Die Verteilung von Entscheidungskompetenzen im Rahmen von Arbeitsverträgen",in:*Ansprüche, Eigentums- und Verfügungsrechte*, ed. M. Neumann, Schriften des Vereins für Socialpolitik, Neue Folge, 140, Berlin, 199-217

---,(1986),"Unternehmensverfassung und Arbeitsmarkt: Die Berücksichtigung von Arbeitnehmerinteressen im Entscheidungsprozeß der Unternehmung", in: *Zur Interdependez von Unternehmens- und Wirtschaftsordnung*, eds. H.Leipold and A. Schüller, Stuttgart.

CODETERMINATION, COLLECTIVE BARGAINING, COMMITMENT, AND SEQUENTIAL GAMES
by
Roger A. McCain[*]

I

When we attempt to evaluate the efficiency of institutions, or to evaluate them from other or more inclusive normative view-points, it is at least helpful to compare the institutions we are evaluating with specific alternative institutions which are real possibilities. It may even be essential that we do this[1] if the comparison is to be meaningful. For economics is not physics. In physics, the efficiency of a heat engine may be, and is, rated by comparison with the ideal of perfect efficiency. Although the ideal of perfect efficiency is unattainable, this procedure is meaningful because efficiency has a quantitative measure. Thus, the substantive meaning of the efficiency rating of a heat engine is a comparison with all other real, rated heat engines: i.e., a comparison of real alternatives. Now, it may be that no such cardinal measure of efficiency is possible in economics. If it is not, then only direct comparison of possible alternatives[2] can supply us with substantive evaluations of efficiency or other normative evaluations of economic institutions. We should recall, however, that cost-benefit analysis aspires to a cardinal measure of efficiency. To the extent that cost-benefit analysis is an actuality, assessments of efficiency relative to an unattainable ideal may have substantive meaning. Even if cost-benefit were altogether successful in attaining this goal, however - which is at best a debatable position - direct comparisons would still be of particular interest in supplying a clear indication of how efficiency might be improved through policy reforms or other innovations.

This principle has often been ignored in discussions of codetermination, especially those associated with the Transaction Cost or Texas[3] School of thought. In these papers, participative firms are unfavorably compared with an unattainable ideal construct sometimes called "untrammeled capitalism." (Furubotn) The "untrammeled capitalist" firm is one in which workers have no say on any managerial decision whatever, so that those decisions are taken strictly on the basis of owner-manager interests. Such firms are so organized as to elicit either the maximal or the

Codetermination
ed. by H.G. Nutzinger and J. Backhaus
© Springer-Verlag Berlin Heidelberg 1989

optimal[4] effort level and yield productivity at least as high, given effort, as any other forms of organization. That is, the untrammeled capitalist firm is an ideal of hierarchical control[5] over labor.

The untrammeled capitalist firm is an unattainable "ideal" for two reasons. First, it is politically impossible in an industrial democracy. That is, the "costs of transaction" for employees to create organizations by means of which they can exert bargaining power over some management decisions, or to create political organizations which accomplish the same ends through regulation and taxation, are less than the benefits that the employees derive from so doing (compare Olson). When these "costs of transaction" are taken into account, "untrammeled capitalist" firms are seen to be unrealizable in an industrial democracy.[6] The actual, practical alternatives in an industrial democracy are different degrees and kinds of worker participation in management. To take the ends of the spectrum, they are collective bargaining and codetermination.

This paper discusses some aspects of the comparative efficiency of collective bargaining and codetermination. The overall argument is that codetermination is efficient in certain ways whereas collective bargaining is not - indeed, that a certain pathology which has been attributed to codetermination, namely the foreshortening of the investor's horizon, is actually present under collective bargaining but absent under codetermination.

To put the argument in the broadest possible terms, I contend that the issue between codetermination and collective bargaining is the issue between cooperative and noncooperative games. Noncooperative games may be defined as games which do not admit of committed agreements for coordinated strategies among the participants; cooperative games do admit of such committed agreements. When committed agreements are in fact possible, rational agents cannot fail to make them, and the agreements cannot fail to be Pareto-optimal if the agents are rational. The institutional and commitment structure of the capitalist firm make action within its framework unavoidably a noncooperative game. (In the case of collective bargaining, it is more specifically a suboptimization game, McCain 1980, 1983a, 1983b). Codetermination is a reform designed to remedy this precise problem, transforming the firm into a cooperative game. To the extent that the reform actually does this, it cannot generate outcomes which are not Pareto-optimal as between the parties to the game, provided that those parties are rational.

Section II will sketch a two-by-two game which seems to capture the essence of the argument. Section III gives somewhat less simple models of collective bargaining and codetermination with the usual apparatus of economic theory - differentiable production functions and utility functions, etc., - augmented by adding some assumptions about bargaining theory and about the commitment structure of the game. Returning to the two-by-two game, the implications of sequential repeated play are considered, in Section IV, in the light of some recent discussions in game theory. Finally, in Section V, I address the question: "if the existence of 'prerogatives of management' is inefficient, why are there any prerogatives of management?" Section VI summarizes and concludes.

II

What are the crucial differences between codetermination and collective bargaining? Both are variants of labor participation in management - differing in degree and kind. Observers of codetermination say that in the codetermined firm, decisions are taken by "Kuhhandel" - cow trading (the idiom in America is horse trading, of course), that is, bargaining. Thus, both are forms of bargaining. There are, however, two crucial differences. First, under collective bargaining, certain decisions are "prerogatives of management," in which the union may not have any say at all. Financial decisions are among these. Under codetermination, since labor representatives it along with owner representatives in the making of management decisions per se (though only at the highest level) the prerogatives of management are not excluded from the influence of the labor representatives. Among important prerogatives of management, excluded from labor influence under collective bargaining but open to labor influence under codetermination, are financial decisions. Second, under collective bargaining, if negotiations break down, a strike is quite likely to occur. Under codetermination, if negotiations (over a change in policy) break down, then business continues as it was before. This difference implies a difference in the "threat point" (Coddington) of bargaining theory and hence in the bargaining outcome.

The two differences together imply a crucial difference in the commitment structure of the interaction between labor and management which produces the firm's allocative decisions. Under codetermination, the management decides how much to invest without any negotiation with the labor representatives, but not independently of them. Investment is a commitment. When they decide how much to invest, the management must (if they are rational) anticipate the effect of the commitment on future wage negotiations. It is clear that there must be some such effects, since the investment by management changes labor's "threat point" for those negotiations. By investing, management offers up to the labor union a more valuable hostage in any future strike. Under codetermination, by contrast, there is no such sequence of commitments. Investment and wage payouts are decided simultaneously, so that management interests in financial decisions can be traded off against labor interests in wages, or conversely.[7] These trade offs take place before any commitment is made - so there is no possibility of exploitation of prior commitment. Investment then offers no hostages for a future strike.

I have argued before that commitment structure is crucial to an understanding of codetermination (McCain 1980). One might suppose that, since labor interests enter into the financial decisions in the case of codetermination, those decisions would be distorted from efficiency, whereas in the case of collective bargaining, they would not be. (Pejovich and Furubotn argue that the decisions would be distorted in the case of codetermination, but do not consider collective bargaining as an alternative). But this prima facie conjecture is diametrically wrong, and it is wrong because it ignores the implications of commitment structure.

When a decision is made by bargaining, we must use bargaining theory to anticipate the result. Unfortunately, bargaining theory remains somewhat controversial. One assumption which is common to most bargaining theories, however - and to all such theories which treat bargaining as a cooperative game - is that the outcome of bargaining must be Pareto-optimal among the participants, subject to the constraints which apply at the time of the decision (including constraints created by prior commitment). If we accept this assumption, then codetermination cannot, in itself, imply any distortion of financial decisions. Suppose, for example, that the tentative agreement between the labor and management representatives provides for investment at a level reflective of a "foreshortened horizon." That is, the marginal revenue product of capital is above its marginal private cost to the firm. Then the management would be able to bribe the labor force to accept a higher level of investment, by offering them a wage increment which would only be some part of the discounted present value of the difference between the marginal revenue product and marginal cost of capital. The owners of the firm would then be net gainers, and so would the workers. Now, what would prevent the negotiators from making such a deal? A theorist who claims that codetermination would lead to foreshortened horizons surely must explain why the deal does not take place. No explanation has been offered. In any case, one cannot appeal to "transactions costs" to explain it, since transactions costs are sunk costs by the time that the negotiators have arrived at a tentative contract.

By contrast, when certain decisions (such as financial decisions) are made prerogatives of management or of labor, trade-offs such as this are excluded. The fact that financial decisions are prerogatives of management is itself the explanation why no such trade is made. We are then left with the question "why are these decisions prerogatives of management," which is to say, "why do we not have codetermination already, except in Germany, and why does its existence require legal enforcement there?" This issue is deferred for now.

The importance of commitment structure for this problem, and the difference between the codetermined firm and the firm under collective bargaining may be illustrated by the following simple "game" in which each of the two parties has just two strategies. The game is, in addition, a two-stage game. Payoffs are in "transferable utility." At the first stage, the "employe" chooses either to invest or not to invest. The amount either invested or not invested is I and, if investment takes place, the investment yields W , the alternative wage of the work force employed, plus B + I. If the firm does not invest, then it can place its capital at the social rate of return, (1+r), and the workers who would otherwise be employed on the project are employed in their second-best opportunities at W. Thus, if investment takes place, the net payoff is B+W, while if investment does not take place the total payout is (1+r) I-I+W = I+W. Clearly it is socially optimal to invest if

(1) $B > rI$

The employees' strategies are to threaten a strike or not to threaten a strike. They have an opportunity to make this choice only if investment takes place, so that they are in fact hired. If they do threaten a strike, they have bargaining power enough to obtain a proportion of B as a supplement to their wages. That is, if they threaten the strike, their wage payout is W+aB, where 0 < a < 1 and a is the proportion of the net return to capital which the employees obtain through bargaining. Consequently, the employers' net payoff in this case is (1-a)B. If the employees do not threaten to strike, they get only their alternative wage W. It will always be in their interest to threaten the strike, if they have the opportunity to do it.

This game is shown in Figure 1 in tree form. Clearly if the employers invest, they must expect that their actual net payoff will not be B, but (1-a)B. Accordingly, they invest if

$$(2) \qquad B > \frac{r\ I}{1-a}$$

Comparison with (1) will demonstrate that this decision rule is inefficient, and moreover the inefficiency takes a recognizable form: the rate of discount is raised. This is precisely the pathology which some scholars attribute to codetermination, but here we find it attributed to the alternative to codetermination, collective bargaining.

But what about codetermination? Codetermination will make the game a cooperative one, i.e. will admit of commitments to trade off investment against wage concessions. The solution to a cooperative game (if the parties are rational) will be on the utility-possibility frontier for the two parties. This is shown in Figure 2. The utility-possibility frontier is the outer envelope of the conditional utility-possibility frontiers for the case of investment and no investment. Figure 2, which shows the case in which investment is efficient, demonstrates that in such a case the conditional utility-possibility frontier for non-investment is interior to that for investment, so that the conditional utility-possibility frontier for investment is the unconditional utility-possibility frontier. The bargainers cannot rationally fail to come to an agreement on it.

To illustrate the point further, consider the particular case of the Nash bargaining solution. That bargaining theory asserts that the outcome of bargaining will be such as to maximize the product of the utility gains of the bargainers, net of their impasse payoffs (Coddington). We suppose that the employer and the employee are bargaining over the reduction in a, that is, the share of B which the employees seize. This reduction in a is offered in return for the employers' assurance that they will indeed invest. Accordingly,

(3) $\max aB ((1-a) B-rI)$

The first-order conditions in a is

(4) $a = \frac{1}{2} (1 - r \frac{I}{B})$

so that

(5) $(1-a) B = \frac{1}{2} (B+rI)$

which is greater than rI whenever B > rI. Thus, with this incentive, the employer will always invest when it is efficient to do so, and never otherwise.

III

In this section I outline a model of investment and subsequent wage bargaining along lines of the simple game discussed in section II, but which makes allowance for continuous variation of the size of the investment and for substitution of capital and labor, both of which are conspicuous by their absence in the simple game. The central construction for this purpose is, of course, the production function. Thus we begin with

(1) $Q = f(K,N)$

Where is output, K is capital, N is labor, and the interpretation of the production function, f, is as usual.

The first stage of the analysis is to solve the second stage of the game, i.e., wage bargaining, and the determination of the labor force, with given capital.[8] Assume that v is the income of a worker who is on strike. It may be (in the absence of costs of transaction in labor markets, but see Okun, McCain 1983) that v is the opportunity cost of labor. Alternatively, v may be the dole. In any case v is what workers get during the strike, if employer-employee bargaining breaks down. Suppose that a strike, if it occurs, shuts the firm down for a given fraction of the period, z, with $0 < z < 1$.[9] If bargaining breaks down, then employees are on strike for z of the period and work for a wage of w for 1-z of the period. (Discounting to present values is ignored within the period). Thus, in the case of a bargaining impasse, the workers' utility for the period will be

$$(2) \qquad V_0 = zU(v) + (1-z) U(w)$$

If the strike is avoided, on the other hand, the employees' utility is

$$(3) \qquad V_1 = U(w)$$

Hence

$$(4) \qquad V_1 - V_0 = z (U(w)-U(v))$$

Since the employers must commit themselves to capital investment before the wage bargaining takes place, they cannot recoup the cost of capital by shutting down the plant. However, workers are not paid (by the employer) when they are on strike. Thus, in the case of a strike, the employers' net revenue is

$$(5) \qquad R_0 = (1-z) (pQ-wN) - rK$$

where p is the price of output and r the cost of capital. If the strike is avoided, then the employers' net revenue is

$$(6) \qquad R_1 = pQ-wN-rK$$

Thus,

$$(7) \qquad R_1 - R_0 = z(pQ-wN)$$

The key point here is that, because investment is precommitted, the total cost of capital does not vary according to whether bargaining breaks down or not, while the total outlay for labor does.

I adopt the Pen-Svejnar (P-S) bargaining theory, which allows for unexplained differences in bargaining power and which nests the Zeuthen-Nash-Harsanyi (ZNH) bargaining theory as the special case of equal unexplained bargaining power. While we would ultimately aim to explain bargaining power on the basis of other variables, the P-S bargaining theory allows us to make relative bargaining power an exogenous variable. This will prove analytically convenient. The P-S bargaining theory implies that the bargaining decision will be made so as to

$$(8) \qquad \max \; (V_1 - V_0)^a \; (R_1 - R_0)^b$$

where a and b are given nonnegative constants and a+b=1.[10] Maximization with respect to w and N yields the following necessary conditions, after some manipulation:

$$(9a) \qquad \frac{a(pQ - wN)}{N} = \frac{b(\; U(w) - U(v))}{U_w}$$

$$(9b) \qquad pf_N = w$$

where subscripts indicate derivatives in the usual way. Note that the length of the strike, z, does not appear in these equations, for it appears on both sides of each equation and thus cancels out. (In ordinary language terms, this simple model is such that an increase in the strike length has the same proportionate effect on the impasse payoffs of the parties, and since the outcome of bargaining depends on the proportionate loss due to an impasse, but not the absolute loss, the length of the strike does not affect the bargaining outcome). It will be helpful to rewrite (9a) as

$$(10) \qquad p - wN = \frac{b \; N \; (U(w) - U(v))}{U_w} = Nh(w)$$

Now, (9a) or (10) is an expression for the equilibrial distribution of quasi-rents between the firm and the employees (while (9b) is familiar as an expression for the optimal work force.) In the form of (10) it bears a resemblance to the "fair rate of return" regulatory norm (e.g. Averch and Johnson).

The second stage of the analysis is to determine the profit-maximizing quantum of investment, subject to the employers' rational anticipation of the outcomes of wage bargaining ex post. One way to do this is to maximize profits in the ordinary way, save for imposing (9a) [or (10)] and (9b) as additional constraints.[11] It is appropriate to report this problem in some detail. The Lagrangean function is

(11) $L = pQ - wN - rK + y_1 (f(K,N)-Q) + y_2 (Nh(w)-pQ+wN)$
         $+ y_3 (pf_N-w)$

where y_1, y_2 and y_3 are Lagrange multipliers.[12]
The first-order necessary conditions then are

(12a) $L_Q = p - y_2 - y_2p = 0$

(12b) $L_N = -w + y_1f_N + y_2 (h(w) +w) + y_3 pf_{NN} = 0$

(12c) $L_K = -r + y_1f_K + y_3pf_{KN} = 0$

(12d) $L_w = -N + y_2 (Nh_w + N) - y_3 = 0$

Manipulation of these results yields the following marginal productivity equation for capital

(13a) $pf_N = \dfrac{r}{1-y_2} + \dfrac{y_3}{1-y_2} pf_{KN}$

Now, this clearly differs from the familiar (and efficient) marginal productivity condition

(13b) $pf_K = r$

Thus the level of investment will not be efficient. It is, however, somewhat difficult to say whether investment will be greater or less than optimum. There are forces operating in both directions. On the one hand, a larger capital stock increases the quasi-rent and so drives the bargained wage upward. On the other hand, substitution of capital for labor reduces the number of workers to whom the bargained wage must be paid. We note that

$$(14) \quad 1-y_2 \; = \; \frac{h(w) \; + \; Nh_w pf_{NN}}{h(w) \; + \; Nh_w pf_{NN} \; + \; Npf_{NN}}$$

which is between zero and one. If, then,

$$(15) \quad f_{KN} = 0$$

i.e., if substitution of capital for labor is excluded, we have

$$(16) \quad pf_K \; = \; \frac{r}{1-y_2} \; > \; r$$

i.e. the rate of discount is raised relative to the market rate. This is in accordance with the simple game example of the last section and with the diagnosis that the horizon of investment is shortened.

Accordingly, in (13a), we may identify the divisor on the right hand side with the forces tending to restrict investment, and the term in the cross-partial derivative with the forces tending to increase investment. The direction of the deviation from optimality thus depends (nonlinearly) on the relative magnitudes of these two forces.

The contrasting model of codetermination is much the simpler. The decision to invest, hire, and on the wage are made simultaneously and all are subject to bargaining. If bargaining breaks down, it breaks down before any commitment to invest has been made. Accordingly, the impasse payoff to the employer is simply zero.[13] Thus the maximand for the bargaining problem is

$$(19) \quad \max \; (pQ-wN-rK)^a \; (U(w)-U(v))^b$$

and there are no constraints other than the production function. Note that a and b may take different values than before, since codetermination is likely to alter the distribution of "unexplained" bargaining power. Similarly, v may take a different value since it cannot be clearly identified with strike income.

The necessary conditions for this maximum, after a bit of manipulation, are

(20a) $\quad pf_N = w$

(20b) $\quad pf_K = r$

(20c) $\quad \dfrac{a\,(pQ-wN-rK)}{N} = \dfrac{b\,(U(w)-U(v))}{U_w}$

    The first two of these are familiar and their optimality properties are well known. The last resembles conditions derived in McCain 1980 and bears the same interpretation.

    This should come as no surprise. Expressions (19) and (20) express the view, previously stated explicitly, that allocative outcomes under codetermination can be described by the theory of cooperative games. Such outcomes must be efficient as between the parties to the game. The role of the P-S bargaining theory in this context is simply to dictate the form of the social welfare function used to choose among the infinitely many Pareto-optima available to a firm which has some potential profits or rents. (Carson) Any other Pareto-type social welfare function would have the same implications. By contrast, the non-optimality of the model of collective bargaining stems from the noncooperative nature of the game interactions in that model, and in particular, from its commitment structure - from the fact that employers must commit themselves to a level of investment and capital before the wage is settled.

IV

    We now return to the simple two-by-two game of section II to entertain some second thoughts. The game as described there is a one-off game; that is, it is played once without any explicit reference to repeated play in the future. In fact, the management and the work force of a company must "live together" through many years and perhaps through many meetings of the codetermined board. This prospect of repeated transactions over the future can make a difference, as everyone knows who has bought some sort of a souvenir at a resort boutique and then found the same item for half the price in a local shop near home.[14] Studies of the Prisoners' Dilemma, for example, suggest that when the game is played repeatedly, its incentive structure is quite different than it would be if the game were played one-off (Aumann). In this section I review some of the recent discussion of the implications of repeated play and explore its implications for codetermination and collective bargaining.

Repeated play is an important complication in the theory of noncooperative games. Much of the early discussion was centered around the Prisoners' Dilemma. In a game like the Prisoners' Dilemma, the outcome is Pareto-non-optimal, so that the participants could benefit by negotiating an agreement to adopt strategies which neither of them would adopt independently of the other. Such an agreement would require commitment to those strategies, however: each participant can benefit by cheating, whether the other participant cheats or not. In the one-off Prisoners' Dilemma game, however, no such commitments are possible - this, of course, is the defining characteristic of a non-cooperative game. However, if the game is played repeatedly, by the same two players, then enforcement of commitments may become possible (Aumann). In effect, each party says to the other: "if you cheat by adopting a noncooperative strategy on the coming round, then I will punish you by adopting a noncooperative strategy on the following and/or other subsequent rounds" (Hofstadter). It seems that this is at least a possible remedy for the problem of a lack of commitment which makes the game noncooperative, and thus that repeated play might have the effect of converting a noncooperative to a cooperative game.

This would be applied to the collective bargaining game as follows. The management and the workers might arrive at an agreement (probably tacit) that the management would undertake efficient investments and the employees would so practice restraint in their bargaining that the employers would find the investment profitable, along the lines of the cooperative-game model of codetermination in Section II. This commitment would be enforced by the threat that, should the employees "cheat" and exploit their bargaining power fully at any round of play, the employers would retaliate in the following period by not investing in that period, and perhaps in subsequent periods. Thus, the noncooperative game of collective bargaining would be transformed into a cooperative game, and would achieve the same (efficient) outcomes as codetermination.

There is, however, an unexpected difficulty. In dealing with games with complicated commitment structures, such as repeated simple games (or indeed the two-stage games of the previous two sections) it seems appropriate to impose a criterion along the lines of Reinhard Selten's "perfect equilibrium."[15] Intuitively, the condition is that each player's strategy for a given stage of the game must be part of an optimal strategy for the remainder of the game. The solutions to the two-stage games in the previous two sections reflect that intuition. In the literature, however, perfectness is usually defined in terms of subgames, and so the details of "perfect equilibrium" concepts depend on the definition of "subgames." This has been a source of some of the difficulty with the concept.[16] The solutions in the previous sections may not be rigorous instances of "perfect equilibrium" for that reason. Whatever the formal difficulties, though, the intuition embodied in the idea of perfection equilibrium is a sound one. If the equilibrium of a complicated game is not perfect (in some sense), then the players are not acting with foresight, and thus not acting rationally.

When we apply that condition to the repeated Prisoners' Dilemma, the argument for efficiency breaks down, as follows. For concreteness, suppose that the game is to be repeated for exactly twenty rounds. Consider the twentieth round. Since there is to be no twenty-first round, there is no punishment for cheating on this round, and the noncooperative outcome occurs. Now consider the nineteenth round. Since the outcome on the twentieth round is predetermined to be noncooperative in any case, there is no punishment for noncooperation on the nineteenth round. This in turn implies that there is no punishment on the eighteenth round, and so on. A trivial application of the principle of mathematical induction establishes that there is no cooperation on any round of play.

Here we have a conflict between two intuitively appealing arguments. On the one hand, the argument that repeated play could enforce cooperation is certainly an appealing one, and might be supported by a considerable amount of casual evidence and some experimental evidence. On the other hand, the argument that the optimal strategy on a given round of play must anticipate (individually) optimal play by all participants on future rounds is also intuitively appealing. Indeed, it is the obvious way of defining "foresight" in the context of noncooperative games. A failure of foresight would seem to be inconsistent with rational behavior, but, more than that, the whole argument that repeated play can enforce commitments relies on foresight - without fore-sight, the argument could not be considered in the first place.

If the participants in the game could commit themselves to some sort of contingent strategy for each future round - for example, "play cooperatively on round n unless the opponent has played non-cooperatively on round n-1" - then the cooperative outcome would occur (Hofstadter, Selten 1978). But no wonder. In that case we would be talking about a cooperative game, that is, one in which commitments are always possible: and in that case, there is no clear reason why the players would not simply commit themselves to cooperative strategies in every round and have done with it. It appears that, if we take seriously the assumption that the participants cannot commit themselves to joint strategy choices on future rounds of play, then we must accept the per-fectness criterion in some form, and reject the idea that re-peated play in the Prisoner's Dilemma, and similar games, will lead to efficiency when the games are repeated for a definite number of times.

This seeming paradox is even sharper in the "Chain Store Para-dox" of Selten. The Chain Store Game is a game of entry-deter-rence. The "Chain Store" has a definite number (in Selten's exam-ple, twenty) of outlets, and on each round of play, an indepen-dent potential competitor has the option of opening a competing store in one of the twenty locations. Once the competitor has de-cided and has committed itself to enter or not to enter, the chain store can either retaliate by pushing prices down so that both take losses at that location, or it can accommodate the new entrant and accept a lower (but still positive) profit on that location. It would be to the Chain Store's advantage, if it could, to commit itself to a policy of always retaliating. But such commitments are excluded by the rules of the game. Intu-itively, it seems that the chain store would retaliate against early entrants in order to create a reputation for vindictiveness and to persuade potential entrants that it would punish them.

But such behavior is irrational under the perfectness prin-ciple, and would not work against opponents who play with game-theoretic rationality. For (once again) consider the twentieth and last round. Since there are no more potential entrants to de-ter, there is nothing to be gained by retaliation on this round, and the potential entrant who knows this would accordingly enter and expect to profit thereby. Now consider round nineteen. Since

it is predetermined that the entry will take place on the twentieth round, there is no point in attempting to deter it by retaliation on the nineteenth round, and the Chain Store accordingly
will not retaliate on the nineteenth round. Now consider the
eigteenth round. Since entry is predetermined on the last two
rounds, there is no point in retaliating on the eighteenth round.
By now the line of the argument will be clear, and the conclusion, that entry will take place on every round and that retaliation will never take place, will be clear. Selten sees this argument as counterintuitive and goes so far as to reject the concept
of rationality embodied in his earlier perfectness principle.

Selten's example serves to demonstrate that the paradox which
we encounter in repeated Prisoners' Dilemma is much more general
than Prisoners' Dilemma examples might suggest. First, the Chain
Store example is not a case of repeated play in quite the same
sense. The Chain Store does not play against the same opponent
again and again, but against a series of different opponents.
Second, there is no question of a cooperative outcome. The Chain
Store fails to attain a policy which is beneficial to it at the
expense of potential entrants. (Both entry without deterrence and
successful deterrence are Pareto-Optima in this game).

But the solution to the paradox must surely be found in some
reasonably plausible set of assumptions which admits the perfectness principle without at the same time preventing cooperation
(in the Prisoners' Dilemma) or deterrence (in the Chain Store
Game). The key to this will be found in the "simplifying" assumptions of the perfect equilibrium model. The assumptions are 1)
that the game is repeated for a definite (finite and known) number of rounds, that utility functions are known and that utility
functions are given. The relaxation of any of those assumptions
will yield a model which reconciles the perfectness principle
with the intuitively appealing arguments for cooperation in the
one case and deterence in the other.[17] Telser's explanation seems
to have the widest application. Telser observes that, if the number of rounds of play is not known, then the argument from mathematical induction cannot be begun. Telser's argument is applied
to the Prisoners' Dilemma. Whenever the probability of another
round to come is sufficiently high, it is optimal for the parties
to cooperate on the current round. However, if for n sufficiently
great the probability of a round n+1 occurring is very small,
then cooperation will never occur. Now, there probably will be
many real interactions in which the conditional probability of a

round n+1 occurring, given that round n occurred, is roughly constant and close to, albeit less than, one. In such games efficient cooperation can be (in Telser's words) self-enforcing.

If we now apply the same reasoning to the two-by-two game of collective bargaining and investment from Section II, we find that we must modify the reasoning of the third paragraph of this section. The collective bargaining and investment "game" shares some characteristics with both the Prisoners' Dilemma, and the Chain Store Game. Like the Prisoners' Dilemma it requires a cooperative solution to attain Pareto-efficiency. Like the Chain Store game, however, the participants in successive rounds of the game are not identical. In particular, the work force in round n will not be identical to the work force in round n+1. Some individuals may remain from one period to the next, while others do not. This fact has been particularly stressed by those who attribute inefficiency and a shortened horizon to codetermination: it is, in fact, the very basis for the claim that the workers' horizon is short (Furubotn).

Consider the extreme case in which workers are immortal and immobile, so that the firm has the same work force from now until the infinite future, provided the firm continues to exist. In that case, the game seems clearly to be one to which Telser's argument can be applied. So long as there is a large enough probability of another round of play, the workers will restrain their bargaining demands so as to assure efficient investment. If the conditional probability of another round of play is small enough, however, then there will never be self-enforcing cooperation. Now, consider the extreme case in which the work force turns over completely from one round of play to the next. It appears that in this case the argument that a self-enforcing agreement for efficient investment will occur clearly breaks down. The workers who are punished at round n+1 for unrestrained bargaining demands on round n are not the workers who made the unrestrained bargaining demands, and so they will not be deterred from doing so by this threat of punishment. Now, finally, consider the intermediate case in which some workers remain in the work force from one period to the next. Then those who expect to remain in the work force will prefer to restrain the collective demands and assure continued investment, while those who expect to leave the firm will prefer unrestrained collective bargaining demands and wage disbursements now. Without constructing an explicit model of collective choice in unions, it seems that a larger proportion of remaining workers, i.e. a lower rate of turnover, would lead to a greater probability of cooperation. It would also appear that, the higher the rate of turnover, the higher the probability of occurrence of round n+1 would have to be to assure cooperation.

Thus, applying both the perfectness principle and Telser's argument to collective bargaining, we come to the conclusion that both cooperation and noncooperation are possible outcomes, depending on such variables as the rate of turnover between rounds and the conditional probability of occurrence of an n+1st round given that round n occurs. We may also observe that collective bargaining has several properties which make the cooperative outcome less likely, than it would otherwise be, which are missing in the case of codetermination. First, bargaining takes place at discrete periods of one or more years. This relatively long interval between episodes of bargaining implies a relatively high rate of turnover in the labor force. Bargaining on the codetermined board would be likely to occur at more frequent intervals, and these intervals might well be less predictible, with issues discussed as they arise. Second, one source of labor turnover is employer layoffs. The tendency of codetermination to restrain these layoffs would also tend to reduce labor turnover, increasing the probability of cooperative outcomes. Thus, the characteristics most distinctive of collective bargaining are unfavorable to self-enforced cooperative agreements. By contrast, even if the codetermined board is not effective as a means of creating enforcible commitments in itself -   does not in itself transform the firm into a cooperative game - it creates conditions relatively favorable to self-enforced cooperation.

V

It remains to confront a question which must be troubling to those of us who defend the superior efficiency of codetermination as a form of business organization. The problem has been clearly put forward by Texas School critics. If, indeed, codetermination is the efficient form, why need legislation establish it? Why do firms not voluntarily convert to codetermination, perhaps by collective bargaining or by unilateral invitation of the employees to elect members to the board of directors and/or to participate in other ways, in the expectation that the consequent increases in productivity will be at least partly reflected in increased profits? We have located the difference between codetermination and collective bargaining in the prerogatives of management - those dimensions of the firm's activity which are firmly "kept off the table" by management for their unilateral decision. These create the commitment structure which leads to inefficiency in non-codetermined forms both in the models of this paper and in my previous paper in codetermination. Thus, the equivalent question is: why would one party to bargaining insist on keeping some dimensions of the joint activity "off the table" in such a way as to create inefficiency?

Unfortunately, existing bargaining theory cannot answer the question. Most bargaining theories, including the Pen-Svejnar theory on which this paper has drawn, are theories of fixed-threat bargaining, which means that they take the impasse outcome as given - determined by the threats of the two bargainers, which are also given. Moreover, this body of bargaining theory (including also Nash's variable-threat bargaining theory) takes the utility-possibility set as a given. As we have seen, the choice of an agenda will in some cases determine the utility-possibility frontier, since the exclusion of one or more dimensions (such as investment) can move the utility-possibility frontier toward the origin. Thus, if the determination of the agenda of bargaining is endogenous, the utility-possibility frontier is not given, and so existing bargaining theory simply has nothing absolute to say about the outcome of bargaining in such a case.

But all is not lost. Nash's line of reasoning in his theory of variable-threat bargaining is instructive. He observes that bargaining can be conceived as a two-stage game. At the first stage of the game, the bargainers choose their threats. At the second stage, the threats being given, the solution to the game is obtained by fixed-threat bargaining theory. It remains to solve the first-stage game, in the light of that second-stage solution: but in Nash's theory, the first-stage game is equivalent to a zero-sum game and so is readily solved. Following this outline, we might construct a variable-threat, variable-agenda bargaining theory by taking both the determination of the threats and of the agenda as the first stage of the game, and the second stage as the solution of a fixed-threat, fixed-agenda game. No such theory yet exists, of course: but if this is a reasonable outline of the theory, then models in terms of fixed threats and fixed agendas would retain a contingent validity, as follows. The solution to the general bargaining game would be the solution to a fixed-threat, fixed-agenda game into which the optimal (presumably actual) threats and agenda had been substituted. Thus, the fixed-threat, fixed-agenda models would be valid if the threats and agendas on which they are based are in fact the optimal ones. It is this contingent validity which I claim for bargaining models here and elsewhere.[18]

In the absence of a variable-threat, variable-agenda bargaining theory, we are free to conjecture, informally, as to why a bargainer might wish to exclude some items from the agenda. It is quite possible that a movement of the utility-possibility frontier toward the origin might leave one bargainer better off, the burden of the shift falling so heavily on the other bargainer as to induce him further to reduce his demands. The following numerical example will serve to illustrate the point. Let A = B = 1/2 (the ZNH special case) and let the unconstrained utility-possibility frontier be defined by

(1) $U = 10 - V$

The solution then is $U = V = 5$. Then let the constrained utility-possibility frontier be defined by

(2) $U = \begin{cases} 3 - 0.2V & \text{if} \quad V \leq 8.75 \\ 10 - V & \text{if} \quad V > 8.75 \end{cases}$

The solution then proves to be $U = 1.5$, $V = 7.5$. Thus the party whose utility is V is better off, despite the fact that the constrained utility-possibility frontier lies everywhere on or below the unconstrained one. Thus, that party has good reason to prefer the constrained to the unconstrained utility-possibility frontier. If the constrained frontier can be imposed by keeping some item, such as levels of employment, "off the table," then that party will presumably attempt to do so.

VI

In summary, an attempt has been made to compare the reasonable theoretic expectation of efficiency for codetermined firms with that for a realistic alternative, collective bargaining. A characteristic aspect of collective bargaining, the existence of prerogatives of management, implies a commitment structure for the collective bargaining "game" which precludes cooperation and thus creates inefficiency, but may also shift the balance of bargaining power sufficiently in the direction of management to more than compensate the management for the loss implied by the inefficiency. Moreover, the form of the inefficiency, in the simplest case, is exactly that which some critics of codetermination have attributed to codetermination - a striking instance of the confusion which can arise from ignoring the commitment structure of a social interaction.

Footnotes:

[1] This is the position of several writers in the Transaction Cost School of thought.

[2] We are left with the mystery of what it means, in political economy, to say that an institution not actually in existence is a possible alternative.

[3] The term "Texas School" reflects the concentration of transaction cost writers on labor participation in management in Texas institutions, and applies to that group more narrowly; the term Transaction Cost School includes writers on many other topics in microeconomics. These terms are my innovations and others are, of course, quite free to reject them.

[4] There is some confusion as to that. Maximal effort is not optimal if effort has a positive shadow price.

[5] For a game-theoretic model of perfect hierarchical control, which demonstrates that such control (like other perfect social forms!) must be Pareto-optimal, see Thompson and Faith.

[6] Recent union "give-back" in the USA may seem to argue against this point, and there is no doubt that they constitute a strategic setback to the apolitical "business union" approach which has long dominated American organized labor. These give-backs have not restored the "untrammeled capitalist firm," however - they have occurred in a period of historically high unemployment, a special circumstance; profit recoveries following give-backs have motivated very large, bitter union demands; give-backs have been largely limited to declining industries and industries in which labor is traditionally weak; and in some cases they have been accompanied by such things as transfers of stock ownership to workers and the seating of worker representatives on the boards of directors - arrangements hardly characteristic of the untrammeled capitalist firm.

[7] This is, of course, not the intent nor the provision of West German law, which requires separate wage negotiations. However, I regard this separation as an imperfection of codetermination, and probably not a very important one. Labor members of boards of directors are generally members of unions which negotiate wages. Are we to suppose that they suffer amnesia after leaving the board? Is it really possible (even were it desirable) to prevent labor and management from trading concessions in the board, on financial decisions, for concessions at the wage-bargaining table, on wage decisions? Given that union leaders and management representatives must live together over the long term (this will be discussed further in section IV), I think not. What is distinctive about codetermination is that it provides a forum within which such trades can be negotiated, even if institutional arrangements require that they be ratified through separate wage-negotiations.

[8] Worker expectations of layoffs are abstracted from. Thus, the model given here is not strictly consistent with rational expectations, a problem it shares with the Illyrian tradition. To allow for rational expectations of layoffs, we might assume that hiring is done ex ante but that the employer may lay off some workers ex post, once the state of the world (and the wage) are known. The results would resemble some models of implicit con-

tracts: note Baily, e.g. However, this modification of the model, which seems realistic, does not change the results quantitatively and adds considerably to the complication of the model. In particular, specific assumptions have to be made about transaction costs in labor markets - "labor market toll" in Okun's phrase - which are abstracted from here. Also, the condition on the supply of labor (or on acceptability of contracts) must be in terms of the expected value of workers's utility, allowing for risk aversion and rational expectations of layoffs on the part of workers. I have written a model of the worker-managed firm along implicit contracts lines in McCain 1983.

[9] Thus, we apply fixed-threat bargaining theory. It would, of course, be better to allow z to be endogenous, but that would require application of variable-threat bargaining theory. The result would probably not be changed. The very limited amount of experience with variable-threat bargaining models, published and unpublished, suggests that the results would not be qualitatively different in such a model. The reasons for this are discussed in section V below.

[10] I follow the "implicit contract" school in assuming that employers are risk neutral while workers are risk averse. If employers were also risk averse, then utility expressions would have to be substituted in 5, 6, and 7.

[11] This method of procedure is valid only if the maximum from 8. is unique. In the case of plural maxima, the first-stage profit maximum need not exist (since the constraint set defined by 10. and 9b. will not then be closed), and the solution to the two-stage game need not in any case be described by the necessary conditions for the constrained maximum as in the text (since, with plural optima, it may be a corner solution of a more complicated problem). This does not mean that the neoclassical model (max profits, constrained only by the production function) is valid, but that the true model is even more complex and non-neoclassical than the one considered here. The uniqueness of the second-stage maximum is assumed here, for simplicity.

[12] It may be asserted that this formulation embodies some assumption about the source of financing, e.g. that it refers to the "pure rental" case. This is not so. We might, for example, assume that the employer begins the period with a certain capital, the proceeds of the previous period's production, which they may divide between lending out at the current market rate of interest and plowing back in the firm. Then, of course, r is the market rate and so the opportunity cost of the firm's own capital. Assuming then that the employer maximizes the discounted present value of the firm, the firm's derived maximand will differ from 11. only by a constant, and the constant is, of course, irrelevant either for maximization or (as previously noted) in the bargaining process.

[13] A better model, no doubt, would take decisions on particular investment proposals and other issues as they arose - with no determinate sequence - rather than simultaneously. If, then, agreement could not be arrived at on a particular investment proposal, that investment would simply not be undertaken, or might be postponed. In any case, the employers would not lose the use of capital good in place in the event of impasse, and that is the key point. Such a model would be at a much more detailed level than is customary in economic theory - but no doubt there is something to be learned by exploring it.

[14] Note Kuhn, Aumann, Lave, Selten 1978, Telser, and Kreps, Milgrom, Roberts, and Wilson for a sampling of the game-theoretic literature on repeated play in such simple games as the Prisoners' Dilemma and in general.

[15] Selten, 1965, 1975, 1978, Kreps and Wilson. Difficulties with Selten's original concept of "perfectness" motivated reconsiderations and revisions, 1975, 1978.

[16] Note the examples in Selten, 1975, for instances of this. Selten does not, however, interpret them in this way.

[17] Telser and Kreps, Milgrom, Roberts, and Wilson, respectively, establish the first two. The latter is from unpublished research by the author.

[18] A limited amount of unpublished work by the author seems to indicate that Nash variable-threat models of strikes and bargaining do not differ from the conditions of Nash fixed-threat models.

References:

Aumann,R. J.," Acceptable Points in General Cooperative n-Person Games", in Tucker and Luce, eds., *Contributions to the Theory of Games*, Princeton: Princeton University Press, 1959 287-324.

Averch, H. and Johnson L.,"The Behavior of the Firm under Regulatory Constraint", *American Economic Review*, 5, Dec. 1962, 1053-1069.

Baily, M.N., "Wages and Unemployment under Uncertain Demand", *Review of Economic Studies*, 1974, 37-50.

Carson, R.G.,"A Theory of Cooperatives", *Canadian Journal of Economics*, 4, Nov. 1977, 565-589.

Coddington,A., *Theories of the Bargaining Process*, Chicago: Aldine 1968.

Furubotn,E.," The Economic Consequences of Codetermination on the Rate and Sources of Private Investment",in: S. Pejovich, ed., *The Codetermination Movement in the West*, Lexington, Mass.: Lexington Books, 1978) 131-168.

Harsanyi,J.,*Rational Behavior and Bargaining Equilibrium in Games and Social Situations*, Cambridge: Cambridge University Press, 1977.

Hofstadter,D.,"Metamagical Themes", *Scientific American*, 248, 5, (May 1983) 16-26.

Kreps,D.M.,Milgrom,P.,Roberts,J., and Wilson,R.,"Rational Cooperation in the Finitely Repeated Prisoners' Dilemma Game", *Journal of Economic Theory*, 27, 2, (Aug. 1982) 245-252.

Kreps,D.M. and Wilson,R., "Sequential Equilibrium", *Econometrica*, 50, 4, (July 1982) 863-894.

Kuhn,H.W., " Extensive Games and the Problem of Information", in Kuhn and A. W. Tucker, *Contributions to the Theory of Games*, (Princeton: Princeton University Press, 1953) (Annals of Mathematic Studies, n. 28) 193-216.

Lave,L., "An Empirical Approach to the Prisoners' Dilemma Game", *Quarterly Journal of Economics*, Aug.1962 424-436.

McCain, Roger A.," A Theory of Codetermination", *Zeitschrift für Nationalökonomie*, 1-2,1980 65-90.
--- , " The Economics of a Labor-Managed Enterprise in the Short Run: An 'Implicit Contracts' Approach", Advances in the Economics of Participatory and Labor-Managed Firms, V. 1, 1983.

Nash,J., " The Bargaining Problem", *Econometrica*, 1950, 155-62
--- , "Non-Cooperative Games", Annals of Mathematics, 2, Sept., 1951, 286-95.
--- ,"Two-Person Cooperative Games", *Econometrica*, Jan, 1953 128-40.

Okun,A.,*Prices and Quantities*, Washington: Brookings Institution, 1981.

Olson,M., *The Logic of Collective Action*, Cambridge: Harvard University Press, 1971.

Pen, J., "A General Theory of Bargaining", *American Economic Review*, 1952,24-42.

Selten,R.,"Spieltheoretische Behandlung eines Oligopolmodells mit Nachfragetätigkeit", *Zeitschrift für die gesamte Staatswissenschaft*, 121, 1965, 301-324.
--- ,"A Re-Examination of the Perfectness Concept for Equilibrium Points in Extensive Games", *International Journal of Game Theory*, 4, 1, 1975, 25-55.
---, "The Chain Store Paradox", *Theory and Decision*, 9, 2, 1978, 127-159.

Svejnar,J. " Bargaining Power, Fear of Disagreement, and Wage Settlements: Theory and Empirical Evidence from U.S. History", Working Paper 285, Cornell University, 1980.
---,"A Theory of Self-Enforcing Agreements", *Journal of Business* 1, Jan. 1980.

Thompson,E. and Faith, Roger L. ,"A Pure Theory of Strategic Behavior and Social Institutions", *American Economic Review*, 3, June 1981, 366-380.

Zeuthen,F., *Problems of Monopoly and Economic Warfare*, London: Routledge and Sons, 1930.

CODETERMINATION, COLLECTIVE BARGAINING, COMMITMENT, AND SEQUENTIAL GAMES: Comment

by

Ekkehart Schlicht

Codetermination and collective bargaining are distinguished, according to McCain, by the existence of certain management pre-rogatives in the latter. These create first mover advantages (Schelling 1960), which explains why capital favors collective bargaining over codetermination. Furthermore, these first mover advantages create inefficiencies of the prisoners' dilemma type: management will take into account that its decisions, regarding investment projects, for instance, might improve the bargaining position of labor and will be exploited by labor accordingly. These positional shifts might lead to socially inefficient deci-sions, that is, to Pareto inferior outcomes. Although repeated negotiations might lead to implicit or explicit cooperative agreements avoiding these inefficiencies, collective bargaining is vulnerable in this sense, and codetermination is more favourable to cooperative solutions since bargaining involves all alternatives from the outset here, and prerogatives leading to those prisoners' dilemma type of inefficiencies are absent.

That is the argument in favor of codetermination forwarded by McCain. My role, as a commentator, is to raise points of criti-cism, and I shall try to do so, although I feel uneasy because McCain's case is well-taken.

I submit, hence, that McCain's argument in favor of codeter-mination unduly neglects possible inefficiencies of codetermi-nation both on the firm level and on the level of the industry, and that collective bargaining might prove superior in spite of some shortcomings.

1. Transaction Costs Under Alternative Arrangements

My first observation is that the firm's constitution does not effect efficiency if behavior can be observed and transaction costs are neglected: collective bargaining, codetermination, or untrammeled capitalism describe different assignments of decision rights among employers, employees, and unions. If the parties in-volved can enter binding contracts, all inefficiencies can be

Codetermination
ed. by H.G. Nutzinger and J. Backhaus
© Springer-Verlag Berlin Heidelberg 1989

contracted away quite independently of which assignment of decision rights prevails, and efficiency arguments cannot be decisive
with regard to constitutional choices. This is simply the Coase
Theorem applied to the issue of industrial democracy.

As long as behavior (or its consequences) can be observed, explicit or implicit contracts can be rendered viable by introducing suitable self-imposed penalties in the case of fraud.[1] But
bargaining, the introduction of penalties, arbitration boards,
and so forth, introduce transaction costs. Hence, for efficiency,
the constitution of firms is to be chosen such that it minimizes
transaction costs. Industry-wide collective bargaining emerges as
the natural systems solution to problems that are similar across
firms, whether codetermination or untrammelled capitalism prevails initially: it solves problems generated by mobility costs,
ex post small numbers, idiosyncrasies, etc., that can only be
partially resolved by the market or other institutions.[2] Hence
the issue between codetermination and collective bargaining is
not necessarily the issue between cooperative and noncooperative
games as McCain puts it; it might be the issue between different
games involving different bargaining costs, which can be played
both cooperatively or non-cooperatively.

As he admits, cooperation is possible and rational[3] under
codetermination and collective bargaining, since both involve repeated negotiations. Both arrangements will lead to efficient
outcomes by the same argument. It might even be argued that collective bargaining is superior to codetermination since the time
horizon of the union is longer than the time horizon of the
worker because the worker changes firms more frequently than the
union (I presume here industry-wide unions).Furthermore, industry-wide collective bargaining saves on bargaining costs. In Germany we observe, for instance, that strikes are restricted to a
sample of firms although the dispute concerns the entire industry. Under codetermination, strikes or strike-equivalents are
necessary within each firm to achieve the same result, that is,
to witness the degree of determination of labor should the employers anticipate it incorrectly. But as long as these informational deficiencies are absent, and given rational behavior,
strikes and lockouts will not occur under either codetermination
or collective bargaining: they are simply threats for achieving
better bargaining results, and similar threats - equivalents
of strikes and lockouts - will emerge under codetermination as
levers for achieving a strong position in bargaining. Indeed,

those threats may cause more harm under codetermination because they might destroy the spirit of cooperation. Conflicts ought to be channelled institutionally in order to minimize their moral havoc, and collective bargaining is not too bad in this respect. Codetermination, however, might require a certain dose of profit sharing to mitigate conflicts of interest.

All this qualifies McCain's argument insofar as he assumes that strikes will occur under collective bargaining but not under codetermination. That assumption gives an undeserved advantage to codetermination from the outset.

2. The Spreading of Welfare

Codetermination means that, within each firm, only the incumbent workers have a say. Hence decisions will be twisted in favor of the employed, neglecting the wishes of the unemployed. If there is a trade-off between higher wages for the incumbent workers or higher employment, decisions will be biased against additional employment, which implies inefficiencies as well as severe injustice to outside workers - whether unemployed or employed under bad conditions elsewhere. In other words, codetermination of industry, considered as a system, lacks the dispersive forces spreading welfare gains throughout the system which are provided under untrammeled capitalism by perfect mobility and utility taking of labor. In view of the increasing impediments to mobility - through various specificities, idiosyncrasies and ex post small numbers - those welfare-spreading forces are paralyzed, however, and untrammeled capitalism tends to run into similar problems. Industry-wide collective bargaining might be viewed as a provisional solution here as long as no institutions and incentive structures are created which lead to an adequate spreading of welfare gains under codetermination, and to avoiding those inefficiencies generated by neglecting the interests of non-incumbents.

3. Miscellaneous Remarks

Let me add, however, some more general remarks regarding McCain's analysis.

I doubt that we should rely too much on game theory and related rationality concepts since experiments suggest that people
behave quite differently from what game theory predicts in many
instances, pursuing heuristic strategies, looking for focal
points, etc.[4] Analytically, this difficulty is reflected by arguments such as "cooperation is more likely" under codetermination
(McCain). Strictly speaking that argument refers to a behavioral
game theory that is still lacking - it has no place in a theory
where people are held to behave rationally with probability one.

Furthermore, we should take the specificity problem much more
seriously: investment in specific machinery as well as investment
in the acquisition of specific skills is to be protected, and
granting prerogatives to those who have made these commitments
might serve this end.[5] Emphasizing the specificity problem in
this context interlinks the issue of codetermination with the issue of labor specificity and introduces further complications
without solving any other problems, of course.

Footnotes:

[1] If behavior cannot be observed, adequate incentives are to be provided anyhow, and cooperative solutions in the bargaining sense are impossible. Prerogatives with regard to these activities as well as noncooperation are unavoidable from the outset here.

[2] See Williamson (1975, ch. 4).

[3] Selten's (1978) "induction argument" renders all finite games of conflict noncooperative, and the game-theoretic proposals for explaining cooperation as rational, which McCain cites, introduce elements of irrationality. Hence there are some analytical problems involved here, but introducing credible commitments through self-imposed penalities might solve some of these problems.

[4] See Selten and Stoecker.

[5] Alchian (1984).

References:

Alchian, A. (1984), Specificity, Specialization, and Coalitions. *Zeitschrift für die gesamte Staatswissenschaft*, 140(1),34-49.

Schelling, Thomas. (1960), *The Strategy of Conflict*, Cambridge: Harvard University Press.

Selten, R.(1978), The Chain Store Paradox. *Theory and Decision*, 9(2), 127- 159.

Selten, R. and Stoecker, R. (1983), "End Behavior in Sequences of Finite Prisoner's Dilemma-Supergames", *Working Paper*, Institut für Mathematische Wirtschaftsforschung, Universität Bielefeld, Bielefeld, Germany.

Williamson, O.E. (1975), *Markets and Hierarchies*. New York: *The Free Press*.

THE IMPACT OF INDUSTRIAL POLICY AND STRUCTURAL CHANGES ON CODETERMINATION IN THE GERMAN STEEL INDUSTRY

by

Alfred L. Thimm

1. Introduction

During the last fifteen years the American economy has been unable to continue the impressive growth that characterized the postwar quarter century. Particularly during the 1970s, the malaise that infected American society had been accentuated by the apparently superior performance of competing countries. First France, then Germany, and finally Japan appeared to have discovered, in turn, a unique policy that guaranteed economic growth and stable employment. Initially it was "Le Plan", the indicative industrial planning by an elite Gaullist technocracy that assigned quantitative and qualitative investment targets to key industries, then German Codetermination,[*] and lastly the mysterious establishment of industrial strategies by Japan's Ministry of Industry and Trade that were held responsible for the successive peak performances of these countries. The apparent common denominator of the French-German-Japanese experiences was government intervention in the market economy: *industrial policy* and employee-union participation in managerial decision making, that is, *codetermination*.

The decline in the economic fortunes of France and Germany, the general worldwide crisis of the welfare state, and the economic recovery in the United States have sharply reduced both the advocacy and the discussion of industrial democracy and codetermination in the American press and in management journals. Among a small but influential group of economists, pundits, and newspapers, the wage rigidity of contemporary labor markets in advanced economies has emerged instead as the most provocative issue of the day.[1] In particular the attention given by the *New York Times* to Martin Weitzman's proposal for a radical reform of the wage payment system has brought this issue of labor market rigidities to the attention of managers and policy makers.[2] Neither the relationship between codetermination and labor market rigidities nor the impact of an industrial policy on codetermination in a declining industry, however, has been explored sufficiently in the past.

Codetermination
ed. by H.G. Nutzinger and J. Backhaus
© Springer-Verlag Berlin Heidelberg 1989

Until the emergence of a Common Market steel policy, the Federal Republic of Germany had demonstrated a greater dedication to the virtues of a market economy than had any other OECD country, and the impact of government intervention on industrial wages, prices, and labor relations had not been an important issue in West Germany.[3] The interaction of industrial policy and Codetermination in a declining industry may generate behavior patterns and expectations, however, that both alter the nature of Codetermination *and* prevent the realization of policy goals by reinforcing wage-employment rigidities.

A closer look at the political economy of Codetermination in the German steel industry during the 1980s will provide a good indication of the sensitivity of existing employee-union participatory institutions to policies designed to institute structural changes in a declining sector of the economy. In particular, any possible impact of the interaction of codetermination and industrial policy on labor market rigidity deserves close attention.

2. Codetermination in the 1980's: Stability and Change

The role and nature of codetermination has not been a controversial topic in Germany during the 1980's despite several half-hearted attempts in recent months by parliamentary leaders of both the governing Christian Democratic-Liberal (CDU-FDP) coalition and the opposition Social Democrats (SPD) to introduce modifications (Novellen) to existing codetermination legislation that would reduce or extend the power of the German Labor Federation (DGB) in the participatory process. There is virtually no chance that the current Parliament will pass the SPD "reforms" that would extend enterprise codetermination to the introduction of labor-saving technology, and only a modest likelihood that the Coalition leadership will push through its legislative proposal that would give a greater voice in the Codetermination process to employees that are not affiliated with the DGB.[4] The last major change in existing Codetermination legislation was the Codetermination Law of 1976, which represented the culmination of an effort by the German Labor Federation (DGB) and its political allies in the Parliament to increase the power of the national trade union leadership in order to influence macroeconomic policy on both an industry-wide and a national level.

German Codetermination, the participation of employees and unions in the decision making of the firm, occurs on two levels: on the plant level through the works councils (Betriebliche Mitbestimmung) and at the top level of the enterprise through the employee and union representatives on the German version of the board of directors, the supervisory boards (Mitbestimmung auf Unternehmungsebeme). The "works council" codetermination exists in all enterprises that have at least five employees, but the supervisory board codetermination prevails only in large corporations. With the exception of the steel industry, the works council codetermination is more significant and enjoys the strongest support in society. Codetermination on the board level has, however, played a significant role in the steel industry and has attracted the greatest attention in the United States.

Having viewed " codetermination " as the equal participation of labor and capital in decision making since the days of the Weimar Republic, the DGB leadership has considered the "Supervisory Board" the most significant forum for union participation in corporate decision-making. It is important to note in this context that Germany has no "union shops" and that, furthermore, all Codetermination legislation applies to *all* the employees of an enterprise, with the exception of top management. Moreover, though the German Labor Federation is the dominant union confederation, other unions exist and often win works council or board seats in employee elections.

The German unions that represented employees in the steel, coal and iron industries - referred to as "Montan Industry" in Central Europe and throughout this paper - had gained equal representation with stockholders on the steel industry supervisory boards in the Montan Codetermination Law of 1951, and with it recognition as the collective representative of all employees in the steel and coal industry. The DGB had been trying since 1951 to extend the Montan law to the entire German economy, and thus obtain explicit recognition that the DGB leadership was the sole legitimate representative of all German wage-earners.

The struggle to extend "equal union representation" to the entire economy resulted in the Codetermination Law of 1976, a compromise that gave employees and unions an almost equal voice with stockholders on the supervisory board without, however, recognizing the unions, *de facto*, as *the* lawful representative of all *wage* earners. After long and bitter discussion in Parliament and in the press, the final bill directly allocated only a fraction

(1/4 to 1/3 depending on the size of the work force) of all employee representatives on each board to union functionaries;[5]
nonetheless, the 1976 codetermination reform strengthened the
role of DGB unions in key industries without, however, eliminating stockholder control of the supervisory boards. In March
1979, the German Supreme Court (Verfassungsgericht) upheld the
1976 law precisely for that reason. Apart from the recent above-
noted attempts to modify existing laws, the legal structure of
Codetermination had disappeared from the media as a controversial
issue by 1979, and the daily routine of employee-management,
employee-union and union-employer relations seem not to have been
significantly affected by the 1976 legislation; at least, on the
many occasions since 1979 when serious union-management conflicts
have arisen, neither management nor union spokesmen have blamed
deficiencies in the Codetermination legislation for labor-
management conflicts.

Yet significant changes in German society have taken place in
the 1980's that most certainly affect the atmosphere in which employee participation takes place on the shop floor and on the supervisory board level. Stagnation in the smokestack industry accompanied by slower growth in the rest of the economy, the generation change in the trade union leadership and the SPD with the
accompanying increase in radical rhetoric, industrial policies
imposed by the EEC and the federal and state governments in key
areas of the economy, and the crisis of the welfare-state in
Western Europe have all made an impact on the contemporary nature
and effectiveness of Codetermination. But only the relationship
between macroeconomic trends and Codetermination effectiveness
has been seriously examined so far.

There are several hypotheses concerning the operations of
Codetermination during different phases of the business cycle.
There are those who believe that Codetermination's positive effects on employee productivity and on union-management cooperation are fair-weather phenomena that are strongest during periods
of economic growth and political consensus but that disappear
during economic recession and devisive political controversy. The
financial and political columnists Günter Götz, Jürgen V. Eick
(Frankfurter Allgemeine Zeitung), Rainer Hahrendorf (Handels-
blatt, Düsseldorf) and Otto Schulmeister (Die Presse, Vienna)
belong to that group along, perhaps, with the economist Eirik G.
Furubotn[6] and others.

Another hypothesis, advanced by Eberhard Witte and his group
from the University of Munich and also shared by *The Economist*,
views Codetermination on both the supervisory and the workshop
level as an essentially stable system that is affected more
severely by institutional, enterprise, and personnel factors than
by macroeconomic variables.[7] The increasingly heavy burden of
welfare state induced employment costs and wage rigidities are
considered a serious factor in Germany's consistently high unemployment during the 1980's, but the high and rigid welfare-state
induced indirect labor costs are deemed independent of the Codetermination institution.[8]

The significant changes that have simultaneously occurred in
the large number of interdependent economic, social, and political variables in which the Codetermination institution is nested
make it desirable to observe the behavior of management, union,
employer, government, and political parties in a well-defined micro setting that excludes extraneous variables. As a first step
toward gaining some testable insight into these complex dynamic
relationships, we ought to draw, therefore, on case studies of
specific industries and enterprises. In particular, understanding
how micro and macro variables interact is necessary for a proper
comprehension of the codetermination phenomenon.

The German steel industry is simultaneously undergoing a secu-
lar decline and a rapid technological change while being exposed
to various types of "industrial policy" directives from suprana-
tional, federal, and state governments; the major goal of European and national steel policy is the elimination of excess capacity in the most politically acceptable manner while provincial
and local authorities strive to shift the burden of redundancies
to other localities. Arbed-Saarstahl, as we shall show, is one of
those marginal steel enterprises in the heart of the German rust-
belt that owe their survival to political rather than economic
forces. A brief look at the recent history of Arbed-Saarstahl and
the German steel industry ought to provide some clinical evidence
for assessing the role of Codetermination in the most critical
sociopolitical environment that exists today in West Germany.

3. Codetermination in the German Steel Industry during the 1980's

The efforts by the European and, especially, the German steel
industry to solve the problems of overcapacity, changing patterns

of demand, and growing competition from abroad have been heavily influenced by employee and union participation in the decision process and by government intervention. In particular, the German steel industry provides an excellent case study for assessing the interaction effectiveness of both "industrial policy" and Code-termination in restructuring an industry.

The major German steel companies, Thyssen, Krupp, and Kloeckner, have maintained their international competitiveness by reducing excess capacity and investing heavily in labor saving technology.[9] Considerable evidence suggests that the German steel industry has been more successful during the past decade in adapting to changing market conditions than have its competitors in the EEC, EFTA, and North America, although successful adoption in today's global steel industry does not necessarily mean running a profitable operation. Since 1981, few German steel companies have made money on their steel operations, and a few key firms, for example, Hoesch and Salzgitter, have shown massive losses.[10] Despite vigorous rationalization and reduction of excess capacity, the German steel industry, on the average, lost $20 (DM60) per ton of steel produced in 1983 and barely broke even in 1984. (Averages have less meaning in 1984, however; Hoesch and Thyssen, with especially heavy labor saving investment, operated profitably, but Kloeckner experienced serious losses, and Krupp barely broke even on its steel operations.)[11] Still, over the past ten years the German steel industry has been able to sharply reduce its crude steel capacity, lower labor cost, shift production from price elastic crude steel to profitable special steel, and modernize its production facilities. The most productive units could compete profitably in the world market if subsidies and tariffs miraculously disappeared.

Much nonsense has been written in the American press about the cost advantage of the German and Japanese steel industries because their old mills had been destroyed during the war. The steel mills that were rebuilt in Japan and Germany in the postwar period nearly forty years ago either have been thoroughly modernized or, more frequently, have been torn down and completely replaced by "new generations" of highly capital-intensive plants. For example, Thyssen, Europe's most efficient steel enterprise, replaced a 10-year-old mill in 1978 with a highly automated plant, and Hoesch, despite its losses during the last four years, is replacing its 17-year-old "Hörde Plant" with an integrated oxygen steel mill.[12]

The constant rationalization of the German steel industry during the last decade has been matched in Europe only by the small, efficient steel entrepreneurs in Northern Italy near Brescia. These cost-reducing efforts have led to a constant reduction in manpower but, until the 1980's, had generally been supported by the steel union, the union representatives on the supervisory boards, and the work councils within the individual plants and enterprises.

German employees, both union and non-union, blue-collar and white-collar, participate through work councils in the management of all enterprises that employ more than five persons and, in addition, elect somewhat less than 50 percent of the supervisory board members in publicly or privately held stock companies with more than 2000 employees. (Though 50 percent of the board seats are allocated to employee and union representatives, one of these seats is reserved for a senior manager; moreover, the chairman, always a stockholder representative, has two votes in case of a tie.) As mentioned above, a special codetermination legislation prevails for historic reasons in the steel industry that permits the national union leadership to select, *de facto*, 50 percent of the supervisory board members in enterprises with more than 1000 employees.[13]

In accordance with the Montan Codetermination law, the stockholders ordinarily elect five board members, and the trade union *appoints* three union officials and selects *de facto* two company employees to serve on the supervisory board. The ten members of the board then elect a neutral eleventh member to avoid ties. It is customary, though not required by law, that a stockholder representative be elected board chairman and the senior union official vice-chairman. The German supervisory board appoints the management executive committee (Vorstand), which, under the 1951 Montan Codetermination law, must include the industrial relations vice-president (Arbeitsdirektor), who has rarely been a part of top management. The appointment of the Arbeitsdirektor requires the approval of the union officials on the board. The Arbeitsdirektor, consequently, is close to the union and is frequently a former union functionary. Since he and his staff work closely with the elected works council, the influence of the unions on work council behavior in the Montan industry is strengthened.[14] Only in the steel and coal industry has the supervisory board become the dominant instrument of codetermination.[15]

The German Trade Union Federation's (DGB) view of Codetermination has always contained a strong corporative strain, in which capital and labor, represented by their collective organizations, the DGB and the employer's association, take jointly the major strategic decision for both the entire economy and individual industries. In 1972, the Social-Democratic Brandt government created a top-level consultative body, quaintly called Concerted Action (Konzertierte Aktion) in which business, union, and government representatives met to discuss economic policy issues.[16] (The similarity of Concerted Action to the NRA of the 1930s and to the views expressed during the last Presidential elections by "industrial policy" advocates Mesrs. Iacocca, Rohatyn and Mondale is striking.) Stagnation and the revival of class war ideology and adversary labor relations in the smokestack industry led to the demise of Concerted Action; at the same time, growing unemployment forced the German government and the Common Market to intervene in the economy on an *ad hoc* basis.

The European steel crisis had forced the EEC commissioner Etienne Davignon to develop a long-run program in the mid-1970's that provided for modernizing the European steel industry; restructuring regional capacity and product mix through production quotas and minimum prices; and social adoption, that is, redundancy payment in excess of the already high minimum separation payments required by law throughout the EEC. The market was to be replaced by an EEC sponsored cartel that would significantly reduce the freedom of action of the steel enterprises.

We have already noted that the German steel industry operated under a special kind of codetermination law that recognized the steel union as the "collective representative of the employees" and gave it equal representation on the board of directors. When the EEC adopted the Davignon plan in 1978, the question arose how the German steel industry would fare under the combined constraints of industrial policy and codetermination during a period of high national unemployment and slow economic growth. In spite of the consistent attempts of German labor leaders, both Social Democratic and conservative governments had refrained generally from interfering in the Codetermination process through industrial policy guidelines (Strukturpolitische Weisungen). The high unemployment in the steel, iron, and mining industries, as well as the high welfare state costs, however, has made market-driven structural change politically difficult, especially if compared with the feasibility of such policy in the United States. The

Christian Democratic government has been forced, therefore, to accompany the industrial policy of the EEC with *ad hoc* efforts to support politically important enterprises and to encourage, simultaneously, a restructuring of the steel industry. Under these circumstances, observers of codetermination must ask three questions:

1. To what extent, if any, did industrial policy and chronic unemployment affect codetermination practices on the shop floor, on the corporate level, and on the national level?
2. To what extent was the formulation of industrial policy affected by the existing institutional patterns of codetermination?
3. To what extent, if any, did the codetermination practices and traditions affect the economic efficiency of the German steel industry and its attempts to adapt to changing patterns of demand?

It is much too early to arrive at definitive answers to these questions.[17] We can look, however, at several cases that might provide initial data for developing a general dynamic model of "codetermination under structural, economic and political pressure";[18] it is precisely the case study approach that will supply the impetus for the further development of a "micro-theory of the firm under codetermination."

4. ARBED-SAARSTAHL: A Case Study

The interaction of codetermination, industrial policy, and market forces in the European Steel Industry is strikingly illustrated by the case study of Arbed-Saarstahl, a medium-sized Luxembourg-German steel and iron enterprise that dominates the economies of Luxembourg and the German province of Saarland.[19] As in all case studies, special historic and institutional factors affect the decision processes; the major economic and political issues in the Saarstahl case, however, have been typical for marginal but politically sensitive firms not only in the German or European steel industry but also in the American.

The German enterprise Saarstahl draws its raw material from the no longer competitive iron and coal resources of the Saar province. It had been an extremely profitable enterprise in the pre-World War I period, had remained viable in the inter-war period, and flourished again in the late fifties and sixties during the boom-days of the German steel industry. The geographical location of Saarstahl, its major asset during the nineteenth and early twentieth centuries, had become a serious handicap by the end of the 1960s since it is no longer close to its markets; moreover, its ties to old, inefficient coal and iron mines have been a cost burden it has not been able to relinquish for political and social reasons. The Luxembourg steel enterprise Arbed has a similar history, and typical of European industrial policy, the governments of Luxembourg, the Saarland, and (West) Germany encouraged a merger of Arbed and Saarstahl under the assumption that combining two weak, struggling enterprises would create one strong industrial combination.[20]

The new enterprise Arbed-Saarstahl received "restructuring subsidies" from Luxembourg and the Saarland in order to close marginal production units that had become redundant through the merger.[21] In most of Europe and particularly in Germany and Luxembourg, the individual employee has a "vested right" to his job that grows with his seniority. The closing of any plant requires the submittal of a "social plan" by management to be approved by the work councils. The social plan provides generous redundancy payments for all employees, early retirement, retraining, and relocation services.

France's occupation of the Saarland during crucial periods after both world wars affected the province's reintegration into the German economy; that historical event as well as the unusual dependence of the Saar economy on its steel industry prompted the German government, the steel industry, and the public to support attempts during the mid-seventies to keep Saarstahl alive. At that time, government and industry were still opposed in principle to any form of "dirigism" - the European term for "industrial policy" - and resisted EEC attempts to meet Europe's overcapacity in steel through production quotas and government restructuring subsidies.[22] The special nature of the Saarland, however, prompted the German public and government to treat Saarstahl as a "special case" that deserved special treatment. Yet even these historical and institutional circumstances are typical of the European steel industry. Dozens of old steel and coal enterprises in Scotland, southeast Austria, Lorraine, and northern Sweden have lost their former location advantages and must rely on high-cost local raw material, but still provide the only source of industrial employment in their regions. Employers, unions, works councils, and regional politicians pressure the central governments to preserve workplaces in those areas by providing subsidies and increasing tariffs. Since there is always another ostensibly crucial election on the horizon, all governments, whether conservative or socialist, provide subsidies or tariffs, or as in France, subsidies *and* tariffs.

The Codetermination system has provided an especially effective instrument for advancing not only the interests of the steel industry's work force, but also management's. In the Saarstahl case in particular, management used the union representatives on the supervisory board to obtain the support of the national steel union and the Social-Democratic legislators in Saarbrücken and Bonn, while the management representatives and the works councils effectively lobbied the provincial and national governments. Reluctantly, and against its better judgment, the federal government agreed to support the Arbed-Saarstahl merger. The initial DM 300 million restructuring subsidy in 1978 had grown to DM 3.4 billion by 1984, and still there is no end in sight to the spiraling cost of this particular piece of "industrial policy", though the federal government, at least, has refused to supply further funds.

Enough evidence can be gleaned from the attempt to keep alive the no longer competitive Saarstahl enterprise to draw a few conclusions that reflect on the political aspects of Codetermination and, simultaneously, illuminate the various efforts to maintain employment through industrial policies.

(1) Management, Labor, and Government in Germany - as in the United States - have underestimated the steady, structural change that has taken place in the world steel industry.[23] The EEC steel crisis program, the so-called Davignon plan, has provided for modernization and restructuring of regional capacity, as well as production quotas and pricing agreements for a so-called transition period; yet the decline in the EEC steel work force of about 150000 workers since 1981 has not been sufficient to bring production in line with shrinking demand and the growing steel output of Brazil, Korea, Taiwan, India, and Eastern Europe that is just now beginning to hit the world market with full force. Ironically, the "turn-key" steel mills Thyssen and Krupp sold amid much fanfare to Brazil and Eastern Europe during the 1970's are just now getting on stream and adding their output to

world capacity. Arbed-Saarstahl and other marginal steel producers - and all but the most efficient producers in the best locations are marginal today - hoped that the end of the world recession would solve their problems. These hopes have not been and
will not be fulfilled, hence, the new demands for further subsidies supported by labor, local management, and regional politicians.

(2) Given the structural changes in the steel industry, mergers
and reorganization will not solve the problem unless significant
gains in efficiency can be obtained by changing the product mix,
adopting new technology, and moving from crude steel to special
steel, high value added production. Even modernizing production
facilities is not enough unless the new product is competitive in
the world market. The high cost of redundancies in Europe, especially in Germany, often undermines the financial stability of
the enterprise or absorbs potential investment funds. The management at Hoesch, for instance, revised its calculations in the
early 1980's and determined that even a new, up-to-date oxygen
steel plant would no longer be competitive and hence would not be
built as previously planned.[24] In the 1970's the French pioneered
a concentration and merger policy in Europe to create an efficient competitive steel industry and nationalized their major
privately-owned firms into two state-owned enterprises, Usinor
and Sacilor. Both companies still lose money although they have
gradually shed one-third of their work force.

Successful consolidation requires tough measures at an early
stage; these measures must include immediate closing of the least
efficient operations and salary and wage reductions for both labor *and* management, as well as significant changes in the production process and production mix. The tough measures that are now
necessary in the Arbed-Saarstahl enterprise should have been carried out at least five years ago, just as the streamlining of
British Steel that has finally been accomplished by its American
CEO, Ian MacGregor, ought to have been pushed through ten years
ago. Considerable savings could have been realized if inefficient
plants had been closed earlier.[25]

It seems quite clear that Krackow, the former CEO at Arbed-
Saarstahl, felt constrained not only by his board, on which the
steel union holds 50 percent of the seats, but also by the pressures of the state government and the national steel union, I.G.
Metall. Similar pressures are felt by all European companies that

are faced with overcapacity and structural change; however, Code-termination, particularly the Montan Codetermination, provides a formal structure and a justification for delaying hard decisions. At Saarstahl, the "Montan" Codetermination has constrained the practical alternatives open to management and must be held responsible for the enormous opportunity cost that the continued support of an unworkable enterprise represents.

(3) During the 1980s, the national trade unions have made it more difficult to reorganize the steel industry effectively and rapidly. The purpose of the trade unions is, of course, the protection of its members and, especially, their jobs. Union opposition to measures that are painful in the short run has damaged the long-run interests of the work force. The Montan-Codetermination, however, has given IG Metall extraordinary opportunities to perpetrate its policies. At Arbed-Stahl, for instance, the union initially opposed the concept of a common raw-iron production unit for all Saar mills because it feared that such a centralized operation would reduce employment.[26] Subsequently, in an extraordinary display of toughness, the union representatives on the board together with the neutral member forced management against its better judgment to build a new mill in 1978.

During major disagreements between stockholder and union representatives on the supervisory board, German Codetermination practices delay decision until a compromise emerges. The search for consensus has been a particularly significant characteristic of the "Montan" Codetermination version. To have a major investment decision decided by the tie-breaking vote of the neutral member was therefore unique, though typical of the unbending attitude of the I. G. Metall leadership in the Saar. In 1982, Arbed-Stahl asked both its Luxembourg and its Saar unions for "give-backs". The Luxembourg steel union agreed, but the regional union leadership in the Saar refused, thus further widening the profitability gap between Saar and Luxembourg mills.

5. The Lessons of the Arbed-Saarstahl Case.

It is the duty of each works council to represent the economic interests of the employees in its shop. The enterprise's gain through the closing of marginal units will not help the employees that face redundancies or the localities affected. Since the German steel industry might gain if its "basket cases" were closed, one might find more sympathy for "global solutions" among national union leaders than among works councils and local politicians. The parochial demands to maintain local work places, advanced by works councils and regional steel union offices, discourage national union officials and the parliamentary leaders of the Social Democrats from considering the long run. The pursuit of short-run gains has damaged the long-run interests of employees and industry. Politicians have been as shortsighted as union leaders during the steel crisis that has hit Germany later than the other European countries inside and outside the EEC. Invariably, politicians on the Saar and in Bonn, and also in London and Washington, take the short-run view to mollify particular interest groups. Thus loan guarantees, subsidies, or tariffs are provided temporarily to give short-time relief, and are invariably followed by demands to make these measurements permanent. In the Saarstahl case, an initial $120 million restructuring support rapidly evolved into a DM 3 billion open-ended subsidy. The true cost of the subsidies, quotas, and marketing agreements lies in encouraging marginal enterprises to maintain their current comfortable way of doing business and in preventing the reallocation of capital from declining to growth industry. Just as no class has ever been willing to abdicate its prerogatives without a struggle, no organization - particularly no previously successful organization - is willing to change its ways voluntarily.

In the German steel industry the current wage-fringe benefit levels can no longer be supported by all but the most efficient enterprises.[27] This inability to survive in a market economy has prompted Arbed-Saarstahl owners, management, and union to look increasingly toward massive government , as strong political pressure has weakened the German government's firm free-market stance.

Arbed-Saarstahl gives an only slightly exaggerated mirror image of developments in the entire German steel industry. Until the EEC accepted the Davignon steel-crisis program and imposed its production quotas and minimum price agreements on the reluctant German steel industry, German management and labor had agreed that its export-oriented industry could only compete successfully in the world market if it consistently strived to reduce its production costs through automation, technical leadership, and a shift to high value-added products. In the summer of 1978, Europe's nationalized steel industries (especially in Great Britain, France, and the non-EEC countries Sweden and Austria) began dumping their government subsidized product on the world market; for the first time steel imports gained more than 40 percent of the German market. Reluctantly, the German government moved toward encouraging a reorganization of its steel industry by attempting to merge its four largest firms into two giant companies. Since 1980, several "steel concepts" have evolved and have been rejected; hence, the top management of German's big four steel companies - Thyssen, Krupp, Kloeckner and Hoesch - has spent much of its energy and time advancing merger combinations that would favor their respective enterprises. Meanwhile the steel union leadership and its representatives on the supervisory board have ceased cooperating with management to reduce German steel capacity and are now looking toward state and federal subsidies rather than increased productivity as a solution to the German steel crisis. In particular, the union's insistence on including weak steel firms in the potential merger of the big four has delayed such a solution for four years.

The IG Metall has, of course, used its influence with the Social Democratic state government of North-Rhine-Westphalia and the Social Democratic MP's in Bonn to ensure that its views prevail. In 1983 a Krupp-Hoesch merger was close to completion. This merger would not only have included the state-owned Salzgitter company, but would also have guaranteed the continued operation of marginal Hoesch mills. The various non-economic constraints placed upon the merger ultimately prompted Krupp to abandon further negotiations. In the late fall of 1984, Krupp and Kloeckner, the number two and number three firms in the German steel industry, came close to merging their steel operations. In addition, the Australian raw material supplier CRA Ltd. - a Rio-Tinto subsidiary - was to have been included in the merger. CRA withdrew since the German government did not provide financial support for the merger: the high cost of closing marginal steel mills made the merger unworkable once it became clear that no major federal or state funds were available.

Despite the increase in difficulties facing the German steel industry, its most efficient mills retain their long-run profitability, though the survival of many smaller enterprises and the less efficient mills among the "big four" is no longer economically justifiable.[28] Still, Germany, has four strong, in the long-run profitable, enterprises and is therefore in a better position than its European or American competitors. The relative strength of the German steel industry is due, however, to the union and works council's support for the management investment policy that increased productivity and reduced capacity during the 1970's. Until 1978, Codetermination in the steel industry had helped management make a relatively smooth transition toward a slimmer, more capital intensive, more sophisticated manufacturing program. But the adoption of the Davignon plan in 1978 by the EEC introduced industrial policy considerations into enterprise decisions which changed the nature of the decision processes in industry. Codetermination and the increasing role of state and federal government has delayed and damaged the adjustment process in the 1980's that had worked rather well in the 1970's.

It has been argued that in the United States, Canada, and elsewhere the political response to world excess capacity in steel and automobile-manufacture was no different from Germany's even though Codetermination does not exist in these countries. The point, however, is that Codetermination was supposed to unchain creative forces by establishing extensive employee and union participation in corporate decision making. The successful cooperation between management and union during the restructuring of the coal and mining industries in the 1950s was, as a matter of fact, advanced by the DGB as a strong argument in its drive to extend the Montan codetermination to the entire economy. The successful closing of inefficient mines, however, occurred during the prosperous 1950s when a dynamic economy would easily absorb all available labor. The, by German standards, nasty steel strikes of 1978-79 and 1984 demonstrated that "equal codetermination" did not produce a new era of union-management relations, though it has given the union greater responsibility and therefore greater accountability for macro-economic issues.

In summary, economic conditions do seem to affect the way Codetermination operates, at least in the steel industry. Smooth union-management cooperation in restructuring the mining industries in the high growth fifties - a cooperation that often clashed with the short-run interests of employees and stockholders - was followed by an uneasy union acquiescence in steel management's rationalization efforts in the moderately prosperous mid-seventies, to be replaced by active union and work force resistance to further capacity reduction. The class-warfare rhetoric that has emerged during the last six years mirrors the adversary relations between union and employer association leadership that has emerged in the steel industry; hostility on the top level must not disguise, however, the successful cooperation of union and management in the marginal enterprises to tap government subsidies in order to maintain their existence. A new unintended feature of Codetermination has emerged which may reinforce the solid routine cooperation between works management and works council on the shop-floor.

Footnotes:

* When referring to the body of laws and procedures that delineate the participation of employees and unions in enterprise decision making, we shall capitalize "Codetermination."

1 Among those who have raised the wage rigidity issue effectively, we can include the Anglo-American economists James Meade, Lester Thurow, and Martin Weitzman; the meta-social scientists Daniel Bell, Irving Kristol and John Waniski; *The Economist*; the *Wall Street Journal*; the *Frankfurter Allgemeine Zeitung (FAZ)*; and the *Neue Züricher Zeitung*. Specific articles from the *Economist* and the *FAZ* are mentioned below. For Americans, the most important publications that discuss labor market rigidity in the 1980's include: J. C. Meade, *Stagflation*, Vol.I: *Wage Fixing*, Allen and Irwin, London 1982; Martin L. Weitzman, "Some Macroeconomic Implications of Alternative Compensation Systems, " *Economic Journal*, Vol. 93, 1983; Daniel Bell and Irving Kristol (eds.), *The Crisis in Economic Theory*, Basic Books, New York, 1981.

2 Martin L. Weitzman, *The Share Economy*, Harvard University Press, Cambridge, 1984.

3 On the other hand, "Strukturpolitik", that is, government policies to encourage industrialization of underdeveloped regions, has had a long and noncontroversial history in Germany and has been pursued actively during the *dirigiste* Weimar Republic, the National-Socialiste regime, and the free market Federal Republic. For a discussion of the impact of "Strukturpolitik" on a major enterprise see A. L. Thimm, "Decision making at Volkswagen 1972-75", *Columbia Journal of World Business*, Spring 1976.

4 In a union-sponsored conference in March 1985 on "Full Employment, Codetermination and Technology" in Cologne, union leaders demanded not only greater presentations of union representatives on the board of directors of German corporations, but also full economic Codetermination through equal presentation on "social and economic counsels" that should be established on a regional and federal basis (cf. *Frankfurter Allgemeine Zeitung (FAZ)* March 28, 1985.) These demands are ritualistically raised at each major union convention. The demand for "social and economic councils" goes back to 1919 and the early days of the Weimar Republic. But the 1986 SPD bill "to strengthen Codetermination" (Gesetzentwurf zur Stärkung der Mitbestimmung) is of much greater interest. Its provisions will give employees a voice in the adoption of new technical equipment and processes. Moreover, further restrictions on employment terminations would be added. Legislation in Sweden and Holland already gives union leaders a strong voice in implementing innovations, and it is quite likely that a further Parliament dominated by the SPD would pass such a law.

The CDU-Liberal coalition, on the other hand, has been promoting legislative changes that would make it easier for independents or independent unions, particularly those that represent white-collar employees, to gain seats in works council elections. See for instance: "Leitente Angestellte sollen eigene Vertretung erhalten" (senior managers shall obtain their own union representation, *FAZ*, April 18, 1985).

[5] All corporations and limited liability companies with more than 2000 employees must have a supervisory board that is composed equally of stockholders and employee representatives. The chairman, who must be a stockholder representative, may cast two votes in case of a tie.

[6] Cf. Eirik G. Furubotn's, "Codetermination, Productivity Gain and the Economics of the Firm", 1985, and his contrbution to this volume "A General Model of Codetermination" above.

[7] Note especially E. Witte, *Das Einflusssystem der Unternehmung*", Institut für Organisation, Munich, *The Economist*, March 3, 1983. Witte's other recent contributions are noted below.

[8] See, for instance, "Down to Earth," a survey of the West German economy, *The Economist*, February 4, 1984.

[9] A. L. Thimm, "The German Steel Strike 1978-79; Implication and Consequences," *Columbia Journal of World Business*, Summer 1979. D. Tinnin, "Reforging an Old Steelworker," *Fortune*, June 16, 1980b. "West German Steel," *The Economist*, May 3, 1980a, pp. 95-96.

[10] With the exception of 1975-77 and 1981-84, the German steel industry as a whole has remained profitable throughout the postwar period. Thyssen, Hoesch and Krupp have been profitable during 1985 (Cf. "German Steel Firms Stage a Comeback," International Herald Tribune, May 30, 1960, p. 15.)

[11] Cf. "Nicht zum Vorzeigen," *Der Spiegel*, p. 136, March 18, 1985; "Stahlindustrie ohne grosse Erwartungen," Faz, April 18, 1985; "Stahlindustire: Falscher Weg," *Die Zeit* April 4, 1985. *Der Spiegel*, in particular, correctly predicted that Kloeckner's recent losses would endanger the much discussed merger between Krupp and Kloeckner. It was finally, however, the DM 700 m cost of closing a steel mill in Lower Saxony that prompted the cancellation of the merger arrangement (cf., "Europe pays on" *The Economist*, p. 72, July 13, 1985.)

[12] From the union's point of view, Hoesch is not modernizing quickly enough. Hoesch had originally planned to build a new $200 million oxygen plant to replace its twenty-five-year-old mill at the same location. The new mill would have provided employment for 65 percent of the current work force. The company decided in 1984 that it did not have the money to build the plant, especially since there was insufficient demand for crude steel, even at the lower prices an integrated modern plant could support, and even with $100 million state aid from the state of Nordrhein-Westfalen. So much for "industrial policy."

[13] A. Thimm, *The False Promise of Codetermination*, D. C. Heath & Co., Lexington, MA, 1982, Ch. 4, esp. p. 110.

[14] Actually, this statement is not quite correct. The V.W. corporation has had a board in which the union and its allies - representatives of state and federal government on the board - enjoyed a majority at certain times, especially in the 1970s. See A. L. Thimm, "Decision-Making at Volkswagen 1972-75," *Columbia Journal of World Business*, Spring 1976, and Wolfgang Streeck, *Industrial Relations in West Germany*, Chs. 4-6, St. Martin's Press, New York 1984.

[15] Cf. A. L. Thimm, "How Far Should German Codetermination Go?" *Challenge*, July/August 1981, pp. 14-15.

[16] A revival of "Concerted Action" may be emerging. The Kohl Government has met with DGB and industry representatives and discussed measures to reduce unemployment (FAZ, July 24/25, 1985).

[17] The Institute for Organization, University of Munich, has been carrying on empirical research on codetermination for the past ten years. Its publications provide a "macro-view" that tends to minimize changes in codetermination behavior. The macro-nature of its surveys tend to smooth industrial and sector variations and are subject to long delays in capturing actual changes since its survey techniques emphasize perceptions. Cf. Eberhard Witte, "The Influence potential of the Employee as the Basis for Codetermination" (Das Einflusspotential Der Arbeitnehmer als Grundlage der Mitbestimmung), *Die Betriebswirtschaft*, Vol. 40, 1980, E. Witte, "The Independence of the Management Board in the Influence system of the Enterprise" (Die Unabhängigkeit des Vorstandes im Einflusssystem der Unternehmung), *Schmalenbachs Zeitschrift für betriebswirtschaftliche Forschung*, Vol. 33, 1981a, E. Witte, "The Influence of the Stockholder on Enterprise Policy" (Der Einfluss der Anteilseigner auf die Unternehmenspolitik), *Zeitschrift für Betriebswirtschaft*, Vol. 51, 1981b.

[18] An important step towards developing a general model of codetermination has been taken by Erik G. Furubotn (cf. his two forthcoming publications "A General Model of Codetermination" and "Codetermination, Productivity Gains and the Economics of the Firm"). The special case studies considered in this paper seem to be quite compatible with Furubotn's conclusion in his second paper (Codetermination, Productivity..etc). To the extent that codetermination policies during the 1980s in the steel industry portray the adaptive behavior of a high-order feedback system, an appropriate dynamic time-variant model would consist of nonlinear differential equations with coefficients that are functions of time. Such a system cannot be analyzed analytically.

[19] The Saarland is actually a state within the Federal Republic of Germany; the term province is used instead of "state" whenever the latter term might be misleading. By 1984 Saarstahl still provided 30,000 jobs and has remained the largest employer in the Saar.

[20] The initiative for the creation of Arbed Saarstahl came from Emmanuel Tesch, Arbed's CEO, who bought the Saar mills in order to increase capacity and provide a full product line. Only the reluctant support of the German government in the form of a subsidy for building a new blast furnace in the Saar made the merger feasible, however. In the meantime, the various efforts of Saarland, West Germany, and Luxembourg to save Arbed-Saarstahl have weakened the corporate ties between the Luxembourg and Saar components. Arbed has linked its production with Belgium's Cockwill-Scumbre and has just made its first profit in 10 years (*The Economist*, Feb. 9-15, 1985, p. 13), and the new SPD premier of the Saarland, O. Lafontaine, has become the godfather of Saarstahl.

[21] The prestigious *Frankfurter Allgemeine Zeitung (FAZ)* referred to Arbed-Saarstahl as a "bottomless pit" (lit: Fass ohne Boden) in a July 5, 1983, front-page editorial that referred to the DM 2.9 billion (ca. $1.16 billion at 1983 exchange rate) subsidies it had already received and the additional DM 5 billion it still

needed to become self-sufficient. The *FAZ* pleaded for a tough approach to the steel problem and warned against the misallocation of resources to keep alive an uneconomical enterprise. By the end of 1984, the total subsidy had reached DM 3.5 billion (FAZ, Dec. 10, 1984).

[22] It is important to distinguish between "restructuring subsidies" advocated by the EEC and offered by the German Federal governments (both left of center until 1982 and right of center since 1982) during the last few years and the operating subsidies that the Austrian, Belgium, British, French, and Swedish governments have poured into their nationalized steel industries to cover their massive losses. In their drive to obtain protective tariffs, American steel management and the steel unions fail to distinguish between operating and restructuring subsidies. Since the latter pay for the social costs of closing plants, it does not affect operating costs.

[23] A. L. Thimm, "The German Steel Strike of 1978-1979. "Implications and Consequences," *The Columbia Journal of World Business*, Summer 1979, pp. 52-68. The structural changes that led to the establishment of the EEC Davignon plan in 1978 have turned out to be even more severe than Etienne Davignon, the EEC commissioner of industries, had assumed.

[24] Cf. "Estel-Steel Group," *The Economist*, June 6, 1981.

[25] Productivity at British Steel has made a remarkable recovery and is now competitive with the best German producers. Still, losses rose once more to 386 million in 1982 from 339 m. losses in 1981; quite an improvement over the 667 in losses in 1980 (equal to about $1.2 billion at 1980 exchange rates) but still not enough to keep British Steel alive without operating subsidies, in spite of the work force reduction from 160,000 in 1980 to 78,000 in 1983. (Cf. "MacGregor of the Mines," *The Economist*, August 27, 1983, p. 36). British steel has continued to lose money in 1984, but is expected to be profitable in 1985; this writer is skeptical, however (cf. "Should Steel be Helpful?" *The Economist*, February 9, 1985, p. 12).

[26] Cf. J. Jürgen Jeske, "Die Fallstricke der Krise," *FAZ*, July 6, 1985, p. 11.

[27] German social legislation and enterprise work force policies apply to *all* employees, from shop-floor worker to group vicepresident. Only the top-management committee called the Vorstand has a different legal status. The Vorstand consists ordinarily of five to fifteen members who are collectively and individually responsible for managing the enterprise and are considered by law to be "the employer". Each Vorstand member receives a contract, ordinarily five years, and is annually "relieved" (entlastet) by the stockholder assembly of his legal responsibility for the past year.

German industries' high fringe benefit costs benefit not only the unionized production workers but *all* employees; a cut-back in generous pension and vacation benefits (the typical German employee has five weeks vacation) therefore, would have to be borne by the entire workforce.

[28] The *Badische Stahlwerke* is one "mini-steel mill" enterprise with about 1000 employees that has combined good management with new elector-furnace technology to make solid profits in 1983 and 1984 (Cf. *Die Zeit*, August 24, 1984, p. 14).

156

References :

Bell, Daniel and Kristol, Irving, eds. (1981), *The Crisis in Economic Theory*, New York : Basic Books

Jeske, J. Jürgen (1985),"Fallstricke der Krise", *Frankfurter All-gemeine Zeitung (FAZ)*, July 6,11

MacGregor, Ian (1983), "MacGregor of the Mines", *The Economist*, August 27,36

MacGregor, Ian (1985),"Should Steel be Helpful ?", *The Economist*, Febuary 9,12

Meade, J. C. (1982), *Stagflation, vol.I : Wage, Fixing*, London : Allen and Irving

Streeck, Wolfgang (1984), *Industrial Relations in West Germany*, New York: St. Martin's Press

Thimm, Alfred L. (1976), "Decision-Making at Volkswagen 1972-75", *Columbia Journal of World Business*, Springer 1976

Thimm, Alfred L. (1979), " The German Steel Strike 1978-79; *World Business*, Summer 1979, 52-68

Thimm, Alfred L. (1981), " How Far Should German Codetermination Go ?",*Challenge*, July/August 1981, 14-15

Thimm, Alfred L. (1982), *The False Promise of Codetermination*, Lexington, MA: D.C. Heath & Co.

Tinnin, D. (1980a), "West Germany Steel", *The Economist*, May 3, 1980, 95-96

Tinnin, D. (1980b) " Reforging an Old Steelworker", *Fortune*, June 16, 1980

Weitzman, Martin L. (1983), "Some Macroeconomic Implications of Alternative Compensation Systems", *Economic Journal*, vol. 93.

Weitzman, Martin L. (1984), *The Share Economy*, Cambridge :Harvard University Press

Witte, Eberhard (1980), "The Influence potential of the Employee as the Basis for Codetermination", *Die Betriebswirtschaft*, vol.40

Witte, Eberhard (1981a) "The Independence of Management Board in the Influence System of Enterprise", *Schmalenbachs Zeitschrift für betriebswirtschaftliche Forschung*, vol. 33

Witte, Eberhard (1981b), "The Influence of the Stockholder on Enterprise Policy", *Zeitschrift für Betriebswirtschaft*, vol.51

THE IMPACT OF INDUSTRIAL POLICY AND STRUCTURAL CHANGES
ON CODETERMINATION IN THE GERMAN STEEL INDUSTRY: Comment
by
Kurt W. Rothschild

Professor Thimm's paper outlines German codetermination procedures and then turns to the steel industry and steel crisis in
order to analyse the working of codetermination in this special
case. Thimm manages to convey a lot of useful and interesting information on the steel crisis, on the problems of structural
change, and on codetermination. I will not try to discuss all aspects covered in the paper (though some give rise to interesting
disputes on the problems of structural adjustment), but will concentrate on codetermination and Thimm's treatment of it.

Codetermination is a complex subject at the heart of present-
day industrial relations problems in all developed capitalist
countries; it is not specific to Germany. German codetermination
has, however, elicited special interest, partly because of its
long intellectual traditions - going back to the interwar period
and beyond[1] - and partly because of its strong tendency towards
extensive legal foundations. Disputes about these laws and their
consequences have attracted special attention to the German case,
but little notice has been taken of the less formalised development of codetermination in other countries. Particularly in the
early days of the debate on German codetermination (in Germany
and abroad) there was a tendency to exaggerate fears and hopes.
These have failed to materialise. German codetermination so far
has not *decisively* changed the German political and social environment. In other countries, labor legislation has had such an
effect. Herein lies a special feature of codetermination. This is
quite correctly seen by Thimm.

This fact makes it impossible to pass broad and general judg-
ments on the effects of German codetermination (though the temp-
tation to do so is always present). What one can hope for and
what is needed are well-defined, circumspective, and detailed investigations of various aspects of codetermination, of its possible aims and its actual effects. Thimm's paper only partly meets
these requirements.

Although Thimm makes several observations on codetermination
in general, he concentrates on a few more limited, but certainly
important, questions: (1) To what extent did industrial policy

Codetermination
ed. by H.G. Nutzinger and J. Backhaus
© Springer-Verlag Berlin Heidelberg 1989

and chronic unemployment affect codetermination practices on the shop floor, on the corporate level, and on the national level? (2) To what extent was the formulation of industrial policy affected by the existing institutional patterns of codetermination? (3) To what extent did the codetermination practices and traditions affect the economic efficiency of the German steel industry and its attempts to adapt itself to changing patterns of demand? These questions set the tone for the second part of the paper to which we now turn.

There can be little doubt that the questions posed by Thimm are relevant. And one can easily agree that "it is much too early to arrive at definitive answers to these question" and that there is still no "general dynamic model of codetermination under structural, economic and political pressure." So one has to be prepared for modest and provisional observations and answers. It is in this respect that I am not sure Thimm has been sufficiently careful in his treatment of the subject.

The first difficulty arises in his attempt to combine the three above-mentioned questions in one single analysis. While some connection between the three questions certainly exists, I would nevertheless maintain that conditions in the world steel industry are so special even in normal times[2] and a fortiori in a period of fundamental reallocations in world steel capacities and production that events there may be sui generis. It is true that Thimm restricts his theme to the steel industry in the title of his paper; but in his actual treatment he tends to indicate that his conclusions may also have some validity for questions (1) and (2) above, viz. the general problem of interaction between recession, industrial policy, and codetermination. Now while I do not want to deny that suggestions for these wider and important questions might be obtained from the experiences in the steel industry, I would, nevertheless, stress that such indications and analogies have to be argued very carefully if misunderstandings are to be avoided. Thimm's paper itself clearly reveals that special mixture of steel industry dynamics, the interplay of national and international structural policy, and general recession that formed the background of the adjustment process in the steel industry since the 1970s. One must be very careful indeed to draw general conclusions from this special segment of economic history. Going too far in this direction would be like drawing general conclusions about the absence of (legal) codetermination machinery from the year-long miners' strike in the crisis-ridden British coal industry.

But even if we restrict ourselves to the steel sector, I am not sure that Thimm does not overestimate the generality of his results. Recognising that the time for a general theoretical treatment has not yet arrived, he hopes that "it is precisely the case study approach that will supply the impetus for the further development of a micro-theory of the firm under codetermination." Building on this hope, he then proceeds to concentrate on the events in ARBED-Saarstahl, an important steel firm that is struggling with difficult economic and regional problems.

Now, I do not want in the least to deny the value of case studies. Like Thimm, I believe that, in the complicated and underdeveloped fields of the theories of the firm and of organisations and industrial relations, case studies are extremely important. Each case study can be important, and so is Thimm's. But a case study is a case study is a case study (Gertrude Stein). And, considering the extraordinary circumstances of the case under review, it would be risky to generalise even for the steel industry without further case studies inside and outside Germany. After all, strong reactions to the problems and industrial policies in the industry were observed in other countries, and quite a number of them were not so different from those at ARBED-Saarstahl or elsewhere in Germany. In other words, Thimm's paper deals with a special firm in a special industry in a special period - an important story in which one can try to isolate the role of codetermination. But the wider question of codetermination in recession and its interaction with industrial policy needs an extensive network of studies.

I now turn to a completely different point. quite apart from the question of the *general* validity of Thimm's observations, he takes too limited a view of codetermination. It is a view favored by most of the newspapers and monthlies he quotes, like the *FAZ* or the *Economist*. We might call it a conservative position. From this standpoint, codetermination either is regarded as undesirable *per se*, because it limits private property rights and the freedom and flexibility of managerial decision making with possible negative effects on productivity, or is accepted insofar as it reduces tensions in personnel problems and increases mobility and acceptance of technical change with positive effects on labour productivity. It is particularly this latter standard that appears to guide Thimm's judgment whenever he evaluates certain activities and results.

But there is another side to codetermination. Labor's advocacy of codetermination has been motivated not only by the hope for efficiency gains but also by the likelihood of achieving some wider political-economic goals, like democratisation in the economic sphere, a greater say in changes in the work process, and a stronger position in employer-employee transactions. From this viewpoint the aim of "democratic and human labour relation" has to be counted as important as economic efficiency and profitability. The two goals need not conflict; but they might. And then conservative and laboristic views will clash. It is this difference in values and goals that makes codetermination such a hotly debated issue.[3]

Thimm fully recognises that organised labor should use codetermination for the protection of the workers: "It is the duty of each works council to represent the economic interests of the employees in its shop." But he criticises labor at higher levels for having opposed the closing down of factories after 1978 when the steel crisis and the recession had abated. This attitude he regards as parochial for putting the short-run interests of the workers before the long-run interests of the industry as well as the workers. But the problem is that - here and elsewhere - Thimm looks at the matter only in terms of cost efficiency and competition. He may even be right: the resistance to some changes may have been short-sighted. But one should at least discuss the alternative. Mass dismissals during severe recession and in certain regions are an enormous social problem, and to slow down dismissals or try to ease the consequences for those who carry the burden of change need not be short-sighted. The social unrest that such changes create in countries where codetermination is minimal or absent shows that the role of codetermination must be carefully evaluated if one wants a full picture of the global cost-benefits.

Footnotes:

[1] See, for instance, A. Shuchman, Codetermination. Labor's middle Way in Germany (Washington, D.C.: Public Affairs Press, 1957), Parts II and III

[2] This explains the early integration of the European Iron sand Steel Industry after the war and the special law of codetermination for this sector in Germany.

[3] It is no coincidence that codetermination was one of the few issues on which the German Commission on Economic and Social Change (consisting of representatives from the employers' federations and the trade unions and of social scientists) was unable to make a recommendation. See Wirtschaftlicher und sozialer Wandel in der Bundesrepublik Deutschland, Gutachten der Kommission für wirtschaftlichen und sozialen Wandel, (Göttingen: Verlag Otto Schwarz, 1977), pp. 442 ff.

CODETERMINATION IN WEST GERMANY: INSTITUTIONS AND EXPERIENCES
by
Hans G. Nutzinger

1. Origins and Notions of Codetermination
1.1 Introductory Remarks

The system of employee codetermination at both the plant and
the enterprise level in West Germany is now older than thirty
years; if one includes earlier regulations before World War II,
it comprises nowadays almost one century. The idea of codetermination whose ambiguity and vagueness will be discussed in one of
the following subsections is, broadly speaking, more or less accepted in the Federal Republic of Germany; the existing legal
regulations are generally accepted and, perhaps to a lesser extent, implemented in practice. After the legal disputes during
the seventies, centering around the constitutionality of the 1976
Codeterminaton Law (cf. subsection I.3 below), a routine practice
of codetermination can be observed in the eighties. To be sure,
conflicts and disputes in certain areas continue to exist, but
practically no major political force argues for the removal of
this system of interest articulation.

On the other hand, codetermination has not been a major focus
of interest or political action during the last five years, although the unions launched a "codetermination campaign"
(Mitbestimmungsoffensive) in Spring 1983. In a similar way, the
issue of "codetermination at the workplace" for rank and file
workers - interestingly raised by both employers and unions -
has remained in the field of theoretical discussion among social
scientists and the labor market parties; so far, it has not become a center of political or legal action. In spite of these
deficits, codetermination has become a normal and central element
in the German system of industrial relations. This gives us an
opportunity to draw up a provisional balance-sheet of its legal
bases, the practical experiences and future steps in both theory
and practice. As observed before, there is a rather long history
of codetermination regulations in Germany; hence it is useful to
start with a short historical overview in order to better compre-
hend the existing legal system of employee participation in the
Federal Republic.

Codetermination
ed. by H.G. Nutzinger and J. Backhaus
© Springer-Verlag Berlin Heidelberg 1989

1.2 Historical Overview

The idea of a constitutional limitation of private property rights - and especially the right to direct other people's work derived from this property - has a long tradition in Germany, starting as early as in the National Assembly of Frankfurt in 1848 *(Paulskirche)*. The development of an institutionalized employee "codetermination" as a modification (or, as property rights theorists would prefer to call it, "attenuation"[1]) of property rights with regard to the use of the means of productions has to be seen on the background of the specific economic and political development of Germany above all in the late 19th and the early 20th century.[2]

The specific features of the German course of events in the frame of the general process of industrialization in Western Europe and Northern America have to be seen mainly in the following characteristics:

- In contrast to the leading European powers in the middle of the 19th century, especially England and France, Germany had not yet overcome the historical splintering of the territory, and its way to a modern nation state was further complicated by the emerging conflict between Prussia and Austria.
- On the level of politics and society, to this territorial splintering corresponded the lasting dominance of the old feudal powers, especially of the territorial princes and the territorial nobility who were mainly involved in the conflict about the course and the conditions of the nation-building process whereby other social groups were largely excluded.
- In accordance with this delayed formation of a German nation state, also the process of industrialization lagged behind France, Great Britain and the United States, further complicated by various constraints for the mobility of the factors of production (e.g. through domestic tariffs, trade constraints, lack of common currency, etc.).
- Based on the factors mentioned before, a relative weakness of the German bourgeoisie is to be observed which was largely excluded from political power, partly even after the unionization in the Bismarck empire of 1871, and which was largely restricted to the initially less developed economic sphere.

- Correspondingly, there was also a delayed rise of an industrial working class, and in addition to that it is also note worthy that traditional guild-oriented and corporatist ideas were effective not only in the nobility but similarly among large parts of the bourgeoisie and the working class which further favored the tendency for an institutional regulation of social conflicts.

Therefore, in a historical perspective we can perceive the specific form of conflict regulation in the field of industrial relations in Germany (and similarly in Austria), namely in the form of institutionalized codetermination, as an expression of a relatively weak position of the German entrepreneurs between the still dominant feudal powers on the one hand and the growing workers' movement on the other hand; this in turn led to institutionalized and basically integrative forms of conflict resolution. So, institutional compromises were needed which tended to increase the area of cooperation and consensus compared with the area of conflict via partial integration of workers into the vertical structure of the firm and in the long run even via restricted participation. This increased ability to consensus corresponded to an increased need for consensus, however: Open and nation-wide forms of industrial conflict, as they became common to England or France, were much more dangerous in Germany, given the unstable and rapidly changing balance among the different social groups. Hence, the emphasis on institutionalized and integrative forms of conflict regulation in Germany is both an expression of strength and weakness.

This general characterization can be substantiated by various historical events, starting with the National Assembly of Frankfurt in 1848 where different proposals for employee participation were based on earlier notions of the guild system. The then rather progressive social policy of the Bismarck empire (legal social insurance, protective and participative trade regulations since 1850, voluntary workers' committees in some factories, etc.) is another expression of this general tendency. The perhaps most illustrative example of state-sponsored employee participation in favor of political stabilization is the "Law on Patriotic Service" *(Gesetz betreffend die Vaterländischen Hilfsdienste)* in the middle of the First World War: In order to insure a steady supply of arms and ammunition, workers' committees in all important enterprises were established (while, at the same time, liability for labor service and restrictions to workers' quitting were also introduced).[3] This ambiguity of the codetermination idea can be further illustrated in the period of the Weimar Republic after World War I. Compared with far-reaching ideas of a direct political and economic democracy in a comprehensive council system, the Works Council Law *(Betriebsrätegesetz)* of 1920 was rather disappointing as it gave workers' representatives - the works council *(Betriebsrat)* - only modest rights in personnel and social affairs and virtually no influence in economic decisions.[4] During the Nazi era 1933-1945 even these very restricted forms of worker representation were annihilated and replaced by a compulsory German labor front *(Deutsche Arbeitsfront)* comprising both the workers as "follower" *(Gefolgschaft)* and the entrepreneurs as "enterprise leader" *(Betriebsführer)*, corresponding to the Nazi authoritarian principle in politics.

1.3 The Existing Legal Structure

The existing legal structure of codetermination in Germany today is partly based on its precedents in Imperial Germany and in the Republic of Weimar. Due to the specific situation after World War II, legal development has been far from systematic.[5] Based on a "voluntary" union participation in the iron and steel producing (not processing) industry which has been offered by the employers themselves after World War II in order to prevent or minimize dismantling and decartelization by the Allies, the first law which was passed by the West German Parliament *(Bundestag)* was the *Montan-Mitbestimmungsgesetz* (Codetermination Law in the mining and steel producing industry) in 1951. Up to now, it contains the farthest-reaching institutional - arrangements with respect to economic codetermination. Whereas the workers do not have direct representation at the annual general meeting of the corporations, an equal number of workers' representatives (mainly proposed by the respective union) is elected to the board of supervision with a neutral member, the so-called "eleventh man", elected by capital owners and workers' representatives jointly in order to avoid impasse situations. According to German company law - and in distinctive contrast to American company law - the supervisory board appoints the board of management and is assumed to advise, to supervise and to control its conduct of business but has no decision-making rights with respect to the management of the company which is incumbent solely on the board of management (§ 111(4) of the German Joint-Stock Company Law). In case of conflict between the board of management and the supervisory board, the former can appeal to the stockholders' general meeting in order to get a three quarters majority to overcome a veto of the supervisory board. Only one employee or union representative, the labor director *(Arbeitsdirektor)*, responsible for personnel affairs, is a member of the board of management. So, even under the farthest-reaching law, there is no direct employee and union influence on the economic decisions and even with respect to the controlling functions of the supervisory board, there is a final majority of the capital owners.[6]

Industrial relations in all enterprises with more than five permanent employees are ruled by the Works Constitution Law of 1972 *(Betriebsverfassungsgesetz)*, based on the earlier law of 1952. With respect to economic affairs, its regulations are far weaker than those of the Codetermination Law. There is only a one-third employee and union representation on the supervisory board according to the 1952 law in companies with more than five hundred employees. The basic institution of the Works Constitution Law is the works council *(Betriebsrat)*. This law distinguishes between rights to codetermination *(Mitbestimmungsrechte)*, consultation and cooperation *(Mitwirkungsrechte)* and rights to information, complaint and hearing. As a rule of thumb, these rights are strongest in social matters and internal work regulations (e.g., working hours); they are mostly of the medium type in personnel matters such as engagement, regrouping, discharges, and transfers. In business questions, the Works Constitution Law mainly gives rights to information, and only with respect to those decisions which directly affect employment or working conditions of employees (e.g., those relating to technical innovation, closing and opening of new plants or major parts of it), more influence is given to the representatives of employees.[7] The Works Constitution Law of 1972 has also increased the individual employee rights in matters concerning his or her own employment, but these rights are more or less confined to legal claims to information and hearing and the right to complaint as well as to employ the members of the works council in case of conflict at the work place (e.g. with superiors).[8]

For employees in public administration, a similar law was introduced in 1955 *(Personalvertretungsgesetz)*. A special group of so-called *Tendenzunternehmen* (enterprises pursuing a "tendency", i.e. noneconomic aims) is partly or fully excluded from regulations of the Works Constitution Law; these are, above all, organizations in the fields of mass media, charitable and religious institutions, political parties, scientific organizations and the like.

In 1952, the unions heavily opposed to the one-third employee representation in the supervisory board according to the Works Constitution Law and proclaimed the *Montan-Mitbestimmungsgesetz* of 1951 as the model for a general regulation of employee and union participation in the supervisory board. A special committee, chaired by Professor Biedenkopf, was established by the Federal Government in 1967 in order to give an account of the practice of the *Montan-Mitbestimmungsgesetz* as a basis for a possible legal extension. Although the *Biedenkopf Report* (1970) was quite favorable in its assessment of the practice of this law,[9] it did not recommend its extension to all large companies: The Biedenkopf committee voted for an increased employee participation in the supervisory board, but below full parity, arguing that although it did not find clear proofs for decreased profitability in the mining and steel producing industry, it assumed that profitability was better secured by capital owners and management. And in fact, both the regulations and the practice of the Codetermination Law of 1976 applying to all large corporations with more than 2000 employees (except the *Tendenzunternehmen* and public administration on the one hand, and the mining and steel producing companies on the other hand) are not very far from the ideas of the *Biedenkopf Report*: In all decisive issues, workers influence, even in the supervisory board, remains short of full parity.

The main differences between the 1976 Codetermination Law and the *Montan-Mitbestimmungsgesetz* have to be seen in the composition of the supervisory board. In corporations with more than 2000 and less than 10000 employees, the supervisory board has twelve members, among them 6 employee representatives. Two of them are nominated from the respective unions, and four are representatives of the working collective. These four "internal" members have to represent the respective subgroups (workers, salaried employees, and the *Leitende Angestellte*, i.e., the salaried management). Thereby each group has at least one seat at the board of supervision which in practice favors the representation of management in the respective committees. In fact, as the salaried management has to be considered at least partly as the representative of capital owners, there is no equal representation of "capital" and "labor" in the supervisory board. But in any case, the breaking vote of the chairman of the supervisory board - in case of conflict elected by the majority of capital owners alone - ensures a majority of "capital" in all voting impasses even if the representative of the salaried management votes together with the other employee representatives. Also, the labor director in the board of management is normally no longer a representative of the employees or the unions as he can be (and frequently is) elected against the majority of employee representatives' votes, in contrast to the older *Montan-Mitbestimmungsgesetz*. Although both the law and the following practice revealed an ultimate power of capital owners even in the board of supervision, the employers brought an action against the new law before the German constitutional court *(Bundesverfassungsgericht)* which was rejected on March 1, 1979, mainly on the ground that the law did not imply full parity (on which assumption the employers' action was based). Still, the legal question is open whether a full parity between "capital" and "labor" would contradict the basic principles of German Civil Law and of the German Constitution, especially with respect to private ownership, liability and the freedom of coalition and profession. Politically, this Codetermination Law has, at least at the moment, brought public discussion and public interest in these questions to an end as there is a broad consensus that there must be a fair time of practice of the new law before any legal changes should be introduced and as questions of unemployment and of the reform of the social insurance systems are much more urgent.

There have been lots of practical disputes and legal actions with respect to the practice of the law since 1978 when the law became practically effective in large corporations.[10] The political positions are quite clear: The unions and the Social Democratic Party consider this law to be only one step in the right direction and demand an extension of the *Montan-Mitbestimmungsgesetz* for all big corporations. The employers, on the other hand, supported by the majority of the Liberal Party and parts of the Christian Democrats, consider the Works Constitution Law (granting only a one-third employee and union representation in corporations with more than 500 and less than 2000 employees) as the model for business-wide economic codetermination. Although in practice employers get by with the Codetermination Laws of 1951 and 1976 (as they confess in private and sometimes even in public talks) they go on to argue against the principle of full parity allegedly inherent in these laws as, in the long run, it could undermine private property, free enterprise and the social market economy altogether.

The system of legal codetermination as summarized in Table 2 (see below) however does not even include the complete legal basis of codetermination: Works agreements *(Betriebsverein-barungen)* between the management and the works council, based on the Works Constitution Law, collective agreements between unions and employers at enterprise, sectoral and regional levels *(Lohnrahmen- und Manteltarifvereinbarungen)* as well as different regulations of the general labor law belong likewise to the basis of practical codetermination. The rather complicated system of institutions within legal German codetermination is sketched in Table 3 (see below).

However, even these elements do not exhaust the complete system of German industrial relations which we might term codetermination in the broader sense. The complete network comprehends - similar to the Japanese system - plenty of informal regulations, gentlemen's agreements, logrolling procedures, corporation guidelines in accordance with employee representatives and the like. Also, in the metal and the chemical industry we have the supplementary shop-steward system which serves an important role for the practical implementation of legal codetermination at the shop-floor level and as a "pool" for recruiting future employee representatives in the works council and in the supervisory board. The major system components of German industrial regulations - or of "codetermination in the broader sense" - are summarized in Table 1. Before over-emphasizing the degree of practical codetermination, given the many possibilities of formal and informal employee influence, however, one must keep in mind that we also face a lack of practical codetermination, above all in small and medium-sized firms even in those cases where it is mandated by law.[11]

Table 1

SYSTEM COMPONENTS OF GERMAN INDUSTRIAL RELATIONS
(GENERAL EMPLOYEE PARTICIPATION)

I)   LEGAL CODETERMINAITON

II) VOLUNTARY WORKS AGREEMENTS
(MANAGEMENT/WORKS COUNCIL)

III COLLECTIVE AGREEMENTS
(EMPLOYERS/UNIONS)

IV) INFORMAL REGULATIONS
- GENTLEMEN'S AGREEMENTS
- COMPANY GUIDELINES
  (in accordance with Works Councils)

V)   SUPPLEMENTARY SHOP STEWARD SYSTEM
(mainly in the metal and chemical
industry)

VI) GENERAL LABOR LAW
(combined with I) above)

AD I): MAIN CODETERMINATION LAWS

I.1 MONTAN LAW
(in the mining and the steel producing industry
- about 40 companies 1951)

I.2 WORKS CONSTITUTION LAW 1952
(now only valid in corporations with 500 to 2000 employees for representation in the supervisory board)

I.3 WORKS CONSTITUTION LAW 1972
(basic law for most firms with more than 5 employees;
employee representation in the supervisory board
according to I.1 or I.2 or I.4)

I.4 CODETERMINATION LAW 1976
(for - about 500 - companies with more than 2000
employees)

TABLE 2

MAIN CODETERMINATION RIGHTS

I) FULL CODETERMINATION RIGHTS
   (= (paritätische) Mitbestimmung)
   i.e. Veto Power by employee representatives in
   the Supervisory Board or by the Works Council

II) CONSULTATION AND COOPERATION RIGHTS

   (= Mitwirkungs- und Beratungsrechte)
   i.e. employer's ultimate decision-making
   rights after formal procedures have been
   observed

III) RIGHTS TO INFORMATION HEARING AND COMPLAINT
   *(= Informations-,Anhörungs- und Beschwerde-
   rechte)*
   i.e. no direct employee participation in
   decision-making

LEVELS OF CODETERMINATION / DEGREE OF PARTICIPATION

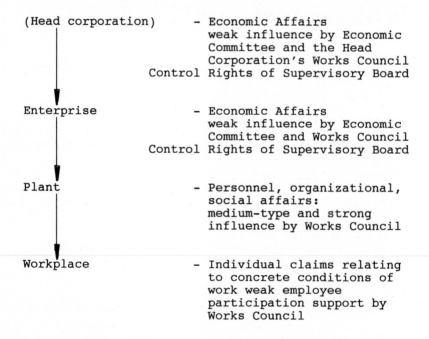

(Head corporation)   - Economic Affairs
                          weak influence by Economic
                          Committee and the Head
                          Corporation's Works Council
                Control Rights of Supervisory Board

Enterprise   - Economic Affairs
                          weak influence by Economic
                          Committee and Works Council
                Control Rights of Supervisory Board

Plant   - Personnel, organizational,
                          social affairs:
                          medium-type and strong
                          influence by Works Council

Workplace   - Individual claims relating
                          to concrete conditions of
                          work weak employee
                          participation support by
                          Works Council

Table 3

INSTITUTIONS OF GERMAN CODETERMINATION

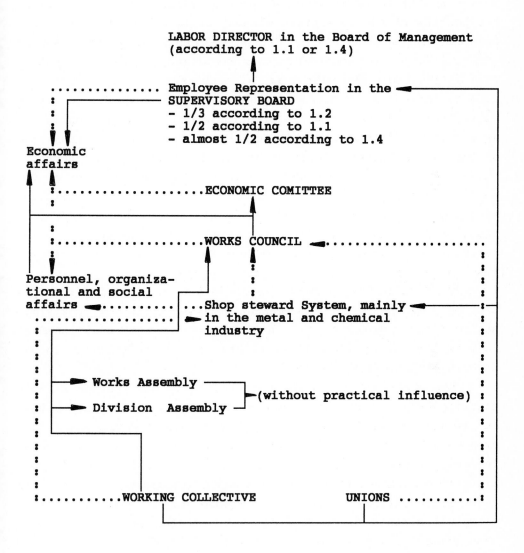

LABOR DIRECTOR in the Board of Management
(according to 1.1 or 1.4)

Employee Representation in the
SUPERVISORY BOARD
- 1/3 according to 1.2
- 1/2 according to 1.1
- almost 1/2 according to 1.4

Economic
affairs

ECONOMIC COMITTEE

WORKS COUNCIL

Personnel, organiza-
tional and social
affairs

Shop steward System, mainly
in the metal and chemical
industry

Works Assembly

Division Assembly

(without practical influence)

WORKING COLLECTIVE   UNIONS

—————— direct influence, e.g. by elections
.... indirect influence, e.g. by proposals

1.4 Different Notions of Codetermination

The notion of "codetermination" in academic literature is used in rather different ways. One group of definitions identifies codetermination more or less with a general notion of *partici-pation* in the sense of employee participation in decision-making and profits of the enterprise without specific regard to the legal or contractual basis.[12] The so-called *Biedenkopf Report* (1970, 1,4) of the codetermination committee (Biedenkopf Committee) defines codetermination as "... the institutional participation of employees or their representatives in shaping and determining the processes of will-formation and decision-making in the enterprise." This broad definition corresponds largely to the definition of general *participation*, for instance by Backhaus (1979, 6) "... as a procedure which enables the gaining of the complete relevant information through participation in decision-making of all people concerned ... by giving all people concerned equal or functionally weighted opportunities of influence and interest articulation, participation furthermore fullfills the function of an information processing procedure."

In this view, codetermination differs from general participation only by the following demarcation: "The notion of codetermination is in general use of language insofar more restricted as it refers to institutionalized rights of participation in industry" (Backhaus, 1979, 12).

A few other authors attempt a deliberate demarcation between participation and codetermination. This delineation cannot help but to use personal evaluations of researchers which makes this procedure subject to broad normative dissent. For instance, Teuteberg (1981, 72f.) argues that "... codetermination and par-ticipation mark somewhat different basic attitudes of the citizen to entire political, economic and social events." Using the ety-mological kinship of "participation" and "partnership" he holds that participation would be cooperative whereas codetermination was based on a conflict view of industrial relations. Hence, the latter were based on group interests, the former, however, on the idea of a "common interest." On this linguistic level, one could easily object that participation of different groups in the deci-sionmaking process should serve the representation of group in-terests whereas the idea of "codetermination" should be based on the idea of a common responsibility for the enterprise and the economy as a whole. However, those linguistic exercises, even if they are substantiated by historical examples, lack an appropriate and hence consensual foundation.

If we look at the notion of codetermination among the people concerned - the employees - then we find in the empirical codetermination research during the last thirty years an even broader and more heterogeneous perception of the issues than in the academic literature. Our own empirical field studies in an automobile plant (VW Kassel) and an electrotechnical plant (AEG Kassel) give an impressive illustration of this diversity. As far as concrete answers are given to the notion of codetermination - the percentage of unclear or refused responses varies considerably among the different studies (cf. Niedenhoff, 1979, chapter V) - the employees mention practically everything: The range of answers encompasses general definitions, particular dimensions of codetermination, e.g., codetermination at the work place, different institutions and representatives of codetermination as well as particular tasks where there is or should be codetermination. Very often, the idea of codetermination is not limited to the enterprise or even the economy as a whole, but comprises political, public and even private life as well. That codetermination is rather a middle-class than a working-class notion is further illustrated by the fact mentioned before that considerable percentages of employees do not have a clear or sometimes even no idea at all about it. This result of our own field studies is confirmed by numerous other empirical research projects.[13] The resulting difficulties in measuring and evaluating the effects of codetermination in the enterprise will be discussed in the following section.

But there seems to be a rather simple way out of all these difficulties, used by various researchers, namely to confine codetermination to its legal regulations in the Federal Republic of Germany. Considering our earlier remarks at the end of section I.2 on "codetermination in the broader sense," it should be obvious that this restriction is quite problematical given the fact that institutionalized employee participation in economic decision-making is not exclusively based on the laws mentioned before, but also on a variety of collective agreements between unions and employers at different levels, on regulations of labor law and social law and on a broad range of informal interest articulation and "harmonized procedure" (i.e., agreed upon between management and employee representatives). In a broader perspective, the representation of employee interests in the political system can be attributed to codetermination in the sense of an institutionalized employee participation in economic decisions. The perhaps most important fact that the relative strength of "capital" and "labor" depends more frequently on the specific economic conditions than on legal regulations, has not yet been analyzed in a systematic manner. The interesting study by Kotthoff (1981) reveals remarkable differences in the influence of the works councils, largely dependent on the size of the firm: In small and medium-sized enterprises, very often paternalistic management principles continue to prevail whereby the works councils are frequently either ineffective or even nonexistent.

The legal definition of codetermination, however, implies further problems for empirical research as the legal norms sketched before are rather heterogeneous. For different groups, different legal regulations apply as explained above: The Codetermination Law of 1976, the Codetermination Law in the mining and steel producing industry of 1951, the Works Constitution Law of 1972, sometimes combined with the former law of 1952, the special regulations for *Tendenzunternehmen* and the *Personalvertretungsgesetze* (laws on staff representation) in public administration at the federal and state levels. For about 13 percent of West German employees, no legal rules for institutionalized codetermination apply, especially in very small enterprises.[14] Again the fact should be considered that there is a big gap between the legal norms and their practical implementations: The actual level of institutionalized employee participation varies considerably among different enterprises, ranging from far below up to remarkably above the legally prescribed degree.

Our short overview leads to the following preliminary results: Codetermination applies to a central part of human life, namely work for living. In principle, it concerns every employee and hence the big majority of the working population. On the other hand, there is no clear idea - neither among the people concerned, the employers, researchers nor the politicians - what exactly has to be perceived as codetermination.[15] Of course, there is a common-sense notion of codetermination related to the most important actors, such as the works council, employee representatives and the supervisory board and the unions.

But knowing actors and institutions does not clarify the role attributed to codetermination. As Muszynski (1975) has shown[16] history and practice of German codetermination is characterized by an ambivalent if not contradictory argumentative foundation.

On the one hand, especially in the legal discussion, codetermination is based on the notion of a trustful collaboration of all members in a *cooperative* enterprise; hence, codetermination is perceived as a legal institutionalization of these opportunities for cooperation within the enterprise. On the other hand, codetermination is also based on the historical experience of a structural conflict between the employer directing other people's work and the employee basically obliged to carry out those directions. In this perspective, codetermination is an attempt to confine the entrepreneurial command by means of institutional regulations aiming at establishing a legal countervailing power in order to limit and control the entrepreneurial command without removing it altogether. The constitution of an enterprise could then be labeled, in terms of political theory, as a "constitutional monarchy."

This normative perception of codetermination (as institutionalized cooperation or as institutionalized conflict) influences the evaluation of the empirical results. Frequently, both ideas are advocated at the same time whereby the mix varies among the different authors. Without claim to a final definition we propose to perceive codetermination as an *attempt to increase the area of purposeful cooperation between employer and employees, based on partly uniform interests, e.g. in the economic success of the enterprise, by means of institutional participation of employees and their representatives within the conflict relationship between "capital" and "labor."* Certain conflicts, such as the implementation of productivity-rising, but labor-saving innovations, will continue to exist in the frame of codetermination, and generally we have to expect that employers' interests are somewhat modified under codetermination, but that they will finally prevail. Within those areas of conflicting interests, both the legal norms and the empirical observations indicate that codetermination has more or less a *defensive* function, namely to mitigate the consequences of entrepreneurial decisions for the employees concerned as far as possible without basically altering the entrepreneurial decision and its implementation, e.g. the technical innovation. Even if in most cases the economic decision is not completely predetermined by outside conditions, international competition with "non-codeterminated" countries puts narrow limits to workers' influence. At least in the long run, codetermination cannot (and one may add, should not) save jobs which have become unprofitable. This, however, does not mean that there is no room for effective codetermination in the short run nor that there might not be considerable differences in the economic conduct of a codeterminated enterprise compared with one not subject to codetermination. The market does not dictate everything but it places boundary-stones to the course of action.

2. Problems of Empirical Research

We have already emphasized that there are considerable differences in opinion and a remarkable vagueness not only in the academic literature on codetermination but also in the perception by the people concerned. This state of affairs leads to a lack of sufficiently standardized and, therefore, comparable research methodology in this field. The two major deficits of empirical codetermination research can be summarized as follows:

(1) There is a remarkble lack of appropriate specification of the topic of research and, related to this, a lack of theoretical foundation (cf. Monissen, 1978, 77-81).
(2) The focus of most empirical codetermination research has not been on its economic effects, but on sociological and psychological consequences; and the few studies which include these implications - especially Weddigen (1962) and the Biedenkopf Report (1970) - do not apply econometrical techniques;[17] they are more or less based on opinion polls.

If we look at the famous sociological studies on codetermination in the fifties[18] we find lots of interesting details about the perception and subjective evaluation of codetermination and works constitution among the people affected by and involved in codetermination (working collective; management; labor directors; members of the works council; shop stewards; union representatives) but they do not say very much about any economic consequences at the plant and enterprise level and virtually nothing at the sectoral and macroeconomic level. Compared with these sociological studies, the first investigations into the economic consequences of codetermination by Otto Blume (1962), Walter Weddigen (1962) and Fritz Voigt (1962) did not receive much attention. Their work concentrated on the activities of the people involved in codetermination (members of the works council, labor directors etc.) and on the relationship between employee repre-

sentatives and the representatives of management and capital owners. However, they were important as they influenced the techniques of the most famous research study, the Biedenkopf-Report;
furthermore, their findings came close to the results of the
Biedenkopf committee.

The Biedenkopf committee gathered its information mainly
through a written questioning of employers' and employees' representatives in codeterminated firms, supplemented by extensive
hearings with a small selected number of those officials. Taken
altogether, the Biedenkopf committee's assessment of codetermination was quite favorable.[19] It focused mainly on the effects of
different compositions of the supervisory board (one-third versus
50 percent representation), on the role of the labor director as
an employee representative in the board of management and his cooperation with the works council and on the effects of codetermination on the objectives of enterprises, especially their profitability. Compared with earlier research, two main results are
worth mentioning:

(1) In contrast to the fifties, the labor director seemed no
    longer to be characterized by a conflict of interests, but
    had found his role as a member of the board of management,
    explaining the firm's policy to employee representatives and
    ensuring a flow of information between management, works
    council (and sometimes shop stewards), and the employee
    representatives in the supervisory board.
(2) The neutral member of the supervisory board normally did not
    use his vote to overcome impasse situations (as the codeter-
    mination law implicitly presupposed) but he either stried to
    mediate between the representatives of "capital" and "labor"
    as he frequently did not feel competent enough to take the
    responsibility for his decisive vote or was "left out" of the
    decision logrolled solely between the two parties in the
    supervisory board.

Although the Biedenkopf Report marks some advance compared
with earlier studies, especially of the functionalist sociological variety, it is still characterized by the lack of a clear
theoretical framework and a shortage of systematic factual evidence. So, important questions, especially about macroeconomic
implications of codetermination, remained not sufficiently an-
swered. The Biedenkopf committee itself acknowledged those

deficits implicitly when it stated that its recommendation for nation-wide codetermination was ultimately based on a *Wertentscheidung* (normative decision).[20]

Even less satisfactory than the numerous research projects in the field of codetermination and works constitution[21] is the arbitrary use of research results in public discussion. Employers, unions and politicians alike tend to quote only those studies - or, moreover, those parts of studies - which they deem useful for their own interests. As Hartmann (1977) in his final evaluation of the practical use of codetermination research has convincingly demonstrated, lack of interest, one-sidedness, fragmentary and biased quotations, and the more or less complete neglect of the narrow limits to the meaning of these studies are predominant. Of course, it is highly unsatisfactory that all parties involved - unions, employers, and even politicians - use empirical codetermination research as some sort of a quarry where one extracts what one wants and leaves behind what one dislikes. This "quarry attitude" towards empirical social research in general and codetermination studies in particular also explains the popularity of the Biedenkopf Report: Its empirical findings pleased the unions to a considerable degree, its political recommendations for the further institutionalization comforted the employers.[22]

This quarry attitude, in particular toward the Biedenkopf Report, culminates in its representation by the employer's institute (Niedenhoff, 1971) where major results were simply misrepresented by misquoting, omitting important parts of quotes, biased or even wrong indirect quotations and so on. This extreme case is illustrative for the public use of codetermination research insofar as more subtle forms of arbitrary application and misrepresentation are, unfortunately, more or less common in this field.

During the five last years interesting research based on a broader sample of both codeterminated and non-codeterminated firms has been undertaken mainly by two research teams, the one led by Witte (1980, 1981, 1982), the second led by Kirsch (see Kirsch et al. 1980, 1984). The main findings of the Witte group centering around the influence system within the firm are shortly reviewed in Kraft's contribution to this volume. The interesting results of the Witte group suffer, however, from their specific investigation period which was mainly during winter 1978/79; at this time the Codetermination Law just started to become effective, and no routine practice and experience of this new law was available. In addition, the at this point undecided legal dispute before the Constitutional Court concerning the constitutionality of the Codetermination Law led to a wait-and-see attitude from the employers' side. The investigations by Kirsch et al. (1984) centered around the interrelationship between codetermination and the firm's full authority for market-related action. Interesting enough they found a positive correlationship between both elements, mainly due to the fact that codetermination increases workers' needs satisfaction and hence increases the room for effective cooperative behavior.

Among the numerous case studies during the last five years I would like to mention the - probably first - comparative evaluation of codetermination at two different time points (before and after the Codetermination Law of 1976) carried out by Diefenbacher et al. (1984) in a big automobile plant and a corresponding research study in a big electrotechnical plant, based on the same research design (Nutzinger et al. 1987). These studies reveal an increased interest in codetermination at the workplace and the importance of work conditions for employee involvement in codetermination: For a variety of reasons, unqualified workers tend to be excluded from direct interest articulation via codetermination and to be shifted to the traditional labor market exit option.

3. Outlook

Our findings about the state of codetermination research and, even more so, its use in political discussion are rather disappointing. Nevertheless, compared with the long time prevailing purely normative and legal discussion of the topic, it marks a modest advance as one at least attempts to gather empirical data about the practical performance and ceases to infer everything from "the nature of property" or the "nature of man" on the one hand or from the legal regulations on the other hand. One important result from the most recent German studies, especially by Kotthoff (1981), Kirsch et al. (1980), Knuth and Schank (1981, 1982) and Witte (1980, 1981), is a remarkable gap between legal norms and practical implementations in the field of the Codetermination and Works Constitution Laws. Remarkable differences

among firms and branches have been found which cast additional
doubts about easy generalizations of field studies.

Given the importance of the issue both in terms of people involved and in terms of the possible positive or negative effects
for economic performance, further progress is called for at least
in three respects:

(1) There is plenty of data and information about various aspects
    of codetermination and works constitution gathered by the
    social science research of the last thirty years mentioned
    before. A systematic representation of the findings of these
    studies - especially of the primary data which are only
    partly published so far - is needed in order to get ad-
    ditional information about changes over time and charac-
    teristic differences between sectors, firms and workplaces.
    So, a much clearer picture of the dynamics of codetermination
    (if there is any) could be gained. This would pave the way
    for the second step:

(2) The modern econometrical attempts at evaluating participation
    and codetermination, started by Cable and FitzRoy (1980),
    Svejnar (1981, 1982) and Benelli, Loderer and Lys (1987)
    should be further pursued and elaborated. These econometric
    studies do not replace the older type of research based on
    interviews, questionnaires and investigations at the enter-
    prise level. Due to differences in the underlying approach,
    there are also differences in the preliminary results derived
    from this type of work: Whereas Cable and FitzRoy reveal a
    positive influence of participation (broader defined than co-
    determination) on firm productivity, Svejnar finds that the
    1951 Codetermination and the 1952 Works Constitution Law had
    no influence on productivity, in contrast to Blumenthal's
    (1956) assertion. Finally, Benelli et al. tried to uncover
    evidence for a reduction in firm values, presumably caused by
    employees' risk aversion, but did not find. Of course, con-
    clusive results about the economic consequences of codeter-
    mination need further theoretical and empirical work.

As codetermination is an important part of the German economy
in general and German industrial relations in particular, more
reliable investigations into the practical functioning and consequences of codetermination seem to be urgent. In this respect,

I would like to mention two major topics related to an appropriate theoretical frame for codetermination research in the future:

- As the empirical findings reveal a rather big gap between legal norms and practical implementation in the field of co-determination, other forms and possibilities of interest articulation, especially in the economic process, should be taken into account. In the frame of Hirschman's exit-loyalty approach, the costs of different forms of interest articulation should be assessed with respect to varying economic conditions, degree of factor mobility, relative importance of human capital specific to the job or to the firm etc.
- An evaluation of the economic consequences of codetermination should furthermore consider the following important fact: The alternative to codetermination is not a situation with non-attenuated private property rights in the means of production, but one with other - and partly expensive - forms of interest articulation through collective bargaining, collective actions such as frequent strikes, low productivity based on low motivation etc.[23]

At the beginning of this paper I have emphasized the specific historical conditions for the rise of codetermination as a predominant form of industrial relations in Germany. So the other question whether one should support or resist the use of codetermination in other countries is even more difficult to answer, even if we had more reliable data about the effects of codetermination in Germany and even if we were willing to base our normative judgment solely on the economic net value of this specific form of regulating industrial conflicts: "Employee codetermination practices and legislation are deeply rooted in a country's history and institutions and cannot be easily exported from one country to the next" (Thimm, 1980, xiii). If the German economy has not operated too unsuccessfully compared with other major industrialized countries, such as Japan and the U.S., this could perhaps be attributed to a considerable degree to its social stability which is both based on and effected by limited employee participation via codetermination.

Footnotes:

1 See section III below for a critical examination of the so-called "attenuation" aspect of codetermination.

2 For an overview of the historical development see Nutzinger (1981) with further references.

3 For more details see Grebing (1974), Muszynski (1975), Nutzinger (1981), Schneider and Kuda (1969) and above all Teuteberg (1961).

4 According to the 1922 amendment, the works council delegated one or two members into the supervisory board of joint-stock companies.

5 For a good survey of existing legal regulations in Germany see Monissen (1978) and the shorter overview by Nutzinger (1977).

6 For head corporations in these industries, an amending law (Mitbestimmungsergänzungsgesetz) was introduced in 1955.

7 The legal basis and practice of "working conditions adapted human need" according to the 1972 law is discussed in Nutzinger (1980).

8 Thimm's (1981) assertion that the 1972 law has decreased the individual participatory rights of the single worker is simply at odds with the legal facts (cf.   81-84 of the law) as well as with the empirical evidence.

9 More on this is in section II below of this paper.

10 For details, see the contributions by Nagel and by Theisen to Diefenbacher/Nutzinger (1981), Nutzinger 1982) and Diefenbacher/ Nutzinger (1984)

11 See e.g. the empirical study by Kotthoff (1981).

12 For an empirical analysis, based on this broader notion of participation, see especially Cable and FitzRoy (1980). One of the rare attempts at an evaluation of the economic consequences of codetermination, the study by Weddigen (1962, 14), defines codetermination "... in the broadest sense as employee participation by means of representatives in cooperation with employers and their delegates with respect to decisions concerning regulations and measures referring to question of social policy, personnel policy or economic affairs."

13 For this see Kißler and Scholten (1981, 189 se.) with further references and Kißler (1982) as well as the earlier studies by Pirker et al. (1958) and by Popitz and Bahrdt (1957).

14 Calculation based on Niedenhoff (1979, 201).

15 This is not an uncommon situation in economics; let us remember only that there is not even a clear definition of economics apart from the comfortable but tautological statement attributed to Jacob Viner that "economics is what economists do."

16 A similar thesis is put forth by Thimm (1981) who, however, uses an alleged break between the 1952 and the 1972 Works Con-

stistution Law to assert a shift from cooperation to conflict. If Thimm were correct, why do German employers favor the Works Constitution Law (of 1972) as a basis of nation-wide codetermination?

[17] Only in the last few years, Svejnar (1981, 1982) and Benelli, Loderer and Lys (1987) have attempted an econometric evaluation of codetermination in Germany based on aggregate sectoral data. For a more detailed analysis of these econometric studies and a research design for a future work in the codetermination area see the contribution by Kraft to this volume.

[18] Pirker et al. (1955), Neuloh (1956, 1960), Popitz and Bahrdt (1957) and the Institut für Sozialforschung (Institute of Social Research, 1955).

[19] For a good overview on the findings, see Monissen (1978, 78-81).

[20] Monissen's (1978, 77) evaluation of the Biedenkopf Report is worth quoting although it seems to us probably too harsh: "A systematic quantitative assessment of the economic consequences of codetermination was not attempted. Subjective criteria, a priori guesses, and idiosyncrasies replace the theoretical analysis and a narrow documentation had to serve as a substitute for an appropriate empirical implementation guided by the methodological standards of a developed social science. Such an approach is symptomatic for the 'empirical' studies in the area of the codetermination problem."

[21] For a more or less complete list of all these research projects, see Diefenbacher (1983).

[22] In fact, the Biedenkopf Report (1970), together with the empirical study of codetermination in the supervisory board by Brinkmann-Herz (1972), are up to now the only codetermination studies more or less commonly accepted in social science.

[23] This aspect is neglected in the discussion of codetermination by Jensen and Meckling (1979, especially section III).

References:

Backhaus,J.: *Ökonomik der partizipativen Unternehmung*, Tübingen: J.C.B. Mohr, 1979.

Backhaus, J. and Nutzinger, H. G. (eds.), *Eigentumsrechte und Partizipation*. Property Rights and Participation, Frankfurt/Main: Haag and Herchen, 1982.

Benelli, G., Loderer, C. and Lys, Th., "Labor Participation in Corporate Policy-making Decisions: West Germany's Experience with Codetermination",in: *Journal of Business*, vol.60 (1987), 553-557.

(Biedenkopf Report), Bericht der Sachverständigenkommission zur Auswertung der bisherigen Erfahrungen bei der Mitbestimmung: *Mitbestimmung im Unternehmen*, Bundestagsdrucksache VI/334, Bonn: Heger, 1970.

Blume, Otto, "Zehn Jahre Mitbestimmung - Versuch einer Bestands-aufnahme," in: Potthoff, E. et al., *Zwischenbilanz der Mitbestimmung*, Tübingen: J.C.B. Mohr, 1962, 55-304.

Blumenthal, Michael W., *Codetermination in the German Steel Industry. A Report of Experience*, Princeton, Princeton U.P., 1956.

Brinkmann-Herz, Dorothea, *Entscheidungsprozesse in den Aufsichtsräten der Montan-Industrie*, Berlin: Duncker and Humblot, 1972.

Cable, J. and FitzRoy, F., "Productivity, Efficiency, Incentives, and Employee Participation: Some Preliminary Results for West Germany," in: *Kyklos* 33 (1980), 100-121.

Dahrendorf, Ralf, *Das Mitbestimmungsproblem in der deutschen Sozialforschung*, München: Piper, 2nd ed., 1965.

Diefenbacher, H. and Nutzinger, H. G. (eds.), *Mitbestimmung. Probleme und Perspektiven empirischer Forschung*, Frankfurt/Main - New York: Campus, 1981.

Diefenbacher, H. and Nutzinger, H. G., "Basispartizipation oder arbeitsteiliges Gegenmachtmodell? Die Praxis der Mitbestimmung in einem Großbetrieb der Automobilindustrie," in: Nutzinger (1982), 447-503.

Diefenbacher, H., *Empirische Mitbestimmungsforschung*, Frankfurt/Main: Haag + Herchen, 1983.

Diefenbacher, H. et al., *Mitbestimmung: Norm und Wirklichkeit*, Fallstudie aus einem Großbetrieb der Automobilindustrie, Frankfurt/M.-New York: Campus, 1984.

Diefenbacher, H./Nutzinger, H.G. (eds.), *Mitbestimmung: Theorie, Geschichte, Praxis.*,Heidelberg: FESt, 1984.

Diefenbacher, H./Nutzinger, H.G. (eds.), *Gewerkschaften und Arbeitsbeziehungen im internationalen Vergleich*, Heidelberg: FESt, 1984.

Diefenbacher, H./Nutzinger, H.G. (eds.), *Mitbestimmung in Betrieb und Verwaltung*, Heidelberg: FESt, 1986.

Grebing, H., *Geschichte der deutschen Arbeiterbewegung. Ein Überblick*, München: dtv, 5th ed., 1974.

Hartmann, H., " Soziologische Ergebnisse zur Mitbestimmung - und die Reaktion der Praxis, " in: *Kölner Zeitschrift für Soziologie und Sozialpsychologie*, Vol. 29 (1977), 331-352.

Institut für Sozialforschung (ed.), *Betriebsklima*, Frankfurt/M : Europäische Verlagsanstalt, 1955.

Jensen, M.C. and Meckling, W.H.,"Rights and Production functions: An Application to Labor-managed Firms and Codetermination", in: *Journal of Business*, Vol. 52 (1979), 469-506.

Kirsch, W. et al., *Werte von Führungskräften und Arbeitnehmervertretern im Einflußbereich der Mitbestimmung*, Research Report, first draft, typescript, University of München, 1980.

Kirsch, W. et al., *Mitbestimmung in der Unternehmenspraxis*. Eine empirische Bestandsaufnahme, Herrsching: W. Kirsch, 1984.

Kißler, L., " *Mitbestimmung auf der Zeitachse* ", in : Nutzinger (1982), 505-515.

Kißler, L. and Scholten, U., "Mitbestimmung als Kommunikationsproblem. Gewerkschaftliche Mitbestimmungsinformation und ihre Rezeption durch die Arbeitenden", in: Diefenbacher/ Nutzinger (1981), 183-218.

Knuth, M. and Schank, G. ; " Betriebliche Normsetzung als Mitbestimmungswirkung - Einigungsstellen als Möglichkeit innerbetrieblicher Konfliktlösung", in: Diefenbacher/ Nutzinger (1981), 177-182.

Knuth, M. and Schank, G., "Die Einigungsstelle: Grenzbereich von Kooperation und Konflikt in der betrieblichen Mitbestimmung", in: Nutzinger (1982), 375-399.

Kotthoff, H. , *Betriebsräte und betriebliche Herrschaft*. Eine Typologie von Partizipationsmustern im Industriebetrieb, Frankfurt/Main-New York: Campus, 1981.

Monisssen, H. G., " The Current Status of Labor Participation in the Management of Business Firms in Germany", in: Pejovich, S. (ed.), *The Codetermination Movement in the West*, Lexington, Mass.: D.C. Heath, 1978, 57-84.

Muszynski, B., *Wirtschaftliche Mitbestimmung zwischen Konflikt- und Harmonie-Konzeptionen*, Meisenheim am Glan: Anton Hain, 1975.

Neuloh, O., *Die deutsche Betriebsverfassung und ihre Sozialformen bis zur Mitbestimmung*, Tübingen: J.C.B. Mohr, 1956.

Neuloh, O., *Der neue Betriebsstil*. Untersuchungen über Wirklichkeit und Wirkungen der Mitbestimmung, Tübingen: J.C.B. Mohr, 1960.

188

Niedenhoff, H.- U.," 20 Jahre Montanmitbestimmung im Spiegel empirischer Untersuchungen", in: *Berichte des Deutschen Industrie-Instituts zu Gewerkschaftsfragen*, Vol.5,Nr.9, Köln 1971.

Niedenhoff, H.- U., *Mitbestimmung in der Bundesrepublik Deutschland*, Köln: Deutscher Institutsverlag, 1979.

Nutzinger, H. G., " Co-Determination in the Federal Republic of Germany: Present State and Perspectives", in: *Economic Analysis and Workers' Management*, Vol. XI (1977), 318- 324.

Nutzinger, H.G., " Betriebsverfassung und Mitbestimmung: Soziale Beziehungen im Unternehmen", in: Robert Bosch Stiftung (ed.): Deutschland-Frankreich: *Bausteine zum Systemvergleich*, Vol. 2: Wirtschaft und Soziale Beziehungen, Gerlingen: Bleicher, 1981, 187-212.

Nutzinger, H.G.(ed.), *Mitbestimmung und Arbeiterselbstverwaltung.* Praxis und Programmatik, Frankfurt/Main - New York: Campus, 1982.

Nutzinger, H.G., "Industrial Relations and Codetermination in the Federal Republic of Germany", in: *Management Under Differing Labour Market and Employment Systems*, (Second Berlin-Toronto Symposium on Comparative Management) Berlin - New York: Walter de Gruyter, 1987.

Nutzinger, H.G. et al., *Mitbestimmung in der Krise.* Fallstudie aus einem Großbetrieb der elektrotechnischen Industrie, Frankfurt/M.: Haag + Herchen, 1987.

Paul, E. and Scholl, W., "Mitbestimmung bei Personal - und Investitionsfragen", in: Diefenbacher/Nutzinger (1981), 115-142.

Pirker, Th. et al., *Arbeiter-Management-Mitbestimmung*, Stuttgart-Düsseldorf: Ring-Verlag, 1955.

Popitz,H. and Bahrdt,H.- P., *Das Gesellschaftsbild des Arbeiters*, Tübingen: J.C.B. Mohr, 1957.

Schneider, D. and Kuda, R., *Mitbestimmung. Weg zur industriellen Demokratie ?*, München: dtv, 1969.

Svejnar, J., " Relative Wage Effects of Unions, Dictatorship and Codetermination: Econometric Evidence from Germany", in: *Review of Economics and Statistics*, Vol. 63 (1981), 188-197.

Svejnar,J., "Codetermination and Productivity: Empirical Evidence from the Federal Republic of Germany", Jones, D. and Svejnar, J. (eds.), *Participatory and Self-Managed Firms*, Evaluating Economic Performance. Lexington, Mass.: D.C. Heath, 1982, 199-212.

Teuteberg, H. J. , *Geschichte der industriellen Mitbestimmung in Deutschland*, Tübingen: J.C.B. Mohr, 1961.

Teuteberg, H. J., "Ursprünge und Entwicklung der Mitbestimmung in Deutschland", in: *Zeitschrift für Unternehmensgeschichte*, suplementary volume 19, 1981.

Thimm, A.,*The False Promise of Codetermination*, Lexington, Mass.: D.C. Heath, 1981.

Voigt , F., " Die Mitbestimmung der Arbeitnehmer in den Unternehmungen", in: Weddigen, W. (ed.): *Zur Theorie und Praxis der Mitbestimmung*. Berlin: Duncker and Humblot, 1962, 87-536.

Weddigen, W. , " Begriff und Produktivitat der Mitbestimmung" , in: Weddigen, W. (ed.), *Zur Theorie und Praxis der Mitbestimmung*, Berlin: Duncker and Humblot, 1962, 9-86.

Witte, E., "Der Einfluß der Arbeitnehmer auf die Unternehmenspolitik",in: *Die Betriebswirtschaft*, Vol. 40 (1980), 541-559.

Witte, E., " Die Unabhängigkeit des Vorstandes im Einflußsystem der Unternehmung, " in: *Schmalenbachs Zeitschrift für Betriebswirtschaftliche Forschung*, Vol. 33 (1981), 273- 296.

Witte, E., "Das Einflußsystem der Unternehmung in den Jahren 1976 und 1981", in: *Zeitschrift fur betriebswirtschaftliche Forschung*, vol. 34, 416-434.

CODETERMINATION IN WEST GERMANY:
INSTITUTIONS AND EXPERIENCES: Comment
by
Derek C. Jones

Professor Nutzinger has written a succinct review of empirical research into German codetermination. In my comments I will dwell on some of his main points and, by reference to recent empirical work on producer (industrial/worker) cooperatives and British retail cooperatives (in which there are worker directors), I will show how these arguments have broader applicability.

Nutzinger's paper begins by noting that, contrary to the impressions gleaned from much of the literature on German codetermination, the postwar legislation does not represent a sharp break with previous practice. There is a long history in Germany of law-making in this area and all acts have imposed constitutional limitations on the rights of private property. Similar observations frequently apply to producer cooperatives. Little of the recent literature on contemporary worker cooperatives in the West is aware of (let alone informed by) the historical antecedents of contemporary cooperatives. Yet in all Western economies, the phenomenon of worker cooperatives has a long history, and there are many examples of legislative initiatives dating back to the nineteenth century.[1]

Nutzinger also notes that existing laws on codetermination are hardly radical: in all industries, both at the board and at the workshop level, the codetermination law provides that the influence of workers and their representatives must be less than parity. Similarly, so-called "worker cooperative" often differ substantially from the textbook "labour-managed firm". Legislation seldom *requires* that all workers in producer co-ops be members and sometimes only a minority of the work force are voting members. For example, among enterprises in France registered as producer cooperatives, the fraction of the work force that are members varies from almost zero to unity. In consultancy and printing co-ops membership averages around 70 percent, whereas in construction the average value is below 50 percent. (See Defourney, Estrin and Jones 1985). Furthermore, the contemporary cooperative scene is often painted with a broad brush that ignores the enormous variability among producer cooperatives of

Codetermination
ed. by H.G. Nutzinger and J. Backhaus
© Springer-Verlag Berlin Heidelberg 1989

institutional features such as mechanisms for worker participation in decision making, in ownership, and in control.[2] In Britain the extent of worker representation on the board of directors varies considerably among both producer co-ops (Jones 1975) and retail co-ops (Jones 1985). Whereas the value of individually-owned capital stakes in Mondragon co-ops sometimes approaches $50,000.00, in Italy the average value in construction co-ops is $800.00 (Jones and Svejnar 1985b) and in long-established British producer co-ops, usually less than $100.00 (Estrin, Jones and Svejnar 1983).

Nutzinger emphasises that, measurement problems aside, in German enterprises covered by the codetermination legislation, there may not be a close correspondence between the degree of de facto participation and that prescribed de jure. He argues that it is measures of actual worker participation that are most relevant for intelligent research on codetermination. Moreover, the values such a variable attains show marked variation among enterprises and reflect the influence of an array of factors other than legal regulations. Nor do most studies on cooperatives include direct measures of workers' involvement in day-to-day decision making. But the voluntary nature of the decision to join the cooperative makes the situation very different than that of state-mandated codetermination. Moreover, it can be argued that the manner and extent to which workers participate in the cooperative is an individual choice problem (subject to institutional and technical constraints). The workers choose whether to join a producer cooperative and, in many cases (e.g. France and Italy), determine how much finance to both stake in and lend to the firm beyond the legally prescribed minima. Consequently, empirical work on cooperatives is aided by the availability of various important indicators of employee participation - such as the fraction of the workforce that are members and the size of the - individually-owned capital stake - and the likely closer correspondence between such de jure measures and the degree of actual participation. In accounting for variation in the degree of participation among co-ops, empirical work on producer cooperatives has probably progressed beyond corresponding work on codetermination. Recent work has assumed that the degree of participation and labor effect, which fixes company output, are in fact jointly determined.[3] While a considerable amount of work remains to be done on this complex issue, the preliminary work makes it clear that participation is determined by a variety of enterprise-specific and extra-organisational factors.

Nutzinger refers to the relative absence of hypothesis-testing studies on codetermination by both economists and sociologists. The notable exception is Jan Svejnar's work, which uses industry level data to provide the best available estimates of the effects of codetermination on productivity and wages (Svejnar 1981, 1982). Although the value of his work is abundantly clear, Nutzinger rightly observes that such work represents only a beginning. (For example, studies at a more disaggregated level are needed.)

In a recent paper, Jones (1985), has provided additional evidence on the productivity debate using as an example British worker directors. The experience of British retail co-ops has been largely ignored in the debate on codetermination. This is an important omission because, in these firms, the practice of worker representation on boards has a long history and there is wide variation among British retail co-ops with respect to the nature and scope of worker representation. In 1978, in about one in five firms a third or more of the board of management worked in the coop; in one firm, two thirds of the board were directors. At the same time, in every sixth firm there were no board members who were working in that firm. Many former workers were worker directors too. In addition, various financial mechanisms exist which, in principle, could produce productivity effects. By using this new firm-level data set and a production function estimating framework, I find in preliminary estimates an overall (though modest) positive productivity effect. This is attributed largely to the effects of worker representation on boards (rather than to financial participation).

Hypothesis-testing studies on producer cooperatives are relatively more abundant and have tackled a greater range of issues than have econometric studies of codetermination. Most attention, however, has been devoted to analysing the relationship between how well the enterprise performs and the amount of worker participation, particularly in western co-ops. In a recent study Estrin, Jones and Svejnar (1983) analyze the productivity effects of worker participation in producer co-ops in Italy, France, and Britain.[4] A variety of production functions (reflecting different forms of production technology) are estimated using model selection tests to choose the production function best supported by the data. A vector of proxies for worker participation is used to augment the production function entered in a disembodied form. Since identical measures of participation variables are used for different groups of cooperatives, the authors are able to report closely comparable empirical estimates for different countries and institutional arrangements.[5] The authors conclude that the productivity effects of various forms of participation differ markedly from one institutional setting to another. But in general they find that the overall effect of participation is positive. (For example, in France, the size of the productivity effect tends to be about 5 percent of output, though it does vary across sectors and over time between -2 percent and +26 percent.) The positive effect is found most uniformly for profit (surplus) sharing and, to a slightly lesser extent, individual capital (share) ownership by workers. Participation in decision making is found to be mostly unrelated to productivity, although in some cases (e.g. Italian manufacturing co-ops) the productivity effect is strongly positive. Individual loans by workers to the enterprise do not show association to performance, and collective capital ownership exhibits an insignificant or a negative productivity effect. Instrumental variable estimates of the main effects are found to be quite similar to their ordinary least square counterparts.

The unsatisfactory and frequently self-serving use of research on codetermination in public discussions is pointed out by Nutzinger. Attention is also drawn to the role played by the early (and faulty) work of economists in influencing the work and subsequent report of the Biedenkopf commission. Again I find much merit in these observations and parallels elsewhere. Thus the extraordinarily critical reception given the publication of the Bullock Report (1977) seldom reflected analysis that carefully drew on published research but resulted from ideological hostility to the proposed "attenuation" of private property rights. At the same time, the Bullock Committee, like its German counterpart, may be criticized for failing to adequately consider the contribution modern economic analysis might have played in their deliberations.[6]

In the main, existing research on worker cooperatives is badly used in public discussions, because enthusiasts tend to oversell. Frequently co-ops are presented as a simple panacea for a variety of social and industrial problems. Cooperative failures are blithely ignored, and the success of contemporary firms is greatly exaggerated. Thus popular accounts of British worker cooperatives usually, on the one hand, overestimate the overall size of the contemporary worker cooperative sector and, on the other hand, fail to appreciate that in the past the sector was larger and that individual firms, which sometimes have ceased to exist, may each have provided employment for more than 2000 workers. This contemporary gung-ho advocacy, however, stands in stark contrast to the sustained opposition to producer cooperatives in the past from quarters that might have been expected to be more supportive, notably the Webbs.[7]

Toward the end of his essay Nutzinger correctly identifies the need for codetermination scholars to be able to publish their primary data so that those resources will be available to others. He also warns against the dangers inherent in a simplistic extrapolation of the results of studies of German codetermination for possible adoption in other cultures. While I agree with both points, I believe that their real importance is apparent only when they are considered together and elaborated upon. That is, what is needed for effective empirical research on codetermination and other forms of worker participation, including producer cooperatives, is an international clearing house comprising both primary data and published studies.[8] Such a resource centre would not only facilitate improved studies of, for example, German codetermination but would also allow careful cross national comparative studies of codetermination.

Footnotes:

[1] For the case of Britain, see Jones (1975) and for the United States, Jones (1979).

[2] For an elaboration of this point that pays particular attention to worker cooperatives in France, Italy, Britain, Spain and the USA. see Estrin, Jones and Svejnar (1983).

[3] See Jones and Svejnar (1985b) and Defourny, Estrin and Jones (1985). For an earlier study see Espinosa and Zimbalist (1978).

[4] For other studies on this issue see the relevant essays in Jones and Svejnar (1982). For empirical work on other issues and on nonwestern cooperatives see the pertinent essays in Jones and Svejnar (1985a).

[5] Moreover, unlike most other empirical work, the study is based on evidence from data sets that are considerably larger than those used in previous work.

[6] Thus there was no attempt to model the economic effects of the 2X + Y scheme as proposed by Bullock. Nor was there any - empirical economic analysis of existing British forms of codetermination, notably in retail cooperatives, where worker representation on boards has a long history.

[7] See Jones (1975) for an account and a partial explanation.

[8] Modest steps in this direction include the establishment of documentation centres, such as at Cornell (Program on Participation). A further step in this direction would be a networking of all institutions where there is on-going research in this field. Members would be expected to exchange (so far as other obligations allowed) resources, such as primary data banks that are held by separate institutions.

References:

Bullock, A. (1977), *Committee of Inquiry on Industrial Democracy*, London: HMSO Cmnd. 6706.

Defourny, J., Estrin, S., and Jones, D.C. (1985), "The Effects of Worker Participation on Enterprise Performance: Empirical Evidence from French Cooperatives",*International Journal of Industrial Organisation* 197-217.

Espinosa,J.,and Zimbalist, A.(1978),*Economic Democracy*, New York: Academic Press.

Estrin,S., and Jones, D.C.(1984),"Production, Workers' Participation and Enterprise Characteristics: A simultaneous equation approach",unpublished manuscript, Hamilton College, Department of Economics, Clinton, N.Y.

Estrin, S.,Jones, D.C., and Svejnar, J.(1983),The Varying Nature, Importance and Productivity Effects of Worker Participation: Evidence for contemporary producer cooperatives in indust-rialied Western economies. CIRIEC Working paper. Liège, Belgium: University of Liège.

Jones, D.C.(1975),"British Producer Cooperatives and the Views of the Webbs on Participation and Ability to Survive", *Annals of Public and Cooperative Economy*, vol. 46,23-44.
---,(1979), "U.S. Producer Cooperatives: The Record to Date", *Industrial Relations*, vol. 18,342-357.
---,(1985), "What Difference do Worker Directors make? Evidence for the Case of British Retail Cooperatives", unpublished manuscript, Hamilton College, Department of Economics, Clin-ton,N.Y.

Jones, D.C., and Svejnar, J., eds. (1982),*Participatory and Self-Managed Firms:Evaluating Economic Performance*, Lexington,Mass.
---, eds. (1985), *Advances in the Economic Analysis of Partici-patory and labor managed firms*, vol.1. Greenwich, Conn.: J.A.I Press.
---,(1985), "Participation, Profit Sharing, Worker Ownership and Efficiency in Italian Producer Cooperatives", *Economica*, vol. 52,449-465.

Svejnar, J. (1981),"Relative Wage Effects of Unions, Dictatorship and Codetermination: Econometric Evidence from Germany",*Review of Economics and Statistics*, vol. 63,188-197.
---,(1982), "Codetermination and Productivity: Empirical Evidence from the Federal Republic of Germany", in: *Participatory and Self-Managed Firms: Evaluating Economic Performance*, eds. D.C. Jones and J. Svejnar. Lexington, Mass.

INSTITUTIONAL REFORM: THE FUTURE OF CODETERMINATION
by
Klaus Bartölke and Ekkehard Kappler
in collaboration with John G. Slade

The future of codetermination is unlikely to be a simple extrapolation of the past. Political decisions determine the scope
of codetermination, whereas managerial philosophies set the context of codetermination and its consequences. It is therefore
hard to forecast what course codetermination will take, although
no genuinely new points of departure have emerged in current developments.

No speculation about the future of the German codetermination
system   - as a paramount example of institutional reform within
capitalist society - can be undertaken without establishing perspectives. One perspective is to review the historical development of institutional reforms in Germany, interpreting them as
previous attempts at institutional reform (accounts of that development can be found in, for example, Alemann 1975; Muszynski
1975; Poole 1978; Diefenbacher 1983; Wachter 1983).
The past

During the decade 1830-1840 there were initiatives to establish
workers' committees in plants. At the 1848 constitutional convention in Frankfurt, held as an outgrowth of the bourgeois revolution, a system of councils was proposed at plant, district, regional, and national levels. These councils would deal with personnel and social affairs, such as ethics in the workplace and
the education of employed children. Nothing came of these proposals, however, because of opposition from the conservation groups
that held the majority at the convention.

As labor unions and workers' parties evolved after 1870, the
ideal was reintroduced. Yet it was not until 1891, after the laws
against socialist movements had been abolished, that the Law for
Protection of Labor included provisions for the optional establishment of workers' committees. Such committees existed only in
industries - like printing - with a strong labor movement. In
1905, in the mining industry in Prussia, workers' committees were
made obligatory in companies with more than 100 employees, a measure that was a reaction to strikes in the coal-mining industry
of the Ruhr district. Neither capital nor labor was satisfied
with these laws. The vast majority of employers rejected the

Codetermination
ed. by H.G. Nutzinger and J. Backhaus
© Springer-Verlag Berlin Heidelberg 1989

ideal of worker participation altogether. In the view of workers' parties and labor unions the scope of these laws fell short of what was desirable, so on the whole workers boycotted them.

During World War I, works councils were required by law for companies with more than fifty employees in industries that supplied the front line and the home front. The law passed in 1916 was an attempt to unify the German population and to deal with growing production problems in the wartime economy, as well as a concession by the majority parties to the Social Democratic Party for the latter's backing the declaration of war in 1914. It nevertheless met objections from employers.

The 1918 revolution derived its impetus from a movement that pursued the ideal of creating a societal structure formed as a hierarchy of councils ("soviet") at the local, district, regional, and state levels. This radical leftist movement aimed at destroying capitalist-bourgeois society. A reformist approach prevailed, however, and led to the 1920 Works Council Act. According to that Act, councils were to be established in plants with more than twenty employees. Councils could exercise some influence in personnel and social affairs, but not in the economic sphere. In 1922, the Act was supplemented by stipulations for including one or two council members on the supervisory board (a short description of the company constitution as prescribed in Germany is given below). The councils were subordinated to the unions. Since the unions pursued centralized policies, focusing on collective bargaining either by industry or nationwide, with the idea of achieving economic democracy, they made no serious attempts to activate councils as channels for representing their own interests.

In 1933, with the advent of the Nazi regime, free labor unions and codetermination practices were suspended.

The present

In 1946, after World War II, the Control Council Law 22 imposed by the allies reestablished workers' representation in companies. Several state constitutions, passed in 1946/47, provided for implementing codetermination and nationalization, but the federal constitution of 1949 does not include any such legislative framework.

In the aftermath of World War II unions quickly recovered. Moreover, all political parties displayed strong anti-fascism. A climate was created in which unions, in revitalizing their earlier thinking about economic democracy, felt encouraged to propose far-reaching reforms. They suggested nationalization of the main industries, central economic planning, and comprehensive workers' participation. With the beginning of the cold war, reforms tending toward socialism met growing suspicion from both the allies and certain Germans within Western occupied sectors. There was a change in the outlook of majority parties - and the managerial elite, among whom were men who had held top managerial positions during the Nazi regime. These developments had the effect of diminishing opportunities for basic reforms. A clear indication of this political shift is that the 1951 Codetermination Law was approved only because the German unions threatened to call a general strike if Parliament did not pass it.

The institutional arrangements set up by Parliament in 1951 and the following years reflect two phenomena. First, they reflect the formal, legalistic tradition established in the middle of the nineteenth century. Second, despite the change in political outlook in the years immediately following World War II, a majority of West Germans considered the arrangements a necessary reform in the direction of democratizing their society and a means of preventing fascist movements from ever again taking power.

The 1951 legislation on codetermination probably reflects the kind of framework identified with the Federal Republic of Germany (FRG). It provides a first variant of participation in decision-making by worker representatives as members of supervisory boards. Understanding this kind of participation requires a short look at the legal constitution of joint-stock companies as a model example.

The main institutions of a joint-stock company are the shareholders' assembly, the supervisory board, and the managerial board. All business activities are performed by and under the sole responsibility of the managerial board. In business transactions, the managerial board is deemed to take into account not only the interests of shareholders, but also those of employees and the public. Members of the managerial board are elected by the supervisory board. The main task of the supervisory board, which is made up of different ratios of shareholders' and employees' representatives, is to exercise some degree of control over the performance of the management but not - with the exception of a few cases - to interfere in its day-to-day activities. In order to monitor management's performance, the supervisory board has information rights that cover business policy and return on investments. Shareholders' representatives are elected by the shareholders' assembly.

The 1951 law applies to mining and steel companies financed by equity capital and having a payroll of 1000 upwards. Today, this covers less than 2.5 percent of the work force, or about 600,000 workers (Niedenhoff 1977). There are three specific features of this law:

a) The benches of owners' and employees' representatives on the supervisory board are equal. In addition, there is a neutral person on the board who is empowered to cast a vote whenever necessary. The neutral person cannot be co-opted without a two-thirds vote of both benches.

b) The unions and the works council (see below) decide employee representation by proposing members for the supervisory board, who are then formally elected by the shareholders' assembly.

c) The managerial board includes a labor director who cannot be appointed against the wishes of the majority of the employees' representatives on the supervisory board. This director is in charge of personnel and social affairs and has equal rights with other members of the managerial board concerning decisions about company policy in general.

The next step in the legal development was the Works Constitution Act of 1952. Despite its revision in 1972, this act contains stipulations still effective today as regards supervisory boards of companies not covered by 1976 Codetermination Law. The law roughly applies to equity-financed companies with less than 2000 employees, excluding completely family owned firms with a payroll of 500 downwards. It applies to about 4 percent of the work force, that is, approximately 1 million employees (Niedenhoff 1977).

The momentum lost in carrying through reformist ideas so strong immediately after World War II and the recovered dominance by owners of the means of production are demonstrated in the law's provision that the supervisory board shall consist of owners' and employees' representatives at a ratio of 2:1.

Leaving aside specific laws concerning the civil service, we now jump forward to the period in which the social Democratic Party in coalition with the Free Democratic Party formed the fed-

eral government. The coalition's first attempt at institutional
reform aimed at establishing " industrial democracy "
- though not a dramatic one -   was the 1972 revision of the
Works Constitution Act. The law applies to all economic enterprises with at least five employees over eighteen years of age,
three of whom have worked in the firm for at least six months. It
covers about 70 percent - or approximately 16.5 million -   of
the employed work force (Niedenhoff 1977).

A works council must be established in all enterprises of the
aforesaid description. The number of council members depends on
the size of the firm. For 301 or more employees, a proportionally
increasing number of council members become full-time councillors. Upper level managers are precluded from serving on the
council. Both white- and blue-collar workers are represented.
Moreover, representatives must be elected from different departments and occupations, and the percentage of male and female
councillors is intended to reflect the overall sex ratio of the
employees of the organization.

Although unions are not formally represented on the council,
they may nevertheless play an important role by electing their
own candidates and by participating in consulting councils.
unions have been particularly successful in electing their candidates in those industries where they have traditionally been
strong, such as the metal and mining industries. Unions also play
an important role in large concerns. As a rule, the legislation
covering large concerns (of more than 1000 employees) provides
for participation rights at the various hierarchical levels at
which company decisions are taken.

The law provides four different degrees of participation in
various areas. The council rarely initiates decisions; rather
joint decision making in social affairs like working hours and
remuneration schemes are the rule. Decisions concerning the workplace and the work environment are made by management in consultation with the council. In personnel matters, like intra-firm
training activities, performance appraisal schemes, promotion and
transfer, selection, and dismissals, the council's approval is
needed. As regards questions of company policy, strategy, and
production technology, the council has only information rights.

In plants with more than 100 employees a special economic committee is established to receive this information.

The works council is supplemented by workers' assemblies at
plant or department level. The council must convene such assem-

blies at least every three months. These assemblies are not public, but a representative from both the union and the employer's
association have a right to be present. These two, as well as the
employer   - who must be invited -   have the right to speak and
to comment on the council's report to the assembly.

This combination of rights and exclusions of rights is further
limited by a number of legal requirements concerning the obligation of a council in its actions:

a) Workers' representatives are required to maintain secrecy.
b) Council and management must cooperate in a spirit of mutual
   confidence and with a serious intention to reach agreement.
c) The works council is forbidden to initiate strikes on plants-
   specific problems.

Strikes cannot be called except by unions in their role as
parties in collective bargaining. During conflicts within plants,
appeals may be made to labour courts or to a conciliation committee.

Whereas there were comparatively small differences of opinion
between Social Democrats and Free Democrats (Liberals) on the
Works Constitution Act, their positions were considerably different on the second reform attempt of that coalition - the Codetermination Law passed in 1976. Social Democrats, as well as the
majority of the unions, favored an extension of the 1951 Codetermination Law, which only applies to the mining and steel industries. The Free Democrats objected. Liberals stressed that unions
should have less direct influence and favored the predominance of
company employees in election procedures. Moreover, they successfully brought into play the group of upper level managers, an
idea opposed by Social Democrats and unions on the assumption
that upper level managerial personnel would be more inclined to
align themselves with shareholders and the managerial board than
would lower level employees and the unions. The 1976 law applies
to all equity-financed companies with 2000 or more employees,
that is, about 20 percent of the workforce, or approximately 4.8
million employees (Niedenhoff 1977).

On the supervisory board, there is parity in the number of
shareholders' nominees and employees' representatives. Shareholders' nominees are elected by the shareholders' assembly; employees' representatives by company employees. The bench of the
employees' representatives includes at least one blue-collar, one

white-collar, and one upper-managerial employee, all of whom belong to the one company. The union concerned has a right to propose noncompany union members as delegates for a seat on the board, but these have to be elected, like all others, by persons on the company' payroll.

As in the 1951 law, the managerial board includes a work director. Election to this office is subject to the same rule as for other managerial board members: at an initial poll the nominee needs two-thirds majority of the supervisory board members. If no majority is attainable, the chairperson of the supervisory council has a tie-breaking vote.

At first sight, the two benches appear equally strong. Several employers' associations have claimed that this aspect, among others, makes the law inconsistent with the West German constitutions. The other main points they referred to are a cumulative effect of workers' participation in councils and supervisory boards resulting in a preponderance of the employee side to the detriment of the constitutionally guaranteed rights of private property, secondly an offense against the freedom of coalition because persons connected with employees might act on behalf of the employers' side in collective bargaining, and thirdly the assumption that the passing of the law introduced an illicit change of West Germany's economic constitution.

In 1979, the federal constitutional court ruled that all these allegations were invalid. Parity between the two benches is precluded by the chairman's vote (because of additional specific stipulations the chairman is normally a representative of the shareholders' bench), the heterogeneity of the employees' bench, and the ultimate right of the shareholders' assembly to decide basic company policy. No cumulative effect is possible because supervisory boards and councils fulfill different functions and are procedurally distinct. Nor is there a constitutionally invalid offense against the freedom of coalition. No specific economic system is prescribed by the constitution, and therefore the Codetermination Law cannot be at odds with it. It should be added that although the court confirms the validity of enactments, the legislative body may be compelled to initiate new laws if existing stipulations prove inadequate (the laws described as well as the court ruling can be found in *Bundesminister für Sozialordnung* 1979).

This set of laws applicable to companies is supplemented by legal provisions for collective bargaining and laws containing preventive and compensatory measures related to employment and unemployment. A highly legalistic structure results, of which the main characteristics are presented in Fig. 1 (Garson 1977, who provides the idea for this illustration, characterizes such a structure as a workers' participation model; more complete descriptions of the German system are given by, for example, Diamant 1977; Hetzler and Schienstock 1979; IDE 1981).

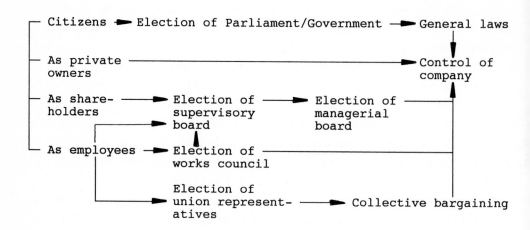

Fig. 1: Main institutions involved in control of companies

This history of industrial relations in the FRG until recently has been characterized by a comparatively low incidence of strikes. A number of points can be made that are related to the strong legalism of the German structure (Conrad 1981):

a) The parties to bargaining are autonomous. The state provides the legal structure but does not directly intervene (although governments do indicate their sympathy for one side or the other). The lack of direct support from outside furthers compromise.

b) The bargaining procedures are standardized. Wildcat strikes and strikes on political grounds are prohibited. Unions are required to poll their members before calling a strike (75 percent of their membership must indicate support).

c) Bargaining issues are limited. They mostly concern one industry in one region. A number of matters relevant to workers are dealt with by legislation and are less subject to collective bargaining. The additional channels of participation described above relieve collective bargaining.

The Future

The additional channels of participation will remain, for the foreseeable future, a major characteristic of the German industrial relations system, but they will also remain controversial. There will always be attempts to diminish the rights of, for example, the works councils through legal changes proposed by employers' associations as well as by sections of conservative and liberal parties in the political sphere. At the same time, unions will continue to press for enlarged codetermination rights for workers and their representatives.

The claims of the political parties can be quickly summarized. The conservative Christian Democratic and Christian Social parties (CDU/CSU) are not interested in extending the domain of codetermination. The worker factions in these parties that are inclined to strengthen codetermination will remain a minority and therefore will not have any major impact of general party policy. The Liberals (FDP) - in coalition with the conservatives at the federal level since 1982 - have never had a strong interest in codetermination and are unlikely to change their outlook. Any change they were to propose today would weaken codetermination rights of employees - in line with employers' associations. The ecological party (Die Grünen) favors direct democracy in general and within companies, but remains unpredictable as regards a concrete program of worker participation in general or institutional forms of codetermination. The Social Democrats (SPD) thus remain the political party most in support of institutional reforms. Traditionally, they have the closest relations with the mainstream of the union movement. There is no updated social democratic program on codetermination, but it can be assumed that this party will to a large degree accept and follow programmatic ideas of the unions.

Although there is no chance of revising the laws on codetermination at the federal level, the federal association of German unions, the Deutscher Gewerkschaftsbund (DGB), began a programmatic initiative in October 1982. On the recommendation of its research center, the Wirschafts- und Sozialwissenschaftliches Institut (WSI), the DGB published a proposed new law of codetermination. In subsequent years additional proposals have been advanced.

That initiative now covers all levels of the economy, namely, the economy as a whole (DGB - Bundesvorstand 1984); the company constitution (DGB - Bundesvorstand o. J.), including public companies and institutions (DGB - Bundesvorstand 1983a) as well as their personnel councils in public service (DGB - Bundesvorstand 1983b); and finally the workplace (DGB - Bundesvorstand 1985).

As regards the economy as a whole, unions complain that at present there are no systematic opportunities for them to participate in decision making. In their view the existing system of chambers of trade and commerce and of handicrafts have either no union representation or too little. The unions' ideal is a system of economic and social councils at federal, state, and municipal levels that would consist of an equal number of delegates from both employer's associations and unions. These councils would have the right to initiate economic policy; consult freely with one another and the federal government; help coordinate economic policy between the three levels; and provide the general public with a clear insight into economic matters, thus maximizing participation of citizens in state action. For the time being, the unions suggest a more moderate solution: reform the chambers already in existence and establish structure councils on the three levels. Union members of the councils would serve on par with those from the employer's associations, and the councils would be entitled to consult governments and parliaments on economic policy and its consequences, industrial policy, and regional economic policy.

At the heart of the programmatic initiative are reforms at the company level. Unions want to include public enterprises and agencies too. They argue for an extension of the 1951 codetermination law for mining and steel (industries that are moribund) as described above to all areas of industry and services. In this context it should be mentioned that early in 1985 a part of the metal workers' union, not the whole union movement, asked for neutralizing equity invested in the steel industry. This demand for the abolition of private property rights is based on the fact that in certain regions the state already ensures the financial survival of steel companies.

The proposed law of codetermination deals with

(1) the companies that should be covered,

(2) the extent of codetermination in the supervisory board and the managerial board, and

(3) the possibility of negotiating through collective bargaining

on codetermination.

(1) All companies displaying two of the following three criteria should be brought within the ambit of the new law: more than 1000 employees, a balance sheet total in excess of 125 million DM, and sales greater than 250 million DM a year.

Enterprises covered by these criteria can choose only one of three legal forms for their company: joint-stock company, limited company, or cooperative. Virtually all requirements enforceable on the joint-stock company are likewise legally binding on the others. Through these enactments the unions want to prevent management from circumventing codetermination by choosing a legal form for the company outside the scope of the law. (Unions are reacting to one interpretation of a loophole in the codetermination act of 1976).

Furthermore, unions do not approve of existing legislation that restricts codetermination to specific industry branches, or that excludes publishing companies or political, denominational, scientific, or art related companies.

The unions' draft prescribes that employees of German firms abroad should be brought within the ambit of domestic legislation. There are also proposals to strengthen the influence of the workers (and especially of the unions) within companies with complex structures, notably trusts, whose headquarters may be outside German jurisdiction.

(2) It is proposed that the election of worker representatives to the supervisory board be similar to the election of members of the works council, but the discretion of the supervisory board should be widened. In the field of codetermination, the owners of firms affected by law have contractually excluded many of the supervisory board's rights and means of influence. The unions have countered by listing decision making items on which the managerial board should be compelled to obtain the concurrence of the supervisory board. Their list includes almost all important managerial affairs from the opening and closing of new plants to periodical planning; major investment decisions; and organizational, personnel, or technological changes that will conceivably have repercussions on more than one plant or more than one division of an enterprise. In the unions' program the influence of the managerial board is approximated to that specified in the codetermination act of 1951.

(3) The law presently in force defines codetermination in prescriptive terms. The new proposal broadens the legal framework to allow for two cases of negotiated codetermination.

(a) Through collective bargaining the new law may be applied to enterprises not within its ambit.

(b) For unions and firms within the domain of the law, negotiations should be authorized in additional areas. The main implications of such an innovation lie in the political possibilities. The extent of codetermination could become the subject of labor disputes and strikes. Further, unions scan try through collective bargaining to extend their influence on the managerial board to the management of divisions and plants. Negotiating on contractual supplements to codetermination addresses the need for legal flexibility in order to adapt codetermination to the peculiarities of different branches and firms. Finally the possibility of negotiating supplements will open the door for further legislative activities on codetermination. Under Swedish codetermination law, negotiable activities and contracts on codetermination are standard procedure, and the law simply offers a framework for the bargaining process. Obviously the contractual elements in the German unions' proposal are of a different quality. The strategy of the unions' demands in the FRG is an institutional one, not a communicative one as in Sweden (for a discussion of German and Swedish regulations, see Gerum and Steinmann 1984).

Several revisions of the Works Constitution Act as well as the parallel act applicable to the civil service are suggested by the unions. Such revisions would extend codetermination rights of the councils, improve their scope of action, strengthen bonds between the councils and the respective unions, bring all employees within the domain of the law (that is, include upper managerial personnel except for a few top ranking officers), and eliminate barriers between white- and blue-collar workers. Unions claim that the law should emphasize employees' interests, and discard terms like "a relationship of trust" to describe a required mode of cooperation between council and management. Unions demand more legally assured, company-paid opportunities for worker representatives to improve their qualifications on subject matters related to their task of introducing employees' interests into company decisions, as well as bargaining rights on social issues.

They ask for fewer restrictions on information for the employees in general. As another indication of a less harmonistic perspective, councils should have enforceable initiative rights. Also, unions demand larger councils to improve the rate between representatives and constituency, a broader coverage of the law (including plants with more than three employees - this number is now five), and the option to substitute the legal solution by a contract between the company and the union.

A new element in the union strategy is codetermination at the workplace. In its programmatic statement, the DGB carefully avoids confusing management tools like quality circles with its intentions. Its goal is to improve opportunities for self-actualization and the quality of work in general. To that end, individual employees should be provided with more information rights concernjobs and working conditions. They should also have suggestions rights on job design and rights of protest and grievance. Employees should be entitled to suspend work when employers do not comply with laws or agreements, and should have the right of assembly in their working section. Legal guarantees of these individual rights should be safeguarded by the council's collective action. This coordinating function of the council is additionally expressed in two other proposals, namely, codetermination at the workplace by intensified contacts between the council and employees, as well as by the council's option to establish committees of employees designed to solve ongoing problems, though the final decision on suggestions by such committees should remain with the council.

Overall these proposals incidentally offer an alternative to modern management methods such as quality circles, information markets, task forces, and learning shops. These techniques, in the eyes of the unions, are only attempts to increase productivity and motivation and largely replace costly cash incentives, besides diminishing the influence of the works council and the unions. In the unions' opinion the workers want jobs that make it possible to shape the organization of their work; increase creativity, responsibility, and social contacts; promote job-enrichments; expand the opportunity to improve qualifications; and decrease permanent supervision and excessive hierarchies. Workers' participation at the level of the job should guaranty enforcement of the general goals of the workers (job security, safety on the job, protection against unhealthy conditions, improved working conditions, and a decrease of supervision and hierarchy), taking all relevant factors into account. To achieve these goals the unions demand facilities that provide more information and insight into the labor process and its various repercussions on workers. It is in line with this perspective that they additionally demand the decrease of division of work, plus other changes in production organization to move employees away from assembly lines and repetitive, monotonous jobs.

The programmatic move by the unions addresses some issues that have been raised by empirical investigations. It takes into account relationships between economic policy and company policy. It underscores codetermination rights in all domains of decisions because information and consultation rights have proved to be rather ineffective. It ventilates the problem of secrecy and the subsequent barriers to employee representatives' actions, thus venturing into a more conflict laden employer- employees relationship. It considers qualifications of representatives as an individual asset necessary to make the legal institutions work as hoped for by the unions. It tries to strengthen solidarity by avoiding institutionalized separation of organization members. There are attempts to provide initiative rights in order to overcome the weakness of simple, one-way reaction to management decisions.

The program nevertheless fails beyond the legal and institutional approach. Codetermination at the workplace seems to be an appendix that is half-heartedly introduced. Workers' problems and actions, singly or collectively, are integrated in a union-dominated process of interest representation through the formal codetermination structure. Such a scheme may well hinder local, spontaneous actions by workers and frustrate unionized workers and those that resent a comparatively centralized union structure.

It is not difficult to infer (Chmielewicz 1983) why the DGB launched this initiative while the government in power has no basic interest in the problem and over two million persons are unemployed in the FRG. The programmatic initiative is designed both to counterbalance conservative attempts directed toward diminishing codetermination rights and to clarify the unions' position on new technologies and their consequences.

Moreover, unions now realize that institutional codetermination is not only a source of influence but also a basis on which they can be made responsible for unpopular decisions (for example, the shut-down of plants). But there are other aspects in this ambivalent argument to which Chmielewicz (1983) drew attention in four points as summarized below.

(1) The unions have problems recruiting new members and retaining existing members' loyality. Present national economic circumstances make it impossible to boost membership figures by activities and success in the (re-)distribution of income. The unions need intangible goals in order to remain attractive to long-term members and to interest potential members.

This argument reflects the union's turn around on participation at the job level. On the one hand, unions in opposition to the DGB or groups of workers in opposition to the leading unions within plants want more democracy at the membership level and less power for the leadership of the unions. By taking this tendency into account, the unions hope to gain new members and to weaken grassroots opposition. On the other hand, the proposed codetermination act promises more influence for the unions' administration than any previous institutional practice.

(2) Since the SPD is in the opposition at the federal parliamentary level, it is quite possible that this party will support the demand of the DGB. That support would involve a political commitment for the future and might imply a strategic success for the unions.

(3) Although there is little empirical evidence about the effects of codetermination on unemployment (an exception is Scholl and Blumschein 1979, 1982; Kirsch, Scholl, and Paul 1984; for some speculations on a theoretical, philosophical, and socio-political basis see Kappler 1981), the unions argue that in times of economic difficulties, stronger rights for the workers and the unions are necessary to mitigate dangerous social tensions.

(4) The codetermination act of 1976 was retrogressive. In 1981 the provisions of the codetermination act of 1951 (Montan-Mitbestimmung) were limited even more. Consequently the initiative of the DGB may now have the function of restating strategic positions that have been attained and goals that have not yet been reached.

In the political sphere the union's ideas have to some extent been put into practice by the Social Democratic Party (SPD).

For example, in North Rhine- Westfalia the Personnel Representation Law (Landespersonalvertretungsgesetz) - a law that applies to the civil service of the state and that parallels the
provisions of the federal Works Constitution Act - was modified
in 1984 in order to establish personnel councils that have codetermination rights with respect to the introduction of new technologies. The Liberal party (FDP) and the Christian Democratic
and Christian Social Parties (CDU/CSU) - consistent with their
general policy described above - do not favor the unions' program. On the federal level, some Christian Democrats are considering presenting a bill for establishing councils of upper managerial personnel which would parallel the works councils. This
initiative contrasts with the unions' views because it separates
the employees within an organization and might therefore weaken
the standing of the works council.

The described programmatic initiative is unlikely to result in
substantial legal revisions favorable to the unions. On the contrary, the possibility is that unions - and their allies in the
political sphere - will fail to influence legal changes. Structural unemployment resulting from technological innovation and
the accompanying loss in union membership may weaken the unions'
power in society. Past experience does not unequivocally demonstrate that codetermination positively affects employment. It indicates rather that employers have successfully used codetermination to cushion the negative effects on employment of rationalization campaigns in companies, especially in the coal and steel
industries. Today the unions are trying to rebate charges that
codetermination has been instrumental in the process of rationalization; it remains to be seen whether supervisory boards and
work councils can prevent jobs from being eliminated. It is more
likely that they will have to apply strategies other than codetermination to the challenges of unemployment.

Might other developments affect the spread and extent of codetermination? Such developments can be observed in three areas,
namely capital sharing schemes for employees, initiatives of industrial companies' personnel, and the alternative sector (the
following description is a development of ideas in Praeger 1984;
Dey 1984; Aumann et al. 1984; and a number of newspaper articles).

A number of firms offer shares of company capital to their employees. In joint-stock companies, employee shareholders with few
exceptions join other minor shareholders who in general do not

have any substantial influence on company policies. In a variety
of employee ownership plans, employees might exert more influence
on management (if a substantial part of the equity is owned by
them), but their motivation changes in the direction of securing
their capital investment. This change in motivation supplants the
idea of codetermination because the latter derives from differences in the interests of employers and dependent employees. It
is doubtful whether in the bulk of employer-employee relations
this development will have more than marginal importance.

Personnel initiatives mainly take two forms both of which are
directed at product conversion. First, employees in the armaments
industry have made a few attempts to suggest production lines,
sometimes combined with suggestions for modified forms of production that meet their criteria of societal usefulness or ecological benefit. Second, in a small variety of companies employees
have proposed changes in product and production to avoid a shut-
down or to stem a business decline. These attempts have not been
very popular with either employers or the unions. Different interests among employee groups and employees without appropriate
qualifications render the long-term survival of these initiatives
unlikely. Whenever initiatives were successful in moving toward
self-management, a direction far beyond codetermination, securing
capital was difficult.

The third development refers to alternative projects in collective forms of production. Statistical information about this
sector is scarce and unreliable. It is perhaps safe to say that,
allowing for an unquantifiable margin of error, there are about
10,000 to 12,000 projects employing some 100,000 plus members,
that is, approximately 0.4 percent of the working population. The
size of the projects is limited; most of them employ .3 to 10
members, a few more than 20, and the largest - a newspaper -
about 100 members. They reject traditional principles of economic
activities. They look for different kinds of products, work organization, and decision-making structures. Property or the means
of production is neutralized, basic decisions are made by the
members as a whole, the division of labour is limited, and role
rotation is employed. Alternative projects often emphasize reim-
bursement of expenses, including the living expenses of their
members, rather than accumulation of profits. This strategy might
contribute to a life-expectancy of just four years. Some projects
try to integrate work and living in general.

It is probably the collectives' social orientation and their neglect of profits, rather than their radically democratic structure, which leads to the phenomenon that only one in three members can live on the economic return of the collective alone; the Kibbutz example has shown that alternative modes of production based on egalitarian, nonelitist, democratic procedures can be economically viable (cf. Bartölke et al. 1985 and references given there). There are, however, indications that the alternative movement is focusing more on economic aspects. The total turnover in recently founded projects is higher, and a network of supportive functions has been created that includes providing expert knowledge and access to banking institutions to minimize restrictions to capital markets.

The question remains whether these alternative projects should be viewed as innovative firms that exploit gaps in the market within capitalist society and, if successful, will because of market competition either become capitalist companies themselves or be taken over by traditional companies.

By and large, all of the developments mentioned - capital sharing, personnel initiatives, collective production - contain an element that focuses on the individual worker. Therefore it is conceivable that, in the next few years, the unions' chances of realizing demands at the workers' level are much greater than those of the initiatives at levels embracing the economy as a whole as well as the managerial or supervisory boards and the works council. The results of workers' participation at the level of their jobs might entail a decline of the unions' influence, which explains the unions' reluctance to support these developments. People will become members of the unions or not. As they become more aware of their individual possibilities, their distrust of institutions tends to increase. And this skepticism will doubtless affect all kinds of institutional reforms. Forecasting the future situation of codetermination from this angle means that a policy of institutional reform is a conservative policy that seems to run into a resurgence of law and order because of the failure of administrative control policies. Even if institutional reform is not by necessity an element of conservative policy, it corresponds with the attitude of the present government in West Germany. This is not surprising: institutional reform has a bureaucratic and thus a hierarchical touch. But what will be the result if institutions demand the reform of other institutions and of their leadership? There has never been more covert authoritarian behavior than in "good institutions". Moreover, many proposals for participative cooperation will find an open door at the management level. The positive effects on productivity are evidence. It would be premature to forecast whether the danger of losing one's job will reinforce one's motivation to join the unions against managerial strategies.

New technologies will require increased participation although it is not clear whether this only holds good for a transitional period. Both exploitation and the difficulty of fostering capital interest are parameters of participation, which indicates the limitations of development. The harder it becomes to gain a satisfying return on investment by rationalization and automatization, the more managers will need participation of their workers. A certain percentage of the workers are becoming experts in operating the new equipment, and managers rely on participation because they are in need of the ideas, the creativity, and the innovative power of the workers. If there is no other way to a higher return on investment, the new technologies will provide workers with a good chance to gain participation rights as a result of the redistribution of property rights in certain fields - for those who remain on the payroll. There is nothing new in this; the establishment of the stock-corporations in the nineteenth century was a similar process. The accumulation of capital was too slow for plant owners, who needed capital from people primarily seeking a percentage of interest and only secondarily seeking managerial positions. Of course, these investors were eager to safeguard their assets, which meant that the new companies needed a supervisory board that included the "new owner". But history shows that the investors' influence gradually diminished.

Perhaps it is vain to predict or to hope that new technologies will confer more influence on the workers. The difficulties of handling technological innovations will decrease along with workers' influence. And the hope that technologies will exert more influence on job security could be balked as well. There is reason to assume that prerogatives resulting from personal knowledge will guaranty purely individual interests. Under given conditions, in the absence of an existential threat, solidarity is no more than a moral slogan. The efforts of the unions toward an encompassing reconstruction of the concept of solidarity has - paradoxically because of the success of social reforms - not met with any substantial backing in the FRG.

A final question remains. What can the social sciences contribute to the improvement of codetermination in the FRG?

The answer is simple: nothing. Social scientists, including
economists, are by and large uninterested in this problem, or
they are interested only in taking a moralistic stance; in other
words, they act less as scientists and more as (moral) philoso-
phers. Obviously, a good philosopher is able to exemplify his
moral stance in a very profound manner, but normally moralistic
social scientists fail to qualify as experts in philosophy. The
morals of social scientists are based on their feeling of being
part of the powerful to the workers as they might be with the sophisticated state of Critical Theory (Horkheimer 1970). To the
extent that the social sciences are incapable of projecting the
critical role of science to society's problems, they will fail to
contribute to the question of participation and codetermination
except by normative prejudice, which could be either negative or
positive in the evolutionary process.

The mainstream of these "scientific" prejudices is irrelevant
to codetermination. This fact is not surprising. The main
methodological and epistemological positions are socio-
technological and not critical points of departure. They are, it
would seem, unconsciously affirmative with regard to the existing
organization of society. This affirmative acceptance of the
status quo is shared by many economists, whose core of belief
postulates that practice must follow theory. At present there are
only a few reflections on the possibility that a specific theory
may in fact be embedded in specific practice, and that critical
theory actually represents an attempt to reconstruct this "theory
in use".

On the basis of an ontological conception emphasizing the
idea of a world organized by recognizable invariances and
patterns and the conviction that the institution of science is in
a position to make these invariances manifest, the only solution
for injecting direction into institutional reform is to confer
leadership status on the "scientific priests." That is, however,
impracticable because it produces a maelstrom of stagnation by
experts. To counteract the vitiating effects of that whirlpool,
science itself would have to become an activity by those
concerned with generalization of common picturing and vitalizing
a reality that person can subjectively experience, but that
cannot be experienced by other persons identically. To take a
simple example, the general practitioner can feel the patient's

head but is precluded from directly feeling the patient's headache; so the relationship of the two is confined to a common endeavor to isolate the cause of the pain. This example provides an illustration of part of the Aristotelian understanding of theory and, if extrapolated to the social sciences, might result in an adequate and substantial scientific contribution to the question of participation and codetermination. By contrast, the building of hierarchies of abstraction (which is another branch of science) that manifest a neopositivistic belief in the objectivity of the ontological foundation will never lead to a scientific answer to questions of codetermination.

The methodological component of such a critical science comprises, for example, action research as a communicative process of authentic participation (Scholl, Gerl, and Paul 1978, p. 166-7), in which - a priori - neither the "scientist" nor the "practical man" has any inherent advantage. It is evident that "action research" in this sense is not a mere technique of organizational development. It is, for methodological reasons, substantially interested in a democratic dialogue unfettered by differences of authority or power. A process based on a communicative understanding of generalization in any specific situation always implies expounding the present from the past without prejudice to the future, a process that creates a non-hierarchical movement and that will of itself constitute participation and codetermination. Only sciences that endeavor to clarify the immanent self-misunderstanding within their (affirmative) production of knowledge possess the prerequisites for a sophisticated exploration of codetermination. In short, the lack of compensatory correctives in their epistemological basis prevents social sciences from hazarding anything other than very tentative empirical conjectures on the medium- and long-range future of (institutional) codetermination.

References:

Alemann, U. v., ed. (1975), *Partizipation - Demokratisierung-Mitbestimmung*, Opladen: Westdeutscher Verlag.

Aumann,Ch., Hofmann, W., Kochs, M., Maletzki, I., and Wagner, B., eds.(1984),*Zukunft der Arbeit*, Augsburg: Universität Augsburg.

Bartölke, K., Eschweiler, W., Flechsenberger, D., Palgi, M.,and Rosner, M.(1985),*Participation and Control - A comparative study about industrial plants in Israeli Kibbutzim and the Federal Republic of Germany*, Spardorf: R. F Wilfer Verlag.

Blumschein, H.(1981), *Personalpolitik, Personalplanung and Mitbestimmung. - Eine empirische Untersuchung*, München: Kirsch.

Bundesminister für Arbeit and Sozialordnung, ed. (1979),*Mitbestimmung*, Bonn: Bundesminister für Arbeit und Sozialordnung.

Chmielewicz, K.(1983),Der Gesetzentwurf des DGB zur erweiterten Mitbestimmung im Aufsichtsrat - Darstellung und Kritik,in: *Die Betriebswirtschaft*, vol. 143, 237-257.

Conrad,W.,(1981),"Federal Republic of Germany",in: *International Handbook of Industrial Relations*, ed.A.A Blum, Westport, Con., London: Andwych Press.

Dey,G.(1984), "Alternative Produktionsmoglichkeiten und Grenzen der Krise. in: *Betriebswirtschaftslehre und ökonomische Krise*, eds., W.H. Staehle and E. Stoll. Wiesbaden: Gabler.

DGB-Bundesvorstand(1983a),*Grundsätze des Deutschen Gewerkschaftsbundes zur Weiterentwicklung des Betriebsverfassungsrechts*, Düsseldorf: DGB-Schriftenreihe Mitbestimmung.

DGB-Bundesvorstand(1983b),*Grundsätze des Deutschen Gewerkschaftsbundes zur Weiterentwicklung des Bundespersonalvertretungsrechts*, Düsseldorf: DGB-Schriftenreihe Mitbestimmung.

DGB-Bundesvorstand (1983c), *Thesen des Deutschen Gewerkschaftsbundes zur Mitbestimmung in öffentlich-rechtlichen Unternehmen* und Einrichtungen,Düsseldorf:DGB-Schriftenreihe Mitbestimmung.

DGB-Bundesvorstand (1984), *Gesamtwirtschaftliche Mitbestimmung - unverzichtbarer Bestandteil einer Politik zur Lösung der wirtschaftlichen und gesellschaftlichen Krise*, Düsseldorf: DGB-Schriftenreiche Mitbestimmung.

DGB-Bundesvorstand(1985),*Konzeption zur Mitbestimmung am Arbeitsplatz*, Düsseldorf: DGB-Schriftenreihe Mitbestimmung.

DGB-Bundesvorstand (o.J.),*Entwurf eines Gesetzes über die Mitbestimmung der Arbeitnehmer in Großunternehmen und Großkonzernen (Mitbestimmungsgesetz)*, Düsseldorf: DGB-Schriftenreihe Mitbestimmung.

Diamant, A.(1977), "Democratizing the Work Place: The Myth and Reality of Mitbestimmung in the Federal Republic of Germany", in: *Worker Self-Management in Industry*, ed. G. D. Garson. New York: Praeger.

Diefenbacher,H. (1983),*Empirische Mitbestimmungsforschung*, Frank-furt: Haag & Herchen.

Garson, G.D. (1977), "Models of Worker Self-Management: The West-European experience", in: *Worker Self-Management in Industry*, G.D. Garson. New York: Praeger.

Gerum,E. and Steinmann, H.(1984), *Unternehmensordnung und tarif-vertragliche Mitbestimmung*, Berlin: Duncker und Humblot.

Hetzler, H.U. and Schienstock, G. (1979), "Federal Republic of Germany", in: *Towards Industrial Democracy. Europe, Japan and United States*, ed. B. C Roberts. London: Croom Helm.

Horkheimer,M. (1970), *Traditionelle und kritische Theorie*, Frank-furt am Main: Fischer Taschenbuch.

Industrial Democracy in Europe (IDE-International Research Group) (1981), *Industrial Relations in Europe*, Oxford: Clarendon Press.

Kappler, E. (1981), *Ökonomische Beurteilung der Mitbestimmung - Gutachten -*, Wuppertal: Bergische Universität.

Kirsch, W.,Scholl, W., and Paul, G. (1984), *Mitbestimmung in der Unternehmenspraxis. - Eine empirische Bestandsaufnahme*, Herr-sching: Kirsch.

Muszynski, B. (1975), *Wirtschaftliche Mitbestimmung zwischen Kon-flikt und Harmoniekonzept*, Meisenheim am Glan: Hain.

Niedenhoff, H. W. (1977), *Mitbestimmung in der Bundesrepublik Deutschland*, 2. ed. Köln: Deutscher Institutsverlag.

Poole, M. (1978), *Workers' Paricipation in Industry*, Rev.ed. Lon-don, Routledge and Kegan Paul.

Praeger, C.M.(1984),*Grundfragen der institutionalisierten Arbeit-nehmer-Beteiligung*, Spardorf: R. F. Wilfer Verlag.

Scholl,W., Gerl,K., and Paul, G.(1978),"Bedürfnisartikulation und Bedürfnisberücksichtigung im Unternehmen - Theoretische An-sätze zur Analyse von Mitbestimmungsregelungen", in: *Arbeits-qualitat in Organisationen*, eds. K. Bartölke, E. Kappler, St. Laske, and P. Nieder, Wiesbaden: Gabler Verlag.

Scholl,W. and Blumschein, H.(1979),*Personalplanung und Personal-politik in der Rezession*, Frankfurt: RKW - Rationalisierung-kuratorium der Deutschen Wirschaft e.V.

Scholl,W.,and Blumschein, H. (1982),"Mitbestimmung und Bedürfnis-befriedigung der Arbeitnehmer", *Zeitschrift für betriebswirt-schaftliche Forschung*,34, 959-978.

Wachter, H.(1983), *Mitbestimmung*, München: Vahlen.

INSTITUTIONAL REFORM: THE FUTURE OF CODETERMINATION:
Comment

by

Warren J. Samuels

1. This interesting and congenial paper is comprised of four parts. The first is a summary of the history of codetermination in West Germany. What the authors have to say comports with my understanding of what happened. In as much as my expertise in that history is negligible, I have no critique to offer. The second is a summary of the initiative, or proposal, advanced by DGB in 1982. I am not certain why this proposal was chosen for presentation: Among rival proposals, including those from employer organizations, it seems to have little chance of adoption. At least this proposal indicates the direction of thought, and the hopes, of one major interest group. The third part of the paper is interpretive. It discusses, first, alternatives and supplements to codetermination and, second, the conditions likely to influence the further history of codetermination. Bartölke and Kappler are so perceptive that I wish this had been the longest section of their paper. Finally, they discuss what social science can contribute to improving codetermination in the FRG. I concur with the substance of what the authors have to say but not with their conclusion. I shall take this conclusion up next and then move on to matters that bear largely on the interpretative framework within which codetermination can be understood.

2. I agree with what the authors appear to be saying as regards the social sciences. Codetermination - and any other policy regarding the organization of production and the treatment of workers - is a normative matter. As such it must reflect and give effect to certain values and to certain power bases and goals. Social scientists qua scientists describe and explain social-economic-political reality. In doing so, they assume either a selective specification of the status quo or a hypothetical specification of society with which to work (for example, to model). An implicit ontological realism is often joined to the scientific desire for determinate solutions to produce an affirmation of the existing organization of society. Only as moralists, that is, as citizens, can individuals who are otherwise also social scientists address the normative questions pertaining to codetermination; except, of course, insofar as they are merely describing

Codetermination
ed. by H.G. Nutzinger and J. Backhaus
© Springer-Verlag Berlin Heidelberg 1989

the events of history, apropos of which many believe that even simple description inexorably gives effect to some normative belief system. Moreover, social scientists generally cannot experience the world as managers or owners or, especially, workers, and this too must limit their effectiveness and adversely affect their "accuracy."

But I think that our authors, while correct so far, fail to recognize two things that social science can contribute; in other words, their answer of "nothing" is too strong. First, social scientists do contribute criticism of the status quo, either from an idealized version of the status quo or from an assumed alternative to the status quo (which may or may not involve idealization of the status quo), and of course there are numerous variants of each: the specifications of the status quo are many, and the alternatives are no less, and probably more, numerous. This critical role, using social science to give expression to the values and ideologies contained within social science, is not to be foreclosed. Historically, it has been a major function of social scientists as intellectuals. Second, social scientists can provide information, hypotheses, models, theories, and so on, which, while not necessarily purely positive, can enlighten the normative process. Social science, in other words, cannot generate policy, but it can facilitate the making of less rather than more myopic choices. While I share the authors' apparent sense that there is a lack of conclusive compensatory corrections of ideological biases, I believe there are viable and sustainable intellectual, scientific elements in the world of praxis.

3. What is the field of human meaning of which codetermination is a part? Any answer must include the organization of production and the wage system.[1] Codetermination - trade union collective bargaining, workers' committees, workers' parties, and employee stock ownership plans, etc. - represents an attempt to make production organizations responsive to all the interests entering into production, specifically to restructure labor-management (-ownership) relations so as to introduce the economic equivalent of political democracy: economic democracy. From one point of view, it makes of labor a more effective partner in production, especially in decision making; from another, it augurs to transcend the historic conflicts between capital and labor by following what is in externality theory called "internalization," namely, merging the two interests so that the interests of the

hitherto excluded can be encompassed within decision making. It may well be, however, that codetermination is not a solution but a new framework within which the old conflict is now somewhat re- structured and is worked out (though never fully resolved) as la- bor seeks more effective partnership. After all, quite apart from more radical changes, there are significant differences (as the authors appreciate) between right of consultation, right of ap- proval, right to information, and right to initiate.

4. There is one important consideration that most advocates of codetermination and comparable systems neglect. That is the widely encountered situation in which the appeal of economic democracy is applauded by workers who are either simultaneously or subsequently disinterested in participating in organized deci- sion making. Even with a fully labor owned and managed production organization, the work force tends to disaggregate into those who are interested and active in decision making and those who are not; in other words, the equivalent of a managerial cadre forms out of the work force itself. American academicians, particularly those who research and write, may support the idea of collegial governance, that the university should be governed by the fac- ulty, but they do not participate therein, preferring to allocate their time and energy to disciplinary intellectual problems and not to university governance. As a result, those not so active in their professions tend to dominate university governance, and ad- ministrators who rise from faculty ranks come to think of them- selves not so much as faculty but as administrators. The differ- entiation of roles leads to the differentiation of perspectives and, in effect, to classes. Role rotation can be a modifying force, but it has not yet negated the differentiating tendencies. And what is true of much of American academia seems also to be true in Yugoslavia and thus to be a likely consequence of systems of labor participation.

5. Apparently, there is an uneasy, unstable relationship between codetermination and collective bargaining and of both with worker participation at the job or workplace level - just as there are tensions between unions and a more or less independent labor party.

6. The authors also make clear that there is a problem which is both interpretive and substantive: when is a system or technique

of worker participation really substantive participation, and in what respects (over what decisions), and when is it a technique of managerial control and incentive manipulation? On the one hand, the answer is never simple; on the other hand, if one has to ask, it is probably not substantive!

7. Let me distinguish between a system in which capital hires labor and one in which labor hires capital. (Notice that this formulation, among other things, dissolves the idea of contractual equality into a more realistic situation in which one party is economically superior.) Traditional labor markets exist because capital hires labor; that is the wage system as we know it. It is possible, however, to contemplate a system in which labor hires capital, which a truly labor-managed system of production would constitute. Whether any such system is really possible and sustainable is another question. The point I wish to make is that the institutional embodiments and consequences of a system in which labor hires capital can possibly serve as an analytically useful benchmark for evaluating worker participation arrangements within the existing system.

Notice, however, two things: first, as implied above, there is a necessity for the organization of production through leadership; and, second, there is a necessity for some system of incentives and rewards that is functional with regard to individual discipline and to the allocation of labor to desired production. These considerations, however, are not themselves dispositive of the crucial issues: there is no unique organization for production, no unique system of leadership and of entry there to, and no unique system of incentives. It is all a matter of whose interests are to count, for example, in determining output definitions, work rules, and so on.

Apropos of the last point, two further points ought to be made. First, I have written here of the organization of production (or producer) interests. But what of the interests of consumers (who are often producers of other products)? Those interests are somehow going to count also; and production units are, after all, going to have to market their output if the production operation is to be viable. Second, most of the issues raised above are readily articulated from a managerial point of view. The logic of the position that worker interests are to count challenges the autonomy, severity, and hegemony of the managerial point of view. But, if I am correct that managerial roles, perspectives and powers will tend to develop from within the work-force itself, the escape from managerialism will not be so easy, however much the personnel may change.

8. Finally, let me say that any consideration of codetermination must appreciate that it is part of a much grander and more complex historical development. This development can be stated without teleology: the increasing pluralization of both economy and polity, including the spread of substantive political and economic democracy. One suspects that this will continue in the future but that is by no means either predetermined or otherwise certain as to direction or substance; indeed, contrary developments are all too evident. While capitalism can be seen as a system of coercion, it replaced a much more coercive system with one arguably more humane, more physically productive, and more free (that is, characterized by a wider diffusion of power). Within capitalism there have been pluralizing developments, two of which are codetermination and unions.

But arguing for such a perspective is an intellectual exercise. The position of those whose interests codetermination allegedly works to promote - the working man and woman - may lead to a different perspective: they will be living their lives as working people, their opportunity set is largely tied to their job situation, and the realization of their pesonal identity, happiness, and way of life is fundamentally tied to their job and through it to the state of the labor market. I say that for several reasons: (1) because of the importance of effective "full" employment policies, (2) because of the inherent and incipient danger that working people will tend (always?) to be the instrument of the realization of the careers and goals of other people, and (3) because after all it is supposed to be their interests as they see them that are to count. It is to the realization of first and third, and the diminution if not destruction of the second, that social science arguably can contribute - but it does not do so only as science.

228

Footnotes:

[1] See Warren J. Samuels, A. Allan Schmid, James D. Shaffer, Robert A. Solo, and Stephen A. Woodbury, "Technology, Labor Interests, and the Law: Some Fundamental Points and Problems," *Nova Law Journal*, 8 (Spring 1984): 487-513; and Warren J. Samuels, "The Wage System and the Distribution of Power," *Forum for Social Economics*, Fall 1985, pp. 31-41.

WORKERS' PARTICIPATION STIMULATED BY THE ECONOMIC FAILURE OF TRADITIONAL ORGANIZATION
An Analysis of Some Recent Institutional Developments
by
Jürgen Backhaus

Introduction and Outline

There is a widely held view according to which labor participation is potentially desirable for political or social reasons, but costly in terms of economic efficiency. The purpose of this paper is to show that contrary to this view recent developments in the institutional structure of works organization should rather be seen as a response to economic failures of traditional organization. Consequently, the postulated trade-off between participation and efficiency is argued not really to exist in the relevant range of institutional development we are currently able to witness.

The paper starts out with a brief characterization of traditional organization. The main features of traditional organizations are (1) intra-firm hierarchical organization, (2) appointment and control of managers by capital and by means of markets for corporate control, as well as (3) the cartelized organization of the labor market and labor's representation through unions in this market, but not in the firm. These features can be shown to conform neatly to the received theories of the firm, corporate control, and collective bargaining (Part 1).

These theories, however, can be shown to suffer from several internal inconsistencies, some of which have given rise to dissenting and differentiating interpretations and new theoretical developments. To name but a few, it has become increasingly apparent that the traditional raison d'être given for the present form of the firm is unconvincing and at least partly fallacious. Monitoring the managers is a more complex process than was previously asserted. Likewise, systems of consensual decisions as opposed to hierarchical direction need to be analyzed in terms of both costs and benefits involved (Part 2).

From this more complex point of view, a number of organizational failures become apparent, of which the following are only examples:

Codetermination
ed. by H.G. Nutzinger and J. Backhaus
© Springer-Verlag Berlin Heidelberg 1989

(1) Incentives to distort information and resist innovation;
(2) Lack of control over intra-firm processes;
(3) Externalization of the costs consequent to firms' decisions
and performance (Part 3).

Industrial practice, in turn, can no longer be argued to conform to the received theory of the firm either. The traditional
organization, worldwide, is undergoing structural changes. By way
of example, the system of labor participation which has developed
in the Federal Republic of Germany is briefly sketched. This example was chosen because Germany has apparently gone farthest
among all Western democracies in requiring companies by law to
arrange for substantial labor participation in firms' decision
taking (Part 4).

The central features of labor participation, works councils,
codetermination, and the labor director are interpreted as organizational responses to the economic failures of traditional organizations discussed above.

From this economic analysis of the failure of traditional organization a dissenting view emerges, interpreting labor participation as a response to organizational failure in the interest
- not at the expense of - economic efficiency.

Undertaking such a study as this one may be thought to be important for two reasons: in order to understand and explain contemporary features of industrial organization and predict changes
they are likely to undergo; and secondly in order to explain and
predict changes in the behavior of firms as a consequence of
changes in their internal structure. While the first issue may be
interesting in its own right as well as mainly for theoretical
reasons, the second is likely to prove most interesting in terms
of policy oriented research. As we are currently able to witness
major changes in the industrial and company law, both in Europe
and in the United States, the task of predicting the likely consequences of these changes becomes a rather pressing one.

1. Traditional Organization and the Economic Theory of the Firm: No Need for Workers to Participate

1. In a non-trivial sense, if we follow standard neo-classical
textbook analysis, the problem under consideration in this essay
is not an integral part of economic analysis. Rather, the topic

might suitably be referred to technical considerations. The firm (which is the technical economic notion for an enterprise embodying several characteristics not common to any enterprise) is represented by a production function, which describes an "entrepreneur's" decision making behavior, as he is confronted with an array of feasible technical arrangements. To quote from Henderson and Quandt's succinct statement:

" The technology may state that a single combination of x_1 and x_2 can be utilized in a number of different ways and therefore can yield a number of different output levels. The production function differs from the technology in that it presupposes technical efficiency and states the maximum output obtainable from every possible input combination. The best utilization of any particular input combination is a technical, not an economic problem. The selection of the best input combination for the production of a particular output level depends upon input and output prices and is the subject of economic analysis. (1971, 54) "

This makes it quite clear that the problem of how to arrive at the most efficient organizational form for combining inputs in order to generate outputs is not regarded by those authors, as an economic but as a technical problem. The approach also presupposes that there is only one relevant decision-making agent in the firm who is confronted with an optimization problem, the details of which may be complex; whatever complexity arises, however, does not stem from alterations in the production function as a consequence of entrepreneurial behavior. The neo-classical theory of the firm thus is devoid of an explanation of the firm's internal organization. Still, the absence of such an explanation has never been anything less than obvious to economic theoreticians of the firm. Far from regarding the lack of treatment of the firm's internal organization as a deficiency of the theory of the firm, its proponents, notably Machlup (1967, 1-33) regarded the abstractness of the model as a virtue, not a vice. The firm was supposed to be a theoretical construct, designed in order to explain the average market behavior of enterprises, and not at all intended to be either a perfect representation of any particular prototype firm nor an exemplification of internal decision-making processes. The optimization problem theoretically attributed to the entrepreneur was likewise not intended to describe a similar optimization problem supposedly being faced by a real entrepreneur:[1]

" The type of action assumed to be taken by the theoretical actor in the model under specified conditions need not be expected and cannot be predicted actually to be taken by any particular real actor. (1967, 6) "

Ignoring for the moment developments in the theory of the cooperative in both its traditional version and its more modern appearance as the theory of the labor managed firm,[2] the traditional theory of the firm is silent on the subject matter under review. The theory of the firm is not designed to, was never intended to, and for methodological reasons cannot be employed to predict changes in firm behavior as a consequence of alterations in the internal organization of enterprises.

2. Which are the features of industrial organization that the theory of the firm in its orthodox version took for granted? Three of them may be singled out for being most important. Unlike markets which rely on coordinated activities to come forth as a result of agreement and prior competition, in the firm individuals are coordinated by means of authority and directive. The firm, although competing with others in the decentralized market economy, is internally built on the principle of centralized guidance. In its external relations, the firm's behavior is dictated by market conditions, where the extent of this dictate depends on the extent of competition and contention (Baumol 1982). Even under the fiercest monopoly conditions the monopolist cannot extract more than consumers are willing to concede voluntarily. Each transaction requires prior consent. Internally, the firm is largely free to establish its own rules, determining, among other things, for each individual what and what not he is supposed to do.

Secondly, the relationship between employee and the firm is based on a long-term contractual arrangement which allows the firm to determine the amount and type of (labor) services to be rendered upon agreement to pay a fixed wage. This unilateral right, on which authority rests in the firm, extends over the entire period during which the contract is in force, irrespective of changes in business conditions affecting the firm. It is this right to determine type, extent, and timing of services to be rendered which establishes the hierarchical order in the firm.

The economic significance of the firm lies in the combination of factors of production: labor, capital, and managerial talent in order to produce a maximum output or, alternatively, a given output at minimum costs. The firm as a structured organization is the means of productively coordinating the different factors of production. In principle, establishment of the firm could be based on any of the factors of production involved, the firm could be labor based, management based, or capital based. In line with major historical developments, however, the typical firm is viewed as being capital based (Chandler 1977). Capital owners form a corporation, the officers of which appoint managers to run the firm which has been set up by the corporation. Whereas the corporation is the peculiarly structured cooperative of capital, with each share carrying one vote, the firm is merely the technical unit in which production actually takes place, for and in the name of the corporation.[3] Following a theoretical conception worked out by Henry Manne (1967), the firm is operated in the interest of capital owners by the capital appointed managers who are competing among each other and with potential outside rivals. Deviating from the corporation's objective to maximize its net present value will result in lower values per share. Consequently, corporate owners will exercise their discretion in order to discipline managers in pursuit of subgoals as soon as their deviation from the corporation's objective has been perceived. It is important to note that taking disciplinary action does not depend on particular capital owners propensity and willingness to intervene. If, and as soon as, managers' deviation from the goals of the corporation has been perceived, and as a consequence, the value of shares have dropped, a takeover of the corporation becomes more likely, endangering the tenure of the management of the (unsuccessfully managed) firm.

Where is labor's place in this theoretical construction? Although formulations vary, the link between the labor market and the firm starkly differs from the conception of the nexus between the firm on the one hand and managerial and capital markets, respectively on the other. Since labor contracts are in force over an extended period of time and involve provision of ex ante unspecified (labor) services in exchange for payment of a fixed wage amount, the wage cannot be an instrument of disciplining the worker engaged in subgoal pursuit. Whereas labor contracts are perceived to be entered when the candidate provides signals (Spence 1974) convincing the prospective employer of his capabilities and preparedness to extend a continuous and able work effort, the wage rate is negotiated in processes of collective bargaining between the firm and the union(s) reresenting the workers. This partition of an otherwise quid pro quo relation disconnects the nexus between effort and reward. Consequently, collective bargaining in the labor market can be seen as being of a largely redistributive nature. In this respect, the labor market is unlike the market for corporate control. The labor market cannot be relied upon to closely monitor worker performance.

Whereas capital markets discipline the corporation, and managerial markets discipline executives, labor markets do not discipline workers. If a corporation chooses inept or unfortunate managers, the shareholders suffer a loss. The shareholders who selected the bad management in turn risk to loose their control of the company. When they choose able and fortunate managers, however, they are rewarded. Their control over the company is reinforced. When managers behave ineptly, their income suffers a setback. And they are under increased risk to be replaced by a rival management eager to take over the job. When managers are successful, they increase their income, render their tenure on the job more secure and, on the basis of their past performance, are likely to receive offers from other firms.

When a worker performs badly on the job, there may be no immediate consequence for him at all. When he performs excellently, there may be no consequence either. While performance is related to income and wealth in both capital and corporate markets, this link is tenuous in the labor market. Disciplining workers is the task of management inside the firm, not of market competition. Still, this arrangement is thought to be efficient, since effective managers are being rewarded. Worker participation is thought to weaken the disciplinary authority of managers over workers, and therefore seen to be a likely source of inefficiency (Furubotn 1978; 1982). Thus runs the basic argument supporting the notion that in a traditional firm there is no need for workers to participate. The argument, although summarized here in an almost ad hoc way, is rooted deeply in the history of thought on micro-economic theory. As much depends on specifics of assumptions and reasoning, let us take a closer look at the conditions under which, in theory, there is no need for workers to participate.

3. While the firm as a locus of private government[4] has for long been part of industrial reality, economists have for quite a while failed to understand the reasons for its peculiar existence. As a matter of fact, the problem was not even seen to be a theoretical puzzle at all, until Dennis Holme Robertson wondered in 1923 why it is that there are

" ...islands of conscious power in this ocean of unconscious cooperation like lumps of butter coagulating in a pail of buttermilk (1923; 1928(2), 25) "

Thus, Robertson has to be credited with at least asking the question. The first answer which seems to have a bit satisfied economists was provided, however, by Ronald Coase, who reworded the problem slightly and asked

" why codetermination is the work of price mechanism in one case and of the entrepreneur in the other? (1937, 389) "

While Robertson would mostly associate social control with the function of risk bearing, Coase took a more general approach. He noted that people will choose those institutions, where for a particular exchange transaction costs can be minimized. Thus, there will be no firm, unless, for particular transactions, transactions cost inside the firm are lower than outside, i.e. in the market place. These are his basic considerations:

a) When economic agents desire exchanges over an extended period of time, transactions costs may be saved by entering into a long-term contractual relationship, which stipulates the conditions for the exchange.
b) If agents desire a long-term contractual arrangement, where an indeterminate service is to be exchanged for a determinate fee, the contract may stipulate that the party receiving the ex ante indeterminate service has the right to determine the service in exchange for a fixed fee (wage).
    This is, in a nutshell, Coase's argument for the existence of the hierarchical firm. Let us take a closer look.
    Indeterminacy of the service to be rendered can refer to the type of service, i.e. the type of work to be done only to a very limited extent; otherwise, it would not be meaningful to enter into one and only one contract with the same agent instead of

profiting from the division of labor provided by the market-place (Smith 1776, Book I, ch. III). Hence, indeterminacy must refer to amount and timing of the service to be rendered, where the amount has an upper limit in the working capacity, and the relevant timespan is given by the duration of the labor contract. While the expected length of an exchange relationship involving rendition of more or less identical services is an adequate reason for setting the conditions of the contract once and for all, it is not sufficient reason for constituting authority. Thus, argument a) can explain why some transactions, instead of occurring in the market, take place in an organization. The argument fails to explain, however, why this organization should be a firm, i.e. a hierarchical governance structure.

Argument b) is rather vague. Let us split it into two parts.

b_1 The service is contingent in frequency and extent on some event "e" which escapes the control of either party. While the worker receives a fixed wage amount, the employer receives the labor service contingent on the needs of the enterprise; the needs, however, are determined by market forces beyond either workers or managers' control.

In this form, the argument may support intraorganizational instead of market exchanges. But it completely fails to establish the need for hierarchical discretion. The situation rather resembles a case where some machine, e.g. a vehicle or a computer, is serviced by a maintenance and support team.

b_2 The service is contingent in frequency, extent and type on some event "e" which escapes the control of either party. When "e" occurs, several reactions are possible, the choice among which determines the profit. While the worker receives a fixed amount the "entrepreneur" determines the precise type, extent, and frequency of the work to be performed.

It should be noted that - while this version looks more encouraging, it begs the question of who the entrepreneur should be and how he should learn the optimal response. Although b_2 narrows down the scope of hierarchical organizations to those exchange relationships where a stochastic event requires an economic choice between alternative courses of action, it does not help us *a priori* to explain where this choice should optimally reside.

4. A completely different explanation was given by Alchian and Demsetz (1972). They are concerned with a *team* of workers who co-operate in producing a particular output. As they work, the input of each worker has only a marginal effect on the output, which is why, if a particular input is marginally reduced, the burden of the ensuing marginal output reduction will be evenly spread over all workers alike. With n workers and an output Y, the marginal output reduction $\Delta_i Y$ consequent to worker i's marginal input reduction $\Delta_i L$ results in a decrease of $\Delta_i Y/n$ in each worker's output share. If at the margin

$$\Delta_i L = \Delta_i Y$$

each worker has a rather strong incentive

$$\Delta_i L - \Delta_i Y/n$$

to reduce his input share marginally. This does not, however, imply that input reductions can be gotten at the expense of only 1/nth of the consequent output reductions. From the point of view of the other workers, it is worth almost

$$\Delta_i Y \ (n-1 \ )$$

to prevent a particular member from withholding his input, *i.e.* "shirking". How this amount will be spent in order to prevent team members from shirking depends on the relative costs and benefits of using alternative policing devices, like mutual su-pervisions, firm specific ethics and codes of conduct, social in-volvement, spectacular "tribunal" in the work place, incentives for individual workers to detect slack and sloth, or any possible combination thereof. Incidentally, all of those forms - and many different others - are being used in one type of work organiza-tion or another. Alchian and Demsetz, in their much acclaimed pa-per, however, do not address the dichotomy of different ap-proaches at all. They center on one approach to reduce shirking:

One method of reduction is for someone to specialize as a mon-itor to check the input performance of team members. Alchian and Demsetz (1972) arrived at this conclusion because they felt there was a need for someone to specialize in the task of determining the individual team members' performance, since with team production it is difficult, solely by observing total output, To either define or determine each individual's contribution to this output of the cooperating inputs (1972, 779). Not any form of organizing production efficiently need require such an explicit measurement. Again, we must conclude that Alchian and Demsetz's analysis is unsatisfactory in establishing a clear cut case for the efficiency of hierarchical organization and the simultaneous inefficiency of workers' participation in the conduct of an enterprise. The measurement problem which they highlighted might, however, provide some clues for understanding recent changes in works organization.

While asymmetry of the employment relationship is largely being denied by Alchian and Demsetz, in a more recent attempt at classification (Lloyd R. Cohen (1979, 580-590)), asymmetric labor contracts are described as promoting efficiency. Inferring from Coase's statement the relative efficiency of intra-firm transactions as compared to inter-firm (market) exchanges (in those cases where we observe transactions typically to take place within firms), he concluded that the renumeration of the factors of production must be higher in the case of the firm. As far as this increase extends to labor, it can consist in either higher or steadier income streams; the latter version follows Knight (1921) in assuming risk-averse labor.

a) In either case, the net present value of expected worker income must be assumed to be higher when employment is sought inside the firm. under risk aversion, calculation of the net present value is to be based on an appropriately higher interest rate.

b) If workers seek employment (instead of freely and independently marketing their services) because they cannot borrow against their high but insecure future income, the argument reduces to a measuring problem as in the Alchian-Demsetz case.

This metering problem Lloyd likewise concludes to be the important area. However, difficulties in measuring output do not provide a clear rationale for establishing hierarchies. With this problem Lloyd deals by referring to hierarchical organization as a common characteristic, not a necessary element of the firm. He writes:

" Perhaps the most commonly ascribed characteristic of firms, which has been mistaken for its definitive nature, is the presence of supervision and overseeing of employees by the employer or his agent. If being an employee entails the receiving of payments on the basis of a measure which does not reflect one's marginal product, then where is the incentive to raise one's marginal product? Here lies the rationale for the overseeing and supervising role of the employer. The option of terminating the contract can be exercised on the basis of a subjective measure of the employee's marginal product. This threat of termination of the contract serves as an incentive for the expenditure of effort on the part of the employee towards the goals desired by the firm's owner (1979, 589)."

It is clear that participating employees typically seek to avoid dismissals of colleagues on the basis of subjective output measures. In order to understand the implications of this analysis for the role of employee participation in the firm, let us look at the options of a typical utility maximizing employee under a firm structure as described by Lloyd.

Given the measurement problems which lie at the heart of effecting production in a continuous organizational framework - although not necessarily within a firm - there are four different outcomes of employee-employer cooperation:

a) the employee shirks and the employer (or his agent) doesn't realize it;
b) the employee shirks and the employer (or his agent) realizes it;
c) the employee fully cooperates, but the employer (or his agent) doesn't realize it;
d) the employee fully cooperates, and this is realized by the employer (or his agent).

In this "game", from the point of view of the employer, outcomes b) and d) dominate a) and c). Outcome a) is, in principle, equally costly as outcome c) which may carry substantial opportunity costs. In the absence of any numbers to be attached to the different outcomes, it suffices to note that the employers or his agent have strong incentives to achieve b) and d) and avoid a) and c).

From the point of view of the employee, b) and c) are dominated by a) and d). Although there is, in principle, an "optimum"
solution d), it is not obvious that it can be attained. As long
as c) may occur with some positive probability, the employee has
to hedge against the risk of this "accident". He can do so in two
ways: he may on the one hand divert some effort from his job to
the task of convincing the employer or his agent of his cooperative effectiveness. To an extent, this is in the employer's interest as receipt of the information helps avoid outcome c). Insofar as the employee cannot be sure that this strategy will be
effective   - and the more so the more risk averse he is assumed
to be -   the employee must divert some additional effort from
his assigned task in order to create an alternative position to
fall back on in the event c) occurs. Expenditure of this second
type of effort (hedging) is not even remotely in the interest of
the employer. The extent of hedging will be a positive function
of the risk aversity of the employee and a negative function of
the reliability with which the employer or his agent can collect
correct information about the performance of employees.

Table 1

	Employer (or his agent)	
	I	II
	Not realize	realize
Employee:		
I Shirk	a	b
II Cooperater	c	d

It is probably worth noting that I and II are not discretely
distinct strategies the employee has at his disposal. From the
employer's point of view, "hedging" is tantamount to what the employer perceives as "shirking". Since a) and d) are roughly
equivalent to the employee and since "hedging" carries better
chances for reemployment than cooperation should the employer
fail to exercise option II, risk averseness will require adopting
option I. Assuming

$$d \geq a > b > c$$

as the employee's preferences and assuming that the employee decides under uncertainty, he will invariably choose option I (hedging/shirking) when either maximizing his minimal gain or minimizing his maximal loss. If the criterion is to minimize the maximum regret, though, the employee may still choose option II when d is intensely more preferred than a. This amounts to saying that those employees are not likely to shirk/hedge, who like their job very much and would deeply regret to have endangered the job by shirking.

This result is somewhat disturbing. It tells us that if there is uncertainty over whether the employer or his agent can properly assess employees' performance - it is optimal for a risk averse employee to shirk on the job unless he very much identifies with the job. Measurement problems are, however, commonly conceived as lying at the heart of team production in the firm. In terms of the preceding analysis we must conclude that - unless measurement problems are of only slight importance, production in the (hierarchical) firm cannot be but x-inefficient.

A related approach was recently taken by Leibenstein (1982) who, in trying to explain *conventions* as rules governing work place behavior, postulated this pay-off matrix for a similar game theoretic situation:

Table 2

Firm Options

Employer Options	W_1 Golden Rule	W_2 Peer Group Standard	W_3 Indiv Maxi
π_1 Golden Rule	15 / 15	17 / 6	20 / 3
π_2 Peer Group Standard	6 / 17	10 / 10	12 / 4
π_3 Indiv Maxi	3 / 20	4 / 12	5 / 5

"Golden rule" refers to cooperative behavior (options II in table 1), while individual maximization would correspond to options I in the preceding table. Since the situation is being depicted as a *prisoners' dilemma*,[5] binding social conventions as social institutions can overcome, in the long run, the inherent instability of work organization. This would constitute a plausible explanation of the firm as a social institution.

Note, however, the stark differences in the incentive structures stipulated in tables 1 and 2 respectively. Table 2 assumes that individual maximizing behavior on the part of the employer (or his agent) would call for the "exploitation" of the cooperating employee, who would be rewarded only in order to prevent him from shirking (or leaving?). Likewise, the employee would rather want to "exploit" the cooperating employer and refrains from doing so only for fear of loosing the job. The monitoring and metering problem, which hinges on the costs of producing reliable information about the effort extended by team members, however, is absent in Leibenstein's analysis, which addresses the issue merely as a distributional problem. According to table 1, the "golden rule" outcome would be stable even in the absence of conventions, if the employee could only count on the employer's ability to discern cooperative and non-cooperative behavior.

In comparing both situations, it seems interesting to note that social conventions binding agents to refrain from individual maximizing behavior (at the expense of others) and to rather engage in cooperative behavior instead, could not alleviate the problem. Under the assumptions of table 1, both employers and employees stand to gain from cooperative behavior and are assumed to abstain from "exploiting" activities. *I.e.*, the employee shirks not because he prefers an easy going life in the work place; rather, he does so in trying to hedge against the risk of loosing his job. While the employer or his agent would gladly acknowledge (and reward) cooperative behavior on the part of employee if he could only tell his cooperative from his non-cooperative subordinates.

A more ambitious game theoretic approach has recently been suggested by Masahiko Aoki.[6] He sees the firm as a team organization where the players are workers, capital owners and management. They are locked into cooperation, which is why firm-decisions can be modeled as outcomes of cooperative games.

In essence, Aoki's theory explains how markets are inter-connected at one point, namely in the firm. As pointed out earlier firms exist because the price-mechanism is inferior to certain administrative procedures (but by no means all such procedures) where increasing returns to scale and collective goods properties are involved. This argument can be developed for both factors of production. As far as capital is concerned, the modern corporation is an institutional device able to behave as an entrepreneur and able to bear risks due to a combined effect of risk-pooling in one firm and risk-spreading on financial markets. The latter argument is based on a seminal paper by Arrow and Lind. They showed that while individual risk costs of investment in a particular firm by a large number of risk-averse investors become negligible with the number of investors becoming large, the sum of risk costs over all shareholders tends to become negligible as well if the number of shareholders becomes sufficiently large, since the individual risk costs diminish in a higher order then the increase in the number of shareholders. This implies that it is the large corporation even more so than the owner operated one that can bear substantial risk. This reasoning also helps explain why the large codetermined firm, due to its being large and due to (instead of in spite of) the codetermination structures, can become a center of innovation.

A symmetric argument can be developed for labor; here, Aoki goes far beyond Gary Becker and scholars working in his tradition. While the Chicago approach assumes that human capital is primarily enbodied in individuals and costs of as well as returns to training can be calculated with respect to the individual, Aoki stresses that human capital is accumulated by means of the collective process of learning on the job. Its returns can only be maximized if shared, and returns can be higher if every employee contributes. Consequently retaining the cooperation of human capital is important for achieving a maximum gain.

Taken together, there are five sources of organizational rent, which form the object of intra-firm bargaining. These sources are: (1) the relatively higher risk-taking ability of the body of shareholders made possible through the corporate institution; (2) the willingness of the employees to cooperate, and the ability of the employer to adapt and monitor effectively under uncertainty; (3) the skills and knowledge formed on the job and enbodied in the employees as well as the ability of the employer to generate and utilize them effectively; (4) the large-scale funds pooled by shareholders and the managers' ability to allocate them internally in an efficient way; and (5) the collective skills formed on the shop floor and enbodied in the team of employees as well as the ability of the employer to generate and utilize these skills efficiently.

Since the firm is made up of several firm-specific resource holders and the firm can therefore no longer be seen, as in the neo-classical case, as a web of pairwise contractual relationships with the owner in the center, there cannot be a single firm objective such as the maximization of profits. Rather, the firm has to be modeled as a bargaining process in which the conflicting objectives of the firm specific resource holders are brought into equilibrium. This is considered a task of management.

Using a cooperative game approach requires not only a cooperative rent, which can be distributed, but also that cooperation is preferable to non-cooperation for each player. The players have to be locked into cooperation for the cooperative game to be robust. This applies to firms with labor participation. Labor as human capital cannot only effectively withhold its contribution to the production of an organizational rent, the owners of human capital are also locked into cooperation since most of their human capital is firm-specific. A parallel result is developed for stockholders of the large corporation; while small stockholders, when they are dissatisfied with the performance of a particular corporation, can withdraw, and by withdrawing will only marginally affect the value of the stock they sell, an institutional investor holding a larger portion of the stock would be in a different situation. Selling would indeed affect the stock value, and this implies that, to an extent, capital owners are locked into cooperation as well.

In order to fully appreciate Aoki's game-theoretic approach, it is helpful to show how it differs from a neo-classical approach to modelling intra-firm behaviour. To the Chicago school in particular we owe models that try to capture the interaction between different resource holders in the firm. Eugene Fama (e.g., in his 1980 JPE article) models an explicit interplay between labor, capital and managers, and his model is even capable of accommodating other stake-holders in the firm such as major clients or financial institutions. Yet the model is set up according to the set of contracts theory of the firm, where the managers, prevented from colluding (against share-holders or workers) by a watchdog-board composed of representatives of the major resource holders, set out to maximize the net-present value of their life-time earnings as determined by an interfirm market for managers. What applies to human capital in general certainly applies to managerial human capital in particular; employment of managerial human capital is likely to be subject to increasing returns to scale and equally likely to possess collective-goods properties. The best market for managerial human capital is therefore likely to be inside the firm, and this raises some doubt on how universally applicable a model such as Fama's might be. Aoki, instead of modeling managers as maximizing their own utility and treating the firm as a mere vehicle for satisfying their own interests, follows a more eclectic approach allowing for managers to have various motivations.

The basic logic of the Aoki model rests on the assumption that the firm employs two factors of production viz labor and capital, both of which are considerably locked into the venture and both of which, while either can threat to withhold the cooperative effort, will produce a substantial rent if and while cooperating. Yet they do not agree on everything, and in particular they do not fully agree on the optimal firm policy. Hence, the model cannot yield a unique result as a neo-classical model would. Some may see this as a disadvantage of his modelling strategy, which, however, has the advantage of capturing a wide range of new institutional developments of which codetermination is only an example.

2. The Economic Theory of the Firm: A Second Look
2.1. The Principal Agent Relationship

The conventional view in the theory of the firm is built around the principal agent paradigm. As Alichan and Demsetz[7] postulated, an efficiently organized firm would bundle five rights in the hand of one owner. These rights involve: (1) the right to control inputs and outputs, (2) the right to compose the team of the firm and determine who will be a member and who won't, (3) the right to control all contracts that are made with the firm, (4) the right to claim the residual after all expenses have been paid, and (5) the right to sell, to close down or otherwise alter the firm in parts or as a whole. This basic paradigm clearly fits a particular view of how an efficient firm is organized, but it is not a view that can be shared across cultures. Interestingly enough, it is not even a view that satisfactorily describes the contemporary large American firm. It is further a view built solely around the problem of monitoring team-members and preventing their shirking, but the equally important problem of creating structures in which innovative and productive behaviour, including learning and teaching, can occur, is not a central focus of the approach.

Beforehand, it should be pointed out that it is irrelevant for the Alchian-Demsetz approach whether labor or capital is the residual claimant and sole owner of the firm. However, capital is normally considered to be the legitimate residual claimant. This implies that capital owners would first have the right to control inputs and outputs. In practice, this performance control takes place within the firm, whereas the overall performance of the firm is monitored by means of capital-markets. Large investors employ analysts, who scrutinize firm data and give early warnings when inconsistencies or indicators of downturns appear that would either stem from the firm itself or important markets in which it operates. The internal structure of the firm will only be relevant if performance turns out to be below par. Hence, for the large institutional investor the question of the internal structure of decision-making is largely irrelevant. Indeed, and sometimes within the same industry, we can observe a profuse proliferation of diverse structures, all monitored by means of the same indicators and by the same industry observers. E.g., the American airline industry until recently had firms that were organized along strictly hierarchical principles side by side with others where unions played a dominant role and again others where employees were dominant, with one firm even being labor-owned. The steel industry provides similar examples. Secondly the model would suggest that capital has the right to hire and fire. Indeed, we observe that for decades large parts of American industry have operated with the closed-shop-principle and hired only at the union hall, leaving the right to determine team membership to organized labour. Empirical studies have shown,[8] that this practice can increase productivity. Unions are not only interested in, but also able to screen job applicants, since the better the performance of workers, the better the productivity of the firm will be and hence the bigger demands at the time of collective bargaining.

Likewise, the same practice illustrates how contracts may indeed not be centralized at one point. Shirking can more effectively be prevented when the working environment created through the firm structure renders shirking detrimental to the shirker's interest.

Again for many decades American industries have worked with various bonus-systems. Currently, the practice of allocating company-stock to even low level employees is very widespread.[9] Firms find it efficient to spread the right to claim the residual over large segments of their workforce.

Plant closings still occur, and in the United States they are less costly to the owner than in Europe, where the worker has to be compensated for the loss of his job. Yet most large American firms either have binding agreements with unions calling for substantial severance payments in the case of layoffs, or they practice such payments without being legally bound. Again, we observe this practice because firms find it efficient to engage in such activities.

The reason why we observe such an ill-fit between the Alchian-Demsetz paradigm and industrial reality is that the paradigm is built solely around the problem of shirking. It is unimaginative with respect to the multitude of contractual relationships into which firms tend to enter.

2.2. Recent Developments in the Theory of the Firm

For several years now, economists have gotten used to describe the relationship between the employer and the employee in terms of an implicit contract.[10] In addition to the explicit exchange of work for pay, there is said to be an implicit agreement that the employer will guarantee employment-security in exchange for a virtual decrease in pay. In theory, the case for such an insurance contract is readily made. Households are risk-averse, because their income generally derives from one main source, their ability to work. Diversification is not feasible nor is open-market insurance (due to moral hazard problems). The employer on the other hand is able to contain the unemployment risk in part - insofar as it derives from the organization of production in the firm. To that extent, the implicit employment guarantee is said to be valid. Beyond the employer's domain, however, unemployment due to general conditions in the industry, the business cycle, structural changes, etc. is not a part of the implicit contract between employer and the firm. The resulting insurance is of the fair-weather variety, protecting against changes in the weather,

but not in the climate. Who would be satisfied with a home-owners' insurance policy that protected against the loss from broken
windows but not against the loss of having the whole house burn
down? As a matter of fact, the opposite type of insurance prevails in the market for home-owners' insurance. Small losses are
deductible, but large losses are covered. Likewise, we should expect similar explicit employment contracts to be observable in
practice.

The standard reasons given in the implicit contracts literature why the insurance contracts assumes the fair-weather-form
turn on the impossibility of writing a labor contract detailed
enough to prevent shirking and, somewhat relatedly, the problem
of moral hazard. Moral hazard refers to a case where the risk to
be insured against increases with the existence of an insurance
contract. The standard way of putting it would then be that a
firm guaranteeing employment-security might be more likely to
find itself in a predicament where layoffs would normally be necessary than a firm that did not. In practice, neither of these
problems seems to be significant. A large number of the best per-
forming industries have explicit employment-guarantees.[11] Employment security is never understood to protect the job of non-per-
forming workers, and the typical way of achieving employment security is expressly not that of writing a very specific contract.
To the contrary: "Companies with no-lay off policies require
something in return from their workers, and most often that something is greater flexibility in the way tasks are assigned and
work-schedules arranged." Significantly, " No-lay off guarantees
occur in both union and non-union situation".[12] Companies adopting no-lay off policies have good business reasons to do so. But
these reasons may differ. Some companies feel that the costs of
lay-offs are too high, in particular in terms of the costs of
training to be borne with future hiring and the time it takes until employees reach their activity-peak. The case of Advanced Micro Devices is illustrative. The company, based in the Califor-
nian Silicon Valley, like others in the semi-conductor industry
faces fierce competition in its labour market for talented engineers. The firm is heavily dependent on these engineers' knowhow,
and inevitably a person who leaves takes some of the company's
ideas with him. According to a company spokesman, the no-lay off
policy paid off particularly during the recent recession that hit
the industry, and when other companies were forced to lay off
personnel. "By reducing hiring, we stuck to our policy and sud-

denly found ourselves witnessing dramatic improvements in production. It was hard to resist the conclusion that the increased efficiency was directly attributable to appreciation for our no-lay off policy. Certainly it was due a large measure to that increased efficiency that we were able to come through it without showing a loss in any quarter. Equally certain, we came through the recession with our production teams intact and able to take advantage of improved demand" (Gutchess, p. 26). At the same company, "the most highly skilled employees are thought not to reach peak production for two years and, even at the lowest skill level, that of hand assemblers, maximum production is not attained for at least six to eight weeks. Automation is eliminating many of the lower skill jobs and thus has the effect of increasing the skill level of the work force as a whole" (ibidem).

2.3. The Productivity of Consensual Decisions

One of the most fiercely contested issues in the literature on codetermination is labor-capital parity in company decision taking. In practice, parity does not appear very often. In the German coal and steel industry, labor and owner representatives have an equal number of seats on the supervisory board of the corporation, but not, of course, in management. An "independent" member is added in order to give the board an uneven number of seats so as to avoid a tie. Likewise, the Bullock Report[13] proposed a similar composition, the 2X + Y formula. The standard view in the literature is that parity compositions of the board should be avoided. Normally they are. The addition of an "independent" board member is supposed to stop short of parity, and so are similar approaches as in the case of the German 1976 Codetermination Act, under which the chairman of the supervisory board, who is normally a capital representative, casts a deciding second vote to break the tie. Surprisingly, even advocates of codetermination adopt a very defensive line of argument when it comes to defending parity decision making. A case in point is the book by Kuebler, Schmidt and Simitis.[14] The authors argue that parity decision making is not required under the 1976 act, and if it were, there is no evidence of such a procedure being harmful. Instead, in what follows I wish to argue that parity decision making, if correctly implemented is not harmful, but productive.

The standard argument against parity is that parity forces the opposing parties into making a joint decision. Hence, in order to avoid conflict, capital owners are said to be forced to make concessions to labour, and these concessions are said to be harmful to the long-run interest of the firm. Although, as mentioned above, parity is rarely found in codetermination arrangements, in what follows I assume that parity is required in order to show what the effects of such a decision-making procedure are on the performance of the codetermined corporation.

One of the standard insights of economic theory is that unanimous decisions are necessarily those that increase the welfare of the decision makers.[15] The reason for this result is simple. A unanimous decision is by definition one that increases the welfare of each decision taker as compared to the case where a decision is not taken. Parity decision making is just such a case of a unanimity requirement, based, of course, on the somewhat counterfactual assumption that labour and capital representatives each form homogeneous groups. This implies that the case of reference, when no decision will be taken, determines how the unanimously agreed upon compromise will look like. If no decision is being taken, the status quo will prevail. This is precisely the reason why in all other contexts but the issue of codetermination unanimity requirements have been criticized as being excessively conservative. Hence, there is indeed no need to agree since the decision is not taken in a vacuum. Agreements are only forthcoming if they involve improvements for at least one party without imposing disadvantages on the other. Not agreeing implies agreeing on the status quo. The party interested in a change has to look for a suggestion which contains improvements, not only for itself, but more importantly benefits for the other party as well. Hence, whatever benefit the consensual decision entails has to be shared among the decision makers. In a committee, operating under the parity rule, only that party has a chance to succeed with an initiative that has thoroughly studied the interests of the other party and is able to offer something of substance. This implies that parity decision making creates incentives to look for new solutions, where the search for the solutions is guided not by one party's interests but by bipartisan considerations. The implication, again, is that the search for information undertaken by members of a committee with a parity rule is drastically different from that search behaviour committee members will show who are not operating under the parity requirement and can impose their view on a dissenting minority. The committee with a parity rule, in order to be able to function, has to provide itself with information that differs in quality from the information needed by a non-parity committee.

For the sake of simplicity, we can distinguish between two cases. The first case may be described as a situation where a particular initiative, while of high priority for one party is of little concern to the other. In such a case, very little is likely to happen. If, for instance, capital owners are not interested in initiatives that the labour side puts forth on the supervisory board, they have the means to withhold cooperation, reducing the significance of the entire board for company decision making. Even under parity, labour can do nothing in the supervisory board without the cooperation of at least one capital representative. This would imply that the managing board would not answer to the supervisory board, but rather to the powerful interests in the stockholders' assembly. This in turn implies that if labour has nothing to offer on the supervisory board, capital can essentially reduce the supervisory board to a perfunctory decision-making body, copying in essence the Anglo-American model of a unified managing board, aided by a few outside directors who represent the major share-holders' interests. The same applies in the reverse case where labour loses interests in the supervisory board, perhaps in order to concentrate on the forum provided by collective bargaining. Again, the significance of the supervisory board would be reduced, strengthening the share-holders' assembly and likely several key subcommittees of the supervisory board in which labour would not necessarily be represented at parity. Only if and as long as both labour and capital representatives are interested in active cooperation on the supervisory board, will that board play an active role in determining company policy. In that case, the ability to arrive at decisions depends upon the extent of having new solutions available. This, in turn, depends on the extent of discretion the supervisory board assumes vis-a-vis shareholders and management. Hence, two rather different scenarios are conceivable. In the cooperative case the committee with the parity rule will increase in significance, whereas in the non-cooperative case its significance will decrease.

This line of reasoning has been criticized[16] for overlooking the fact that the status quo may indeed be subject to change. The firm is, of course, subject to events that may affect labour and

capital differently. If the status quo changes, the benefits derived from particular decisions will change as well, and this is
true for both parties. The most extreme case is given where the
status quo is expected to change at the expense of one party. Let
us assume this party is the capital side. Labour may wish to pursue a strategy of withholding cooperation, expecting that capital
will thus become increasingly more willing to make concessions.
Whether labour would be wise to follow such a strategy is subject
to doubt. As capital continues to suffer losses, the room for
making concessions is certainly shrinking. A lack of agreement
between labour and capital in a situation which is expected to
worsen for capital alone can only be explained by different expectations about the extent and profile of the losses to be expected. If both parties share roughly similar expectations, all
the losses can be similarly anticipated and joint decisions be
based on those common anticipations. On the other hand, if anticipations differ, parity creates incentives to share reliable information in order to arrive at common expectations. Such incentives are not present if unanimity is not required. The same line
of argument, of course, applies when labour is expected to lose
over time.

A similar criticism of codetermination based on a neo-Austrian
model has been put forward by Ludwig Lachmann:[17]

" We now come to the main issue. Economists distinguish between
flows and stocks, between streams of goods and services and the
sources of these streams. While workers sell their services, capital owners entrust the sources of capital services to the enterprise of their choice. In adverse circumstances, they suffer not
merely, as workers also might, a loss of income, but a capital
loss. It seems evident that he who entrusts his capital, the
source of his income stream, to others must be able to demand
that these are responsible to him for their conduct, in particular where he lacks the ordinary rights of a creditor and cannot
withdraw his capital. If, however, managers are responsible for
their management of the (durable and other specific) capital instruments of the company, they bear such responsibility towards
owners, and not towards somebody else. Otherwise responsibility
has no meaning. The worker members of the supervisory boards
share in the control of management, but do not share in this responsibility."

In practice, the distinction between stock and flow does not coincide with the distinction between labour and capital. Labour entrusts its human capital to the corporation in the same way as capital owners entrust their assets. Both have an active interest in monitoring the use of their assets. In both cases, stocks are involved just as well as flows. Employees receive remunerations continuously. But these wages or salaries need not necessarily reflect the true extent of current productivity, since the entire lifetime earnings profile has to be taken into account. It is quite common for employees to accept wages that remain far below their current productivity in the expectation of future higher remunerations. The human capital entrusted to the corporation has to be considered a stock in terms of Lachmann's analysis. On the other hand, capital involvement is hardly confined to entrusting a stock of assets once and for all. In a dynamic and thus Austrian perspective, the stock actually distintegrates into many flows. As the corporation continues to operate, it is constantly contracting on its markets, constantly hiring new labour at various levels and in varying quantities, continuously repaying credit and taking in new loans, issuing new stocks and paying dividends at varying levels, reflecting how capital owners evaluate company performance. If, e.g., a company finds itself in difficulty due to adverse labour relations, it will be forced to increase (instead of decrease) dividend levels in order to remain attractive for new investments. If dividends have to be paid above the true level of current earnings, the stock invested is actually reduced. On the other hand, if the company is profitable, and its prospects are good, dividends may well remain below current earnings, stockholders preferring to store wealth in the corporation and thus increasing the stock of capital invested there. Hence, the size of the stock is constantly varied depending on the performance of the corporation, which in turn depends upon the extent to which labour and capital can productively cooperate. A similar reasoning applies to labour. Here too, when the company falls upon hard times, wages and bonuses may have to be increased in order to prevent key employees from leaving, while favorable company prospects tend to entice confidence and further investment in human capital.

In summary, the requirement of unanimous agreement reflects the realistic situation of labor and capital being locked into cooperation. Where this is the case, i.e. where substantial capital assets are combined with significant amounts of human capital, the parity rule is an adequate institutional response to the problem of organizing production efficiently.

3. The Failure of Traditional Organization
3.1. Barriers to Information Flows

Having human capital available in the firm is not the same as making an optimal use of it. The larger the corporation, the more likely there will be bureaucratic behaviour within the firm. In Fama's model, resource owners have a right to monitor management in order to ascertain an optimal use of the resource. This does not take into account, however, that resource owners may be able to derive utility from opportunistic activities. We may note Tullock's[18] explanation of bureaucratic behaviour in order to highlight the problem. While Tullock had political bureaucracies in mind, it is obvious that the cases apply to private bureaucracies as well. In a chain of subordination, and where remunerations are dependent on performance, information flows will reflect opportunistic behaviour. This reflection takes on three forms: (1) Overreporting of successes will occur and will have to be checked by either mechanism of competition within the bureaucracy[19] or appropriate accounting methods. (2) In polities, underreporting of failures is likely to resurface in town hall meetings, but is also likely to resurface with a lag. Similarly, the business press can be expected to pick up some gross instances of underreporting of failures by corporations, forcing adjustments in stock values. While information on failures cannot totally be suppressed, a true picture of causes and extent of these failures may take time to be visualized. This path is well under the influence of whoever caused the failure. Since democratic governments in western societies tend to change administrations after four or at most eight years, there is always a good chance that failures can be attributed to the party that was in opposition while the failure occurred. Likewise, the current management will at least try to blame its own short-comings on its predecessor. (3) Spreading of responsibility insures that failures cannot be attached to persons. The method is important since it allows to avoid what in a market system would have amounted to a liability. In particular, this method will be combined with overreporting of successes and under-reporting of failures. Successes will be claimed and failures will be blamed (on adversaries).

All three instances of failures in information flows lead to deficiencies in coordination. As Ronald Coase[20] pointed out long ago, firms have to be seen as a substitute for market coordination. Market coordination requires three basic legal institutions, namely property rights, the ability to contract and the existence of liability. Inside the firm, basically the same institutions have to resurface. The requirement of property rights inside the firm demands a provision of precise definitions of tasks and obligations, contracts translate into intra-firm agreements, and liability amounts to holding employees responsible for their activities. Spreading responsibilities undermines all three institutions. Precise definitions of tasks will be blurred by sharing tasks among different departments and subordinate to different purposes. Overreporting of successes is possible due to participation in interdepartmental programs. The same approach facilitates underreporting of failures. Under these circumstances, coordination within the firm will require additional efforts in order to overcome the aforementioned barriers. These efforts can only be based on information enbodied in persons who have incentives to reveal organizational failure. It would be farfetched to suggest that works council members always have optimal incentives to play this role. They don't. Their time horizons do not necessarily match those of their constituencies and their career paths tend to differ from theirs. Nevertheless, important incentives do exist. The influence of a works councilor depends on the web of information he can use. The more information he has which is not available to management, the more likely he is to open up "surprising" avenues for new development and hence the more likely he is to transform his committee into a forum of innovation.

3.2. Inefficiencies in Control

In a market economy, property, contract and liability are instruments of performance control. Since the same instruments are not available within an organization, substitutes have developed. In this instance, the use of human capital is most relevant. We rediscover the problem on the agenda of works council meetings, where decisions have to be taken about advice on hiring, firing and promotions. On these questions, colluding is unrealistic since decisions have to be made within the same constituency.

Hiring adds to the productivity of the permanent staff (in different degrees, hence the distributive problem), promotions affect the ability to perform differentially, and firing has obvious distributive effects. Since colluding is unrealistic, works councilors face important inducements to correct for organizational failures.

3.3. Externalization of Costs

Externalizations of costs occur if capital, management, and labor can collude at the expense of a third party, e.g., environmental pollution is a textbook case. Externalization of costs can also occur within the firm. This is the case when capital use is interrupted or impaired. Capital use can be impaired by opportunistic behavior of management, as e.g. in the Baumol[21] case of the firm that maximizes output at the expense of profits. Human capital use of management can be impaired by either insufficient capital supply or adverse labor relations. Human capital use of labor is, of course, interrupted when firing occurs. As we have seen earlier, this method of externalizing costs becomes increasingly less viable since companies face the costs of training and since employees tend to take the more time to reach their productivity peak the more skills their job requires. A more important impairment occurs when management interests conflict with those of workers. In this case, the traditional model of the firm as in the Alchian/Demsetz case has management resolve whatever conflict occurs. This dissolution cannot always result in optimal capital use. As we look through the list of rights of works councilors in the various western societies, we note that they concern themselves primarily with precisely this issue. It would be wrong to argue that works council representation is an optimal way to insure proper human capital use. We noted earlier that there is a collective goods problem involved here requiring a club-like institutional response. While works councils do not represent workers according to human capital endowments, they can be regarded as such club-like institutions.

4. Works Councils, Codetermination, and the Labor Director: Three Forms of Labor Participation

4.1. Works Councils and the Environment of the Work Place

Works councils codetermine the environment of the workplace, in general, and in particular where technical progress is involved. The textbook view of such legal provisions (which we find in most any Western society either by law or through collective bargaining agreement) is that they lead to constraints of efficient firm behavior. It may e.g. be argued that an optimal technology cannot be chosen due to labor withholding its agreement. Such a view disregards the importance of optimally combining human capital with appropriate technology. Quite obviously, the optimal use of human capital critically depends upon the technology of machinery with which it is combined. The value of human capital in turn depends on this combination. Hence, it is up to the owners of human capital to codetermine technology choice. Again, capital and labor are locked into cooperation in the way Aoki has modelled.

4.2. Codetermination: Differentiating Between Distributional and Allocational Decisions

It is typical for textbook discussions of labor issues to assume that labor can be adequately represented by unions operating within the context of collective bargaining. Such a representation can work adequately where labor is fairly homogeneous. In that case, stipulations about pay and working conditions can be reasonably general and uniform. A completely different case arises when human capital endowments are taken into account. The more complicated the technology with which the firm operates, the more human capital intensive the production process will be, and (likely but not necessarily) the more heterogeneous human capital endowments will be required. In these cases, uniform agreements can only lead to imposing constraints on optimal human capital use. Since human capital use is determined by management choice, and since human capital use determines the level of pay, it is appropriate that codetermination begins where collective bargaining ends. In practice, this is precisely what we see. On the one hand, we notice that collective bargaining agreements establish a floor for wages and fringe benefits. Substantial differences oc-

cur across a particular industry as far as the wage drift is concerned. It must be emphasized that two completely different negotiating strategies have to be used in order to arrive at these
two distinct decisions, setting the wage and choosing the optimal
human capital-machinery combination. Collective bargaining is obviously a zero-sum game, hence the familiar instruments of strike
and lock out. Human capital-machinery choice requires a cooperative effort, since both parties can gain by an appropriate
choice. This is why a two-tier system of labor representation is
absolutely essential for good industry performance. In several
western countries, such as the United Kingdom and the United
States, neglect of developing the second tier, i.e. excessive reliance on unions, has caused severe problems. A union representative sitting on the board of e.g. Chrysler or Eastern Airlines
has to wear two hats and hence cannot perform either role in an
optimal fashion.

4.3. The Labor Director: Participative Personnel Management

Sometimes we have noticed the appearance of a lonely figure:
the labor director. His strongest position is in the German Coal
and Steel Industry, where he is an equal member of the managing
board, and responsible for personnel. He may not be appointed
against the vote of labor representatives on the (supervisory)
board. Some critics have seen this institution as an extension of
union power into management. In fact, we noticed at least the
possibility of the opposite influence. The labor director depends
on the cooperation, not only of the works council members, but
also of his colleagues in management. He will invariably find
himself in a position of minority, and hence can only exert influence by introducing innovative alternatives into management
decisions (see 2.3 above). On the other hand it is up to the
labor director to communicate and translate management views into
labor and union purposes. The labor director's stock in trade
crucially depends on his ability to combine management objectives
with labor aspirations. In addition, he often serves a third
purpose. Where government is an important customer or subsidizer,
the labor director allows management to play the political game
on both sides, government and the opposition. Where the labor
director tends to be affiliated with the socialist party,
management is likely to have close links with conservatives,

which amounts to saying that the board is connected to both government and opposition irrespective of who is in power at the
time.

5. Labor Participation: A Dissenting Interpretation[22]

In this short essay I have tried to argue that the labor representation structures that are variously developing throughout
the western world amount to an efficient response to organizational failures. By "efficient" I understand not the best imagin-
able response, but a response that has indeed materialized in
practice and meets the needs of the organization. There is no
doubt that organizational change will continue. Imposing organizational change, however, can lead to dramatic failures. It is
perhaps appropriate to refer to a recent case in order to illustrate the problem.

Inspired by the positive experience with labor representatives on (supervisory) boards of major private industrial corporations in West Germany, the British labor government in 1974 set
up a committee under the chairmanship of Lord Bullock to propose
means of introducing worker representation at board level in the
private sector of industry. The Bullock Committee thoroughly
reviewed the German experience but suggested a some-what different approach, taking into account the differences in legal corporate structures and the position of the British trade unions. As
we have seen above the main rationale for the German system of
codetermination lies in the notion that corporate boards face two
types of decisions: firstly those that involve some measure of
distribution of rents or rewards between the factors of production, and secondly those that turn on the most efficient way of
running the corporation. While the first type of problem needs to
be dealt with through the channels of collective bargaining, in
the second labor's voice may be important because workers are
needed for the implementation of organizational measures. Hence,
it is only reasonable to tap their knowledge and experience which
obviously may differ from the perspective of management. The Bullock Committee argued similarly that "the difficulties in decision-making at the board which might arise from differences of
view between worker directors and other board members would be
more than compensated for by the easier implementation of
jointly-agreed decision" (p. 160). However, one should keep in

mind that the basic premise of the West German approach, namely distinguishing between allocational and distributional issues, does not resurface in a proper institutional distinction in the British context. British corporations do not know the sharp distinction between a managing board and a (refereeing) supervisory board, nor the equally important distinction between labor representatives organized in works councils and meeting with management inside the firm, on the one hand, and union officials on the other engaged in collective bargaining at industry level.

Against that background, this is what happened at the British Post Office. In 1978 and 1979, Britain embarked on what was called an experiment in industrial democracy in giving union representatives parity with management on the corporate Board of the Post Office. Union representatives were also nominated to advisory boards at the regional and (local) area level. The Post Office had always been heavily unionized. But more than half a dozen unions represent different groups of workers, centrally but separately bargaining for wages and working conditions. A Council of Post Office Unions existed, but was able to act only if there was unanimous agreement among unions (p.12).

The auspices under which the experiment was launched were highly unfavourable. Since at the same time, the Post Office was expected to act more commercially, thus threatening benefits and labor practices unions had long fought for, unions had no interest in helping to prove that a commercialized Post Office was a viable institution. Given the traditionally strong role of unions in the Post Office, "the unions themselves had nothing to gain from the experiment," which was said to be akin to "putting an overcoat on over a raincoat" (p. 100). The experiment was also imposed on an unwilling management and limited to a two-year duration. If successful, the experiment would be continued. Management had no interest in proving this scheme of "industrial democracy" a success.

In describing the course of the experiment, it is important to note that the Post Office was a government monopoly with several organizational objectives, its statute requiring attention to both the welfare of its staff and that of the general public (p. 22). In addition, political targets were set which could be at variance with the statutory service obligations: "there was thus considerable room for the Post Office to negotiate targets and to play one off against another" (p. 46). As a consequence of putting union members on the Board, managers began to weaken the

Board's position. "In the eyes of full-time Board members, the union nominees prevented the Board from playing a more powerful role" (p. 69). Formerly, management had used the Board as a sounding board or a think tank (p. 69), but with union members present, that practice was largely discontinued. Managers complained all along that the union nominees were really not qualified for Board membership. They were probably right, since the general secretaries of the unions were unwilling to serve on the Board for fear of undermining their position with membership (p. 105); hence, less senior union representatives were sent to the Board.

The role these representatives could play on the Board was limited. "Many managers (including Board members) admitted that the style and content of some Board papers had been substantially altered in an attempt to exclude 'sensitive' matters from debate because of the presence of the union member" (p. 70).

Still, union members were not inactive during Board meetings. While "union members made more proposals than did the other Board members," the "majority of the proposals did not lead to any change of policy or action" (p. 83). But occasionally, "the collective opinion of the Board was such as to dissuade the full-timers from a course of action which they had intended to follow, or to persuade them to take a new initiative" (p. 61); Union members seem to have seen their role as specialists in industrial relations: "In the shorter term union nominees saw part of their role as preventing 'management from making stupid industrial relations decisions'" (p. 36). In this sense, union representatives on the Board disappointed management. While management expected union nominees to help in the "problem solving" task of the Board (p. 126), "union nominees went into the experiment unsure of the details of their involvement, but clear on two broad principles: the new scheme was to be used to advance union policies, and to reinforce rather than substitute the existing collective bargaining arrangement" (p. 127-128). Since Board involvement remained constrained (p. 139) essentially to furthering collective - bargaining ends with new means and labor nominees were anxious not to endanger their credibility with the union base (p. 136), it is not surprising that the marginal effect of the nominees was very small indeed. One negotiator "argued strongly not only that he obtained nothing more through the union nominees than he received through the consultative machinery, but also that he received it earlier through the established channel" (p. 141). Under these circumstances, it comes as no surprise that the experiment was discontinued after running its course. Unions made a weak effort to continue the scheme, but management "had become increasingly convinced that it had disrupted the proper role of the Board" (p. 154). The minister required a consensual proposal from both unions and management as a precondition for the continuation of the experiment. Such a consensus was impossible to reach, and the experiment was unceremoniously ended.

This "experiment" is interesting for demonstrating some of the basic pitfalls of engineering schemes of labor participation. The experiment only appeared to follow Lord Bullock's proposal of parity representation between labor and capital. Instead, parity between managers and labor representatives was instituted, with capital owners absent. Secondly, by appointing union leaders as labor representatives, unions were asked to fulfill two different roles at once. Given the circumstances under which the experiment had been initiated, it is not surprising that unions chose to stick with their original task, that of collective bargaining, instead of assuming additional responsibilities in the Post Office. Thirdly, by appointing outside directors to an executive board, no attempt was made to distinguish institutionally between the different functions of managing and refereeing. This was fourthly all the more troublesome since clear criteria for refereeing were lacking, the Post Office being a government monopoly with various conflicting tasks. Finally, insufficient incentives were present for the parties subjected to the "experiment" to support its course. As the authors themselves conclude, "the overall impact of the union nominees was marginal. They can best be seen as an irritant rather than as a major obstruction for management, while for the unions, they brought only limited gain" (p. 177). It would be unjustified to claim that the optimistic Bullock thesis does not, then, receive much support from the Post Office experiment. The Bullock model pays insufficient attention to the specific contests in which board representation is located. 'Strong' schemes of worker directors tend to reflect, rather than resolve, the underlying patterns of conflict and cooperation in industry" (p. 177). This "experiment" was clearly a political exercise in almost every possible respect unfit to show how a codetermination scheme conceived along the lines of the Bullock report might work in a major industrial corporation in Britain.

On summary, I have argued, in this essay, that worker representation on company boards can be an efficient response to organizational failures. Much depends, as this last section has shown, on institutional details. Not any form of worker participation can be expected to yield benefits, and care should be taken to avoid that corporate structures are turned into a political football.

Footnotes:

[1] Machlup further exemplified the problem by referring to his wellknown example of a theoretical car driver (1967 ibidem).

[2] See e.g. Backhaus, J. , Ökonomik der partizipativen Unternehmung I. Tübingen; Mohr/Siebeck 1979, chapter 6.

[3] This distinction, although generally neglected in economists' discussion, turns out to be important for the discussion infra 4.2.

[4] Williamson (1981, 1539 et passim) refers to "the firm on governance structure."

[5] See Harvey Leibenstein "The Prisoners' Dilemma in the Invisible Hand: An Analysis of Intra-firm Productivity," American Economic Review 72(2), May 1982, pp. 92-97.

[6] Aoki, M., The Cooperative Game Theory of the Firm, New York, Oxford: Clarendon Press, 1984.

[7] Alchian, A. A., and Demsetz, H., "Production, Information Costs, and Economic Organization," American Economic Review 62, 1972, pp 777-795.

[8] See e.g. Freeman, R., and Medoff, J., "The Two Faces of unionism," Public Interest 57, 1979, pp. 69-93.

[9] This is not done because companies thereby want to stimulate performance. The performance effect on company employees is likely to be very small. Instead, owning stock in a company gives employees an excellent chance to use their inside information on the stock market, creating a positive externality for the entire group of shareholders. Secondly, inducing company stock ownership also induces complementary human capital investments by employees.

[10] Azariadis, C., "Implicit Contracts and Underemployment Equilibria," JPE Bd. 83, 1975, pp. 1183-1202.

[11] "Job-Guarantee Contracts Are Becoming More Common: unions Increasingly Refocus Priorities on Security, Despite Pitfalls," WSJ, June 29, 1987.

[12] Gutchess, J. F., Employment Security in Action: Strategies That Work, New York, Pergamon Press, 1985.

[13] Lord Bullock (chairman). "Report of the Committee of Inquiry on Industrial Democracy," London HMSO, 1977 (Cmnd. 6706).

[14] Kübler, F., Schmidt, W., and Simitis, S., Mitbestimmung als gesetzgebungspolitische Aufgabe: Zur Verfassungsmäßigkeit des Mitbestimmungsgesetzes 1976, Baden Baden, Nomos, 1978.

[15] See in particular; Buchanan, James M., and Tullock, G., The Calculus of Consent, Ann Arbor, The University of Michigan Press, 1965.

[16] Bonus, H., Zur Transformation der Marktwirtschaft durch Sozialkomponente und Demokratisierung. In: O. Issing (Ed.), Zukunftsprobleme der Sozialen Marktwirtschaft. Verhandlungen auf

der Jahrestagung der Gesellschaft für Wirtschafts- und Sozialwissenschaften, Verein für Socialpolitik, in Nürnberg 1980
Berlin: Duncker + Humblot (Schriften des Vereins für Socialpolitik N.F. 116), 1981.

[17] Lachmann, L. M., "The Flow of Legislation and the Permanence of the Legal Order," Ordo 30, 1979, p. 69-77 (74).

[18] Tullock, G., The Politics of Bureaucracy, Washington, Public Affairs Press, 1965.

[19] See recently: Breton, A., and Wintrobe, R., The Logic of Bureaucratic Conduct: An Economic Analysis of Competition, Exchange, and Efficiency in Private and Public Organizations, New York, Cambridge University Press, 1982.

[20] Coase, R. H., "The Nature of the Firm," Economica 4, 1937, p. 387-405.

[21] Baumol, W. J., "On the Theory of Oligopoly," Economica, 25 1958, S. 187-198. Baumol, W. J., Business Behavior, Value and Growth, New York, Harcourt, Brace & World, 1959.

[22] The following account is based on: Batstone, E., Ferner, A., and Terry, M., Unions on the Board, Oxford, Basil Blackwell 1983, and page numbers in this section refer to their study.

References:

Alchian, Allen A. and Demsetz, H. (1972), " Production, Information Cost, and Economic Organization·", *American Economic Review*, vol. 62, 777-795.

Aoki, Maschiko (1984), *The Co-operative Game Theory of the Firm*,
New York, Oxford: Clarendon Press.

Azariadis, C. (1975), " Implicit Contracts and Underemployment
Equilibria", *The Journal of Political Economy*, vol. 83, 1183-
1202.

Backhaus, Jürgen (1979), *Ökonomik der partizipativen Unternehmung
I*, Tübingen: Mohr/Siebeck.

Batstone, E., Ferner, A., Terry, M. (1983), *Unions on the Board*,
Oxford: Basil Blackwell.

Baumol, William J. (1958),"On the Theory of Oligopoly",*Economica*,
vol. 25, 187-198
---,(1959), *Business Behavior, Value and Growth*, New York, Harcourt: Broce & World
---,(1982), "Contestable Markets : An Uprising in the Theory of
Industry Structure", *American Economic Review*, vol. 72, March,
1982, 1-15.

Bonus, Holger (1981), " Zur Transformation der Marktwirtschaft
durch Sozialkomponenten und Demokratisierung", in: Issing, O.,
ed, Zukunftsprobleme der Sozialen Marktwirtschaft, Berlin:
Duncker + Humblot.

Breton, A. and Wintrobe, R.(1982), *The Logic of Bureaucratic Conduct: An Economic Analysis of Competition, Exchange, and Efficiency in Privat and Puplic Organization*, New York: Cambridge University Press.

Buchanan, James M., and Tullock, G. (1965), *The Calculus of Consent*, Ann Arbor: the University of Michigan Press.

Chandler, Alfred D. (1977), The Visible Hand: The Managerial Revolution in American Business, Cambridge, Mass.:Belkamp Press.

Coase, Ronald H. (1973),"The Nature of the Firm", *Economica*, vol.
16, 387-405.

Freeman, R., and Medoff, J. (1979), "The Two Faces of Unionism",
Puplic Interest, vol. 57, 69-93.

Furubotn, Eirik G. (1978), "The Economic Consequences of Codetermination on the Rate and Sources of Private Investment", in:
Pejovich, S., ed, *The Codetermination Movement in The West*:
Labor Participation in the Management of Business Firms, Lexington, Mass.: D.C. Health & Co., 131-167.
---,(1982), "Information, organisatorische Struktur und die mög-
lichen Vorteile der Mitbestimmung",in Backhaus, J., Nutzinger,
H.G., Hrsg.(1982), *Eigentumsrechte und Participation*: Property
Rigths and Participation, Frankfurt / Main: Haag und Herchen,
203-237.

Gutchess, J.F. (1985), *Employment Security in Action: Strategies
that Work*, New York: Pergamon Press.

Henderson, James M. and Quandt, Richard E. (1971), *Microeconomic Theory: A Mathematical Treatment*, New York: McGraw-Hill, Inc..

Knight, F.H.(1921), *Risk, Uncertainty and Profit*, Published 1971, Chicago.

Kübler, F., Schmidt, W., Simitis, S. (1978), *Mitbestimmung als gesetzgebungspolitische Aufgabe*: Zur Verfassungsmäßikeit des Mitbestimmungsgestzes 1976, Baden-Baden: Nomos.

Lachmann, L.M. (1979),"The Flow of Legislation and the Permanence of the Legal Order", *Ordo 30*, 69-77.

Leibenstein, Harvey (1982), "An Analysis of Intrafirm Productivity", *American Economic Review*, vol. 72, 92-97.

Machlup, Fritz (1967), "Theories of the Firm: Marginalist, Behavioral, Managerial", *American Economic Review*, vol. 57, 1-33.

Manne, Henry, Hrsg.(1969), *Economic Policy and the Regulation of Corporate Securities*, Washington, D.C.

Robertson, Dennis H. (1928), *Control of Industry*, 2.edition, London.

Smith, Adam (1776), *The Welfare of Nations*, 6.reprint, 1978, Harmondsworth, Middlesex: Penguins Books.

WORKERS' PARTICIPATION STIMULATED BY THE ECONOMIC
FAILURE OF TRADITIONAL ORGANIZATION: Comment

by

Frank H. Stephen

Jürgen Backhaus's paper is a brief survey of how the "theory of the firm" has changed in the last fifteen or so years and how the "new theory of the firm" can be applied to analyze a policy proposal. What passed, before 1970, under the name of theory of the firm was really "price theory". The "firm" was simply the interface between two sets of markets (factor markets and product markets). In the intervening period, however, the "new institutional economic" has developed, and many economists have come to recognize that not all resources in a market economy are allocated by the market. Many microeconomists now concern themselves with the hierarchical nature of firms: their internal organization. We have also come to recognize that the market does not always operate through discreet transactions between more or less anonymous agents. Many exchange relations are of a long-term nature, where the identities of the parties concerned is of material significance. One case where the significance of the "identity" of agents has been highlighted is that of transaction-specific investment (Williamson, 1975, 1985). Contracting problems arise where either or both parties have undertaken investments which outside that particular transaction have significantly reduced value. Backhaus's model of codetermination is largely driven by one class of transaction specific investment: firm specific human capital. It will be argued below that while I accept that firm-specific human capital gives employees a "stake" in the firm, even if firm-specific human capital is absent, workers can still have such a stake. That stake should be recognized in the "constitution" of the firm.

Before turning to this point, I would like to discuss briefly a wider question relating to the nature of property rights which is implicit in Backhaus's analysis. This is his discussion of the unanimity rule, which of course, represents an institutional embodiment of the Pareto criterion: that a change is only an unambiguous improvement in social welfare if at least one person is made better off (as judged by him/herself) and no-one is made worse off (again as judged by themselves). Such a rule is viewed by some (including the present writer) as a rather conservative

Codetermination
ed. by H.G. Nutzinger and J. Backhaus
© Springer-Verlag Berlin Heidelberg 1989

criterion since it is biased towards the status quo. It is, on the face of it, an interesting reversal of positions to see the proposal of a unanimity rule (and therefore the Pareto criterion) being opposed as too radical when it takes the form of parity codetermination. However, the opponents of the parity rule are, in fact, objecting not to the parity rule as such but to the change in property rights which is implied by its adoption, that is, the recognition that employees have a stake in the firm. As Warren Samuels (1974) has written in a different context, property rights are merely a recognition of what is to be counted in a particular context as a "cost" of the decision under consideration. The objection to the unanimity rule is really an objection to recognizing the employee's stake in the firm as a legitimate property right. The usual context in which the unanimity rule is discussed is one in which every citizen is recognized as having a legitimate interest or property right in the State. The Pareto criterion is the basis of the concept of efficiency used in neo-classical economics. Efficiency is, as has been pointed out by Victor Goldberg (1974), conjectural. It depends on the particular configuration of costs and benefits of the action under investigation. These costs and benefits are themselves dependent on the distribution of property rights recognized by society: change which "right" are recognized as property rights and you change the effects of a proposal which "count."

The introduction of an unanimity rule via a system of parity codetermination essentially recognizes a new property right held by employees. Their interests must now be considered in making long-term decisions on behalf of the firm. As Backhaus argues, this means that any proposal which secures the support of the supervisory board must therefore be a Pareto improvement. More important, however, is his insight that the parity-rule requires each side in the capital/labor dichotomy to understand the other's point of view and to search for mutually advantageous solutions to problems. The search for such solutions will also encourage the sharing of information in order to achieve common expectations. This is essential in order to overcome mutual suspicion that the "other side" is behaving "opportunistically." Much industrial conflict arises because employees believe employers' statements in collective bargaining negotiations or in terms of adjustments to be made to the company's method of operation as having some strategic motivation behind them. There is a basic lack of trust. Recognizing the employees' stake in the firm through a system of codetermination could have significant implications for "efficiency" due to improvements in what Oliver Williamson (1975) refers to as "atmosphere." In addition, recent evidence (Rubinstein, 1982; Roth and Murrighan, 1982) suggests that when information is symmetric and bargainers' pay-offs are common knowledge, bargaining quickly reaches a solution with which there is little disagreement. Codetermination, because it encourages the disclosure of information and should engender a better understanding of the other side's welfare function, should reduce conflict and enhance the attainment of mutually beneficial solutions.

Codetermination, of course, is not the only means by which an atmosphere of mutual trust and recognition of the stake employees have in the firm can be engendered. The system of lifetime employment in certain sectors of the Japanese economy can be seen in these terms. Formal recognition of the employees' stake in the firm through codetermination is unnecessary because that stake is recognized and the employer's responsibilities to the employees is one element of a social obligation. (One could perhaps see traditional forms of academic tenure in universities in similar terms.)

A consequence of my earlier argument concerning the relationship between efficiency and property rights, however, is that one can no longer appeal to "efficiency" as a justification for a change in property righ since efficiency can only be judged once property rights have been delimited. The allocation of property rights is essentially, therefore, a value judgment. One can, however, be led to making a particular value judgment because of the effect it will have. I would judge that parity codetermination will produce desirable results because it will lead to decisions being made on the basis of their effects on both employees and shareholders. Thus it will internalize effects which would otherwise be external to the decision maker. Employees as well as shareholders have a stake in the firm; codetermination recognizes this.

I would, however, argue that employees have this stake even if they have no firm-specific human capital. It is to this which I now turn. Backhaus has presented us with a discussion of worker participation and parity codetermination in the context of a recent contribution to the theory of the firm. Codetermination fits neatly into Masahiko Aoki's (1984) cooperative game theory paradigm of the firm. Aoki (1984) models the firm as a bargaining process in which the conflicting interests of firm-specific resource holders are brought into equilibrium by management. The firm-specific resource holders concerned are the owners of human capital (workers) and financial capital (shareholders) who are locked into the firm and whose cooperation is necessary to maximize the organizational rent to be distributed between them.

In the Aoki/Backhaus model of the firm a crucial role is assigned to the firm-specific nature of the human capital embodied in workers. It is this which locks labor into the firm and provides an incentive for cooperation: outside this firm an employee's earnings will be lower because his/her firm-specific human capital is worthless to other firms. One of the sources of organizational rent is the willingness of employees to cooperate. Backhaus sees the importance of such cooperation for the generation of organizational rent as a justification for worker participation within a scheme of codetermination.

It would appear that the firm-specific nature of human capital carries the main burden of Backhaus's argument. This is the only contribution labor makes to the organizational rent. Having a stake in the organizational rent is what guarantees labor's cooperation. Codetermination makes that cooperation more informed and more effective and thus improves efficiency. However, if human capital is only firm specific to an insignificant degree, within the terms of this model labor's cooperation is less essential, and the case for participation is somewhat weakened. The extent to which human capital is firm specific is largely an empirical question on which I can shed little light. What I can suggest is that it need not carry as much of the burden of the argument as Backhaus puts on it. There is another reason why labor is locked into the firm which can justify its participation. It is the relational nature of contracts made in internal labor markets.

Relational contracting is discussed by Macneil (1978, 1980) and developed in the context of the employment relation by Goldberg (1980, 1984). The line of reasoning here is developed from that of Goldberg (1984), who argues that as a means for obtaining the cooperation of workers, firms have increasingly in the twentieth century used deferred compensation. Internal promotion ladders, incremental salary scales, non-verted pensions, etc., can be seen as such means of ensuring - cooperation. The workers' current wage, at least in the early years of employment with a given firm, will be less than the value of their marginal product because of the provision of these deferred benefits. Workers who walk away from the firm lose such benefits. Workers dismissed from the firm similarly lose their benefits. Internal labor markets with their associated promotion ladders also promote cooperative behavior. Such deferred compensation, however, exposes workers to opportunism on the part of the employer: dismissal leads to a loss of these deferred benefits and a gain to the employer. In the Backhaus/Aoki terminology this deferred compensation is a component of the organizational rent.

It is, to use Klein, Crawford and Alchian's (1978) term, an "appropriable quasi-rent" an opportunistic employer can capture by finding grounds for dismissing the workers. It should be noted that this rent does not arise from firm-specific human capital. The worker is not necessarily more productive in one firm than another because of on-the-job learning; but at a given point in time his/her earnings will be higher in one firm than in another because these future earnings are in some measure a reward for past cooperation etc. The worker may earn less than his/her VMP in the early years of employment but more than VMP in later years of employment. This deferred compensation may be thought of as a form of bonding. It may not, however, be an explicit element of the worker's contract. Thus it cannot be "cashed in" if the worker leaves or is dismissed. The contract is implicit or, in Macneil's phrase, "relational." Macneil contrasts relational contracting with neoclassical contracting in which third parties adjudicate on disputes between parties to a contract.

By contrast, with the neoclassical system, in which the reference point for affecting adaptations remains the original agreement, the reference point under a truly relational approach is the "entire relation as it has developed ..." through time. This may or may not include an 'original agreement,' and, if it does, may or may not result in much deference being given to it" (Macneil, 1981). In a sense workers have an investment in the firm (they have foregone income in anticipation of a future return), but the return on that investment is contingent on the worker remaining in the firm. But the investment is not one in human capital - no firm-specific skills need be acquired.

Goldberg (1984) has argued that job security, grievance procedures and collective organization can be seen as a response to the employer's potential for opportunism. Deferred compensation cannot have an effect in attaining worker compliance if workers do not see themselves as remaining in the firm long enough to qualify for it. Formal procedures will develop which provide checks on employer opportunism. I would argue that a case for codetermination can be made along similar lines.

The employment contract is relational in nature. Remuneration is not in terms of current productivity. Workers build up stocks of unpaid income. They also enter into an employment relation, frequently on the basis of future prospects for promotion, earnings, etc. Their future prospects, however, are contingent on decisions made by management which will affect the viability and prospects of the firm. Just as shareholders entrust their financial capital to managers so employees entrust their future income prospects to managers. The conventional view disregards their employee interests because employees are implicitly assumed to suffer no loss by having to return to the external labor market. Once, however, we recognize the importance of internal labor markets (and indeed the less than universal occurrence of full employment), we can see that workers are entrusting a great deal to managers. Furthermore, the fact that labor cannot diversify such risks means that a greater share of its wealth is tied to the fortunes of a single firm. Essentially the point being made here is that the employment relation is not adequately captured by the neoclassical theory of labor markets. When the true nature of the employment relation is recognized, it can be seen that labor has a stake in the firm which needs to be protected in a manner akin to that of capital.

These comments do not, I believe, detract from the arguments set out in Jürgen Backhaus's paper. They are supplementary to them. His paper is a good illustration of how the modern theory of the firm can be used to understand issues which as he recognizes were formerly not seen as part of economics.

References:

Aoki, M., *The Cooperative Game Theory of the Firm*, Oxford: Oxford University Press, 1984.

Goldberg, V. P., " Institutional Change and the quasi-Invisible Hand" , *Journal of Law and Economics*, vol. 17, 1974, pp. 461-92.

Goldberg, V.P.,"Relational Exchange : Economics and Complex Contracts" , *American Behavioural Scientists*, vol. 23, 1980, pp. 337- 52.

Goldberg, V. P., " Relational Exchange Perspective on the Employment Relationship ", in F. H. Stephen (ed), *Firms, Organization and Labor*, London: Macmillan, 1984.

Klein, B., Crawford, R. A. and Alchian, A. A., "Vertical Integration, Appropriable Quasi-Rents and the Competitive Contracting Process", *Journal of Law and Economics*, vol. 21, 1978, pp. 297-326.

Macneil,I.R.," Contracts: Adjustment of Long-Term Economic Relations under Classical, Neoclassical and Relational Contract Law", *Northwestern Law Review*, vol. 72, 1978, pp. 854-95.

Roth, A. and Murrighan, J.,"The Role of Information in Bargaining: An Experimental Study", *Econometrica*, vol.50, 1982, pp. 123-42.

Samuels,W.J.,"Commentary:An Economic Perspective on the Compensation Problem", *Wayne Law Review*, vol. 21, 1974, pp. 113-34, reprinted in W.J.Samuels and A. A. Schmid (eds.), *Law and Economics: An Institutional Perspective*, London: Martinus Nijhoff Publishing, 1981.

Williamson,O.E.,*Markets and Hierarchies*,New York:Free Press, 1975.

Williamson,O.E.,*The Economic Institutions of Capitalism*, New York: Free Press, 1985.

EMPIRICAL STUDIES ON CODETERMINATION:
A SELECTIVE SURVEY AND RESEARCH DESIGN

by

Kornelius Kraft

1. Introduction

In recent years economists have evinced a growing interest in
codetermination in Germany. Examining this special institution
reveals the effects of laws that increase the decision rights of
workers. As such laws are discussed in many countries, an evaluation of the German experience can be valuable and relevant to
many other circumstances.

Economists' expectations on the effects of codetermination
are controversial. Alchian (1984, p. 46) concludes that "The campaigns for 'worker participation' or 'industrial democracy' or
codetermination on boards of directors appear to be attempts to
control the wealth of stockholders' specialized assets in the
coalition a wealth confiscation scheme."

Other researchers view codetermination as one reason for the
relatively good industrial relations and therefore as one source
of the success of the German economy after the Second World War.
McCain, for example (1980, p. 89), asserts that "Codetermination
permits improved efficiency by creating a context of joint management decision ...."

With such a diversity of views empirical evidence is needed on
the consequences of the Codetermination Laws. With this motivation as a background, several research projects have been undertaken in recent years. The approaches and results of these investigations are the topics of this article. The empirical projects
can be broadly differentiated into two groups. One group of investigations takes a behavioural approach. These analyze the behaviour of management and workers when codetermination is exe-
cuted by the employees. The other group tries to quantify the effects of codetermination on productivity, wages, and profitability. These econometrically orientated investigations intend to
test how codetermination affects the welfare of an economy.

Codetermination
ed. by H.G. Nutzinger and J. Backhaus
© Springer-Verlag Berlin Heidelberg 1989

2. Behavioural Studies on the Effects of Codetermination
2.1 Institutional Facts

In Germany the top executive level of stock companies is divided into a board of management and a supervisory board. The board of management is responsible for the usual leadership decisions of top management, such as marketing, replacement of machinery, work organization, and minor changes in employment or product and price policy; only very important decisions must be approved by the supervisory board. The supervisory board meets four or five times a year to approve essential decisions and to appoint the top management.

Codetermination rights in Germany are based on three different laws. The first was passed in 1951 and regulates only the coal and iron-ore-mining and the iron and steel industries.[1]

The Works Constitution Act of 1952 granted employees a third of the seats on the supervisory board of corporations with more than 500 employees. Although even a minority representation might affect the outcome of a process of repeated negotiations, the assumption that labour has more power within companies in the coal and iron-ore-mining and the iron and steel industries than in others seems appropriate.

The Codetermination Law of 1976 extended employees' rights in companies with more than 2,000 employees; companies below that size are still covered by the Works Constitution Act of 1952. The 1976 Codetermination Law grants employees 50 percent of the seats on the supervisory board, but the chairman can only be elected by the shareholders' representatives if no majority is achieved. The chairman has two votes in disputes within the supervisory board, a guarantee that the capital representatives will enjoy majority rights. Despite this majority of the capital owners, employee representation on the supervisory board may have influence, even if the supervisory board is not explicitly controlled.

2.2 The Impact of Codetermination on the Independence of Management

It would seem obvious that codetermination would restrict management's independence. Studies by Witte and by Kirsch and Scholl have investigated this question empirically. Witte (1980a, 1980b, 1981, 1982) used a sample of eighty-two stock companies that are independent of other companies and are subject to the Codetermination Law of 1976. The investigation was undertaken before the Codetermination Law was in effect in all the companies (Witte 1980a, 1980b, 1981) and repeated after the law was implemented (Witte 1982).[2] The data was collected in personal interviews with a member of the board of management, a member of the works council, and outside experts from banks and the unions.

Witte (1980a) began with an account of factors that potentially determine the employees' influence. He examined the negotiated rights of employees or their representatives to participate in decisions, the number of employees on the supervisory board, the ratio of members on the works council who are also members of the supervisory board, the existence of works councils in all parts of the firms, the participation rate in elections of the works councils, the bargaining power of the works council, the number of members of the works council exempted from their work duties, the number of members on the work council, the qualifications of the members of the works council, and the influence of the unions based on the percentages of the work force unionized, and the number of external members of the supervisory board. Interestingly only 15 percent of the eighty-two companies studied abide by the legal minimum rights prescribed in the Works Constitution Law.[3] The majority of firms grant their employees decision rights above the level demanded by law.

Witte (1980b) questioned experts from banks and unions as well as members of management and the works council about the influence of the employees in the companies. Their answers were used to construct a scale of employee influence. On average management attributes less influence to the employees than the members of the works council do. The employees themselves assess their influence more highly than others do. Employees have the most influence on decisions concerning internal organization. The strongest factors in determining how much influence employees exert are internal agreements on employee rights, the influence of the unions (percentages of employees unionized, external members of the unions on the supervisory board), and the number of employees on the supervisory board.

Witte (1980b, 1981) could not find a significant correlation between the level of the employees' influence and the profits or cash flow of a firm. Hence, the hypotheses that worker participation decreases or increases profitability are not supported. Witte (1980b, 1981) showed a positive correlation, however, between the level of the employees' influence and the wages and fringe benefits paid. Furthermore, the more influence employees exert, the fewer layoffs occur.

After interviewing experts from banks, members of the unions and the works council, and the management themselves, Witte (1981) measured management's independence on a seven-point scale. He found no significant correlation between the influence of the employees and the discretion of the management.

In a later study Witte (1982) repeated his investigation by again approaching the eighty-two companies that had participated in his first study. The first study had been undertaken before the Codetermination Law took effect: the second analyzed the effects of the Codetermination Law on the employees' level of influence and management's level of independence. In the first investigation information on eighty-two companies was received; in the second, the number of opinions varied from seventeen (from the unions) to sixty-eight (from the banks). The investigations are hence not directly comparable.

The influence of the employees increased from 1976 to 1981 if all answers are taken for an unweighted index. With this index, however, the works council members realize on average a decrease in the influence of the employees, whereas the other respondents indicate an increase. Summarizing controversial answers is not without problems.

The independence of the directors has decreased slightly. Both results could be caused by codetermination, but this seems unlikely. The simple correlation between the directors' discretion and the employees' influence is positive but insignificant for the 1976 and 1981 studies. The employees' high level of influence does not cause the directors' low level of independence. But the capital owners' high level of influence is negatively correlated with the level of the directors' independence. Hence, the overall decrease in the independence of directors from 1976 to 1981 is caused by the growing influence of the capital owners.

Kirsch and Scholl (1983) and Scholl (1984) used another method to reach a similar conclusion. They asked specific questions on personnel and investment policy, the answers to which were used to construct an index of freedom of behaviour within top management. Their index was constructed for companies operating under the Codetermination Law of 1951 (parity), the Codetermination Law of 1976 (quasi-parity), and the Works Constitution Act of 1952 (one third of the seats for employees) and for those with no employee representatives on the supervisory board. The surprising result is that the exercise of discretionary power is increasing as the power of codetermination rights increases. Companies with parity codetermination in the coal mining and the iron and steel industries report the highest level of freedom of behaviour. Freedom of behaviour is positively correlated with the number of conversations between the employer and the works council and negatively correlated with the frequency of strikes and management's attempts to enforce their opinion. According to Witte's and Kirsch and Scholl's studies, codetermination has not led to a reduction in freedom of behaviour for top management. This finding is unexpected, given that Codetermination Laws were intended to redistribute power more evenly between the capital owners and labour. Jürgensen's (1981) view that decisions are retarded and von Weizsäcker's (1984) that decisions are short-run orientated by codetermination are not empirically supported. But one has to admit that Witte's and Kirsch and Scholl's studies are based on the perceptions of the interviewed persons. Their method has its justification, but there may be an explanation for why interviewees incorrectly perceived that management's level of independence was unchanged.

2.3 The Realization of Codetermination on the Firm Level

The Codetermination Law of 1976 leaves open some possibilities of determining the effective level of decision rights for the employee representatives. The individual company has the right to define which decisions need approval by the supervisory board. Gerum, Richter and Steinmann (1981) and Steinmann, Fees and Gerum (1984, 1987) have described the influence employees have, given that interlocking directorships and contracts between companies on dependencies exist, and have investigated how companies determine the "essential" decisions that must be approved by the supervisory board. Gerum et al. (1981) have reviewed the situation that management and the representatives of the employees face in applying the Codetermination Law of 1976. Two hundred and eighty-one stock companies that are subject to the Codetermination Law were investigated. Only 7.8 percent of these are independent of other firms. Thus it becomes obvious that companies might implement the Codetermination Law differently. To investigate this point, Steinmann et al. (1984) compared companies that are controlled by foreign owners with those that are German-owned. The Codetermination Law has attracted attention in other countries. Many business leaders disapprove of the extensive participation rights of workers in Germany. Steinmann et al. (1984) attempted to determine whether this aversion leads to different behaviour in foreign controlled companies. In those companies covered by the Codetermination Law of 1976, they investigated whether management must submit any of its decisions to the supervisory board, and if so, what kinds of decisions must be approved. Steinmann et al. (1984) found that foreign-owned companies give their supervisory boards less extensive decision rights than German-owned firms do. The authors concluded that the companies controlled by foreigners do not follow the doctrine of "good corporate citizenship", that is, adjustment to individual features of the rules a society develops. Those companies do not accept codetermination, a major part of the German Works Constitution.

In a second study Steinmann et al. (1987) investigated whether managerial companies differ from owner-controlled ones in their application of the Codetermination Law. The theory of managerial capitalism has stated that in stock companies with broadly distributed shares the management has more opportunity to follow its own interests than otherwise. The supervisory board has the task of controlling management. If because of a broad distribution of shares direct control is difficult, the supervisory board probably has extended responsibilities that, as a side effect, increase the employees' power in codetermined companies, as they are represented on the board.

3. Econometric Studies on Wages, Productivity, and Profitability
3.1 Codetermination and Wages

Svejnar (1981, 1982a) tries to determine if codetermination in coal-mining and the iron and steel industry has led to a wage increase in those industries. Coal-mining and the iron and steel industry were chosen as a research unit because employees within these industries have stronger participation rights than those in other industries. Codetermination rights in other industries are much more limited. Employees in other industries do not have the same number of votes as the capital side and have no influence in the choice of a labour director. It is reasonable to assume that even a minority representation has an impact on the result of a repeated bargaining process, but Svejnar's assumption that labour has more power within firms in the coal-mining and the iron and steel industry than in others seems appropriate. It is also important to investigate whether workers' rights influence the wages of the employees in the fully codeterminated industries.

Svejnar (1982a) develops a theoretical model that leads to a wage function that incorporates a "bargaining-power" factor. The higher the employees' bargaining-power, the higher the wage will be compared to possible remuneration for other jobs. The average hourly wage of male workers in coal mining and the iron and steel industries is explained out of the average wage in the total manufacturing industry, a dummy variable indicating that the Codetermination Law of 1951 was enforced and in some regressions the lag of the dependent variable. With this carefully developed specification, Svejnar intends to estimate whether alternative wage opportunities and the Codetermination Law can explain wages in the coal mining and iron and steel industry. Svejnar does not try to compare the wages between industries, "since there are numerous industry-specific factors such as sex composition, the extent of employment of foreign workers, the industry unemployment rate and the degree of unionization...." Including the manufacturing wage as an explanatory variable is not much different from comparing codetermined wages with others, or an interindustry investigation. The advantage of using wages in other industries is that human capital and other factors that are not available directly are incorporated through their effect on wages. The disadvantage is that, for differences over time in human capital, sex composition, union coverage and other variables between the industries are not controlled.

The more important point is the value of the dummy variable, indicating the Codetermination Law. Svejnar uses data from 1946 to 1972. The law was passed in 1951, so the dummy has the value zero for the years 1946 to 1951 and one otherwise. Some might aruge that comparing wages immediately after World War II not only with wages during a more prosperous period but with a different currency is not very enlightening, but this is not the most serious criticism.[4] Codetermination was not introduced by the German government, only given the force of law in 1951. The allied forces, especially the British, introduced codetermination into the steel and iron industries in 1947 to counteract the German employers' former support of the Naziregime.[5] When the German parliament regained power, it codified in the law of 1951 the partial codetermination rights that then existed. Hence the dummy variable measures the impact of a legal framework, not the effect of codetermination. Svenjar's estimation that codetermination has led to an increase in the wages of the iron and steel industry by 5.3-5.5 percent (Svejnar 1982a, p. 300) has to be treated as tentative. No effect in the coal-mining industry can be found. In a second approach the ratio of gross revenue to total wage payments is used as a proxy for bargaining power. This variable is introduced twice, once multiplied with the above mentioned codetermination dummy and in its original form. Again, no significant effect can be found.

Svejnar's second study (1981) on wages is more general. He uses a different data set that covers the period 1905 to 1976. His intention was to estimate the effects of unions, the Hitler regime, and codetermination on wages. Svejnar (1981) found that, through codetermination, wages in the iron and steel industry have increased by 6.5 percent. No result could be estimated for the coal-mining industry. Hence, the results of both studies are similar. This second study has essentially the same weakness as the one discussed above: the time period before codetermination was introduced into the iron and steel and coal-mining industries can hardly be compared with the later time period.

Svejnar's study is an example of a well-prepared investigaion. Both the theoretical and the econometric design meet a high standard, but the derived hypotheses cannot be tested by the data used.

3.2 Codetermination and Productivity

In another study, Svejnar (1982b) investigated the impact of codetermination on productivity, perhaps the most important topic in the area of codetermination. The hypotheses referred to in the introductory part of this paper may have shown that expectations on the effects of codetermination on productivity are rather controversial. In a world of perfect competition and full information, any restriction of the market by a participation law must reduce efficiency. But as the world is imperfect, codetermination can provide a channel of communication as well as information on workers' interests and opinions, both of which can improve adjustment to a changing environment.[6] Svejnar differentates worker participation rights according to three laws: the Codetermination

Law of 1951, which applied to the coal mining and iron and steel industry; the Works Constitution Act of 1952; and the extension of the Works Constitution Act in 1972.

After a description of the institutional facts Svejnar (1982b, p. 203) described his econometric model, admitting that the "empirical strategy of this chapter is guided by the availability of data." He used a pooled cross-sectional time series approach, where fourteen industries observed from 1950 to 1976 are the data base. Both Cobb-Douglas and CES-production functions are applied. The dependent variable is the log of value-added divided by the number of hours worked by production workers. The exogenous variables are, of course, the production factors capital and labour in logarithmic form, where capital is divided by worker hours. The coefficient of labour indicates the returns to scale. In the CES-production function the term square of log of capital divided by labour is added as the Kmenta (1967) approximation of the CES-production function. Intercept-dummies for the different industries are used, and a time trend is added to estimate technical progress.

To capture the effect of worker codetermination, Svejnar introduced three dummy variables. The first variable has the value one for industries covered by the 1951 Codetermination Law in the coal mining and iron and steel industries. The second dummy variable estimated effects of the Works Constitution Act of 1952 by having the value one from 1953 on in industries not covered by the 1951 Codetermination Law. Finally, the extension of the Works Constitution Law of 1972 is represented by a dummy variable that has the value one from 1973 on. In the estimates of the coefficients of the codetermination variables, only the dummy variable "1972 Works Constitution Act" was significant. A 3 percent decrease of productivity is estimated. Svejnar admits that "while this productivity decrease is statistically significant, its magnitude is too small to allow a clear interpretation...." This is certainly true, given that this dummy has a value of one in periods of worldwide reduced growth in manufacturing industries; hence, the interpretation of a codetermination effect might not be justified. That capital has a negative but insignificant coefficient in the Cobb-Douglas specification would imply a negative marginal product of capital. The reason for this uncomfortable result might be the difficulty in accounting for the capital stock of an industry. A further surprise are the decreasing returns to scale, with a value of 0.766 for the Cobb-Douglas production function - an unusual result.[7]

In a further step Svejnar (1982b) investigated a subsample out of the fourteen industries, namely, coal mining, iron-ore-mining, potash and rock-salt mining, and other mining. The industries in the subsample share technologies, as well as employ labour forces of similar sex composition and skill qualifications. And only one union represents the interests of all workers in these industries. Svejnar mistakenly assumes that only coal mining is subject to the 1951 Codetermination Law, but iron-ore-mining is also covered. Hence his differentiation is not very useful for testing for an effect of the 1951 Codetermination Law.

Svejnar found a significant negative coefficient of the 1972 law and an "almost significant negative impact" of the 1952 law. Again one might argue that the dummy variable for the 1972 law estimates a change of growth rates in technical progress instead of codetermination.

Apparently the driving force in explaining productivity is the time trend, which is found to be highly significant for all industries. If the dependent variable is Q/L, that is, valued-added per hour, and the independent variables are only the constant α and a linear time trend βt, we have:

$$Q/L = \alpha + \beta t + \epsilon$$

ϵ denotes the residual. If the growth of total factor productivity is declining over time, and a linear time trend with a constant β is used, the residual e is negative for late years.[8] A dummy variable for the years 1973 to 1976 then has a negative bias just for the reason of nonlinear technical progress. Svejnar might have experimented with polynomials in the trend variable as the growth of technical progress does not have to be linear. With that more flexible form of time trend, he could have investigated the stability of the coefficient of the codetermination dummy for the 1972 law.

Svejnar was very careful to discuss the weak points in his study and to apply advanced methods to correct for deficiencies; but the data is of limited use here. It is always problematic to compare different time periods. An increase or decrease in productivity can be caused by many factors omitted in the estimates. Svejnar and others use industry data and a codetermination dummy as if all companies in an industry were covered by the Codetermination Laws. But this is not true. Hence, using industry data can only be regarded as a second best approach, a point discussed in detail later.

3.3 Codetermination and Financial Decisions

The proponents of property rights theory view codetermination as "a wealth confiscation scheme" (Alchian 1984, p. 46). With such an exposed opinion it is natural to look at financial decisions within codetermined firms. Questions of relevance are the development of investment, the amount of dividends paid out or the variance of profits. A theoretical foundation must be established before these topics can be examined. A broad literature exists on the financial structure of a labour managed firm,[9] but relatively little has been written on the codetermined company. Benelli, Loderer, and Lys (1983) undertake to fill this gap by presenting some empirical evidence that is consistent with their theory.

Furubotn (1987) developed a model of joint-investment of capital and labour into firm-specific assets. He pointed out that workers with firm-specific skills have undertaken an investment in sunk costs like the capital owners have done. Furubotn (1987) argues that investment in firm-specific skills leads to a risk-bearing of the employees. Because both the capital owners and the employees bear risk, the two parties should decide on essential topics by codetermination. Similar arguments are made by FitzRoy and Mueller (1984). The extension by Furubotn (1987) and FitzRoy and Mueller (1984) to regard not only financial investment but also human capital investment by the worker is useful. Investment in specific skills is relevant for all firms, and the risk-bearing of employees by holding specific assets is a valid argument to grant decision rights.[10] Benelli et al. (1983), however, disregard investment by employees and look only at the effect of Codetermination Laws on financial investment. In their analysis only investment in capital goods exists, and codetermination has no foundation in risk bearing by workers.

Benelli et al. (1983) investigated the effects of two codetermination laws: the Codetermination Law of the Mining and Steel Producing Industries and the Codetermination Law of 1976. In describing the provisions affecting mining and steel producing, they wrongly assert that the neutral member of the supervisory board "can be elected against the workers' but not the shareholders' will".

Actutally three of the five members of both groups must agree to the neutral member. Thus the power of the employees is even greater than Benelli et al. assumed.

The Works Constitution Law of 1952 granted participation rights to workers on the supervisory boards of corporations that employ more than 500 workers. The Codetermination Law of 1976 extended these rights, giving employees half the seats on the supervisory board in corporations employing more than 2,000 workers. But the chairman can be elected by the shareholders' representatives only if no majority is achieved. If no decision can be reached, the chairman has two votes within the supervisory board. This rule guarantees the capital representatives' majority rights. Despite the capital owners' advantage, Benelli et al. are right that employees on the supervisory board can influence decisions.

Benelli et al. developed a theoretical model on the effects of codetermination on financial decisions. Although a worthwhile effort, their approach is only partially satisfactory. In their model the value of a labour contract is determined by the variables firm value, wage rate, length of the wage contract, number of wage payments, variance of the firm value, and a risk-free rate of return. The arguments are treated as independent variables, but in the following discussion it turns out that they are dependent on each other. The firm value determines the wage and the probability that the contract is terminated because of bankruptcy. The contract should be dependent only on the length of the contract, the wage, and the risk of default, which means an earlier end of the contract than expected. This approach is found in the implicit contract literature.[11] The firm value and the variance of the firm value determine the wage rate and the risk a worker has to bear, but do not themselves influence the value of the contract.

On the basis of their contract model, Benelli et al. discussed the role of debts. They assumed that workers are opposing a debt financing because secured debts have a claim on the company's assets prior to that of wages. Unsecured debts, then, are competing with labour on the firm value, if the company defaults. Benelli et al. concluded that debt financing is reducing the value of the workers' contract and that codetermination will therefore reduce debts. They have implicitly assumed that lended capital is unproductive and hence decreases the value of the company. Their analysis contradicts a tenet of the theory of finance: in perfect competition, the structure of capital sources is irrelevant to the value of firms.[12] Increasing debt financing increases the risk of leverage and must also increase returns per unit of capital (equity as well as debts). In equilibrium the firm value is determined by the balance between risk and return per unit of capital. Furthermore, according to German laws, labour is usually satisfied ahead of capital.

Benelli et al. implicitly assumed that workers do not immediately find alternative employment. But it might be advantageous for workers to increase debts that are paid out as wages, let the company go bankrupt, and look for a new job. Because the workers do not bear the risk of losing capital, they should show an interest in high debts and high risks, just to increase wages in the short run, provided the chance of alternative employment is not zero. Benelli et al.'s analysis of debts leaves some questions open. They develop their hypotheses that codetermined companies pay out low dividends and produce capital-intensive and that capital owners undertake investment with a negative net present value to decrease the variance of the firm value.

The empirical tests that Benelli et al. conducted are based on industry data as were the studies Svejnar made. Compared are the industries subject to the Codetermination Law of 1951 - coal-mining and iron and steel industry [13] - with the other industries. In a time series analysis as a second investigation, the behaviour of industries in the period before 1976 when the extension of the Codetermination Law became valid is compared with the behaviour after 1976. The first point investigated is the ratio of debt to total assets. The ratio is decreasing in the industries covered by the Codetermination Law of 1976 but not in the iron and steel industry. Benelli et al. conclude that this is evidence in favour of their theory. This is surprising, as the iron and steel industry is subject to a stronger Codetermination Law than the other industries and should therefore have a lower debt/asset ratio. But the iron and steel industry has a higher debt to asset ratio than the manufacturing sector as a whole. The second point investigated is the dividends per net income ratio. No systematic difference occurs; nevertheless, Benelli et al. (p. 23) concluded that, "Taken altogether, although we cannot provide a measure of statistical significance, the findings seem to be consistent with our model".

Benelli et al. also compared the prices of stock before and after the introduction of the Codetermination Law, but without using any control variable. No significant results were found, but they concluded that "Taken together these results suggest that codetermination reduces the wealth of the firm owners".

In a last test, the variance of annual stock returns was investigated. The authors hypothesized that codetermination leads to a reduction of the variance because the employees prefer less risky projects, which in turn affects the profits of a firm. Benelli et al. ranked this variance over different industries for Germany and four other European countries. They analyzed whether the ranking of the coal mining and iron and steel-industry (covered in Germany by the Codetermination Law of 1951) differs over the countries. This approach seems promising as it is similar to a cross-sectional test. But why were Austria, Belgium, France and Spain chosen as comparing units? Why not choose, for example, all OECD members? The coal mining and steel and iron industries are heavily subsidized in most countries. A subsidy-free stock return is difficult to find. Austria shows a high variance in the metal industry (which industry by the way is not identical to the German iron and steel industry), but the big firms there are owned by the state. Are Benelli et al. suggesting that state ownership is superior to codetermination? The results of their comparisons are not significant, but are again interpreted as "support to our model" (p. 35). A time-comparison, however, shows a significant decrease in the return variance after the Codetermination Law of 1976. Coal-mining and iron and steel industries show the highest variance among industries surveyed. Does this mean that codetermination by the 1976 law decreases the variance, but that more powerful worker rights like the Codetermination Law of 1951 increase variance? As the theory is not convincing to me, I cannot credit the empirical "evidence." Interpreting insignificant results as support of a theory is also puzzling. Overall this study has raised some interesting questions; perhaps other investigators will find the answers.[14]

3.4 A Research Design[15]

The main shortcoming of the studies by Svejnar and Benelli et al. is their use of industry data. The Codetermination Law of 1951 applies only to companies with more than 1,000 employes; em-

ployee participation on the supervisory board in other industries is restricted under the 1972 law to companies with more
than 500 employees and, under the 1976 law, to companies with
more than 2,000 employees. Looking at industry data, the effects
of codetermination are observed only with a lot of noise. The
studies of Witte, Kirsch and Scholl, and Steinmann, Fees, and
Gerum, are here more useful by investigating only codetermined
corporations and by showing what differences exist between companies that are covered by the same law. But it is certainly interesting to study the quantitative effects of codetermination on
wages, productivity, and profits. How such an approach should be
designed will be described for the example of productivity.

The analysis should be based on data gathered at the company
level, not the industry level. With company data, it is possible
to undertake a cross-section or a pooled cross-section time series analysis. If, for example, a Cobb-Douglas production function is used, and output is denoted with Q, labour with L,
capital with K, a time trend with t and t^2, a codetermination
dummy with D, industry dummies with ΣI_i and the error term with
ϵ, we have:

$$\ln Q = \alpha + \beta_1 \ln L + \beta_2 \ln K + \beta_3 D + \beta_4 \ln LD$$
$$+ \beta_5 \ln KD + \beta_6 t + \beta_7 t^2 + \Sigma \beta_{8i} I_i + \epsilon.$$

An F-, likelihood-ratio or Lagrange multiplier test can give a
result on $\beta_3 + \beta_4 + \beta_5 \neq 0$ or on $\beta_3 <> 0$, $\beta_4 <> 0$, $\beta_5 <> 0$.
Instead of the time trend, the growth rate of the industry or to-
tal manufacturing industry can be used to control for exogenously
given technical progress. This specification can only be applied
if the companies are small compared with the whole industry or
manufacturing sector. It can also be used in a pure cross-section
analysis, where of course no time trend or growth rate of the industry is needed. Other functional forms like the CES- or
translog production function can be tested for their explanatory
power. Nested or non-nested hypotheses tests can be used to discriminate between the different production functions.[16] Output
and capital should be deflated (in a time series). Another alternative is the inclusion of material as an exogenous variable and
the use of sales as a dependent variable. Therewith substitution
effects between material and the production factors can be analyzed. Alternatively to the test with dummy variables on $\beta 3 + \beta 4$
$+ \beta 5 \neq 0$ one can use a Chow-test. The full sample S is divided

into two samples, S1 and S2, where one sample consists of the codetermined companies and the other sample includes all other companies. The Chow-test can now investigate whether or not the coefficients - and therefore the two samples-are the same.

It is frequently argued that a production function should not be estimated with a single equation system, as the production factors are not really exogenous. The argumentation is that the decision on output and factor input is made simultaneously; hence, the value of the production factors should be substituted by instrumental variables. A test on the validity of these hypotheses can be undertaken by the Hausman (1978) approach.

In time series another possibility of the estimation of productivity effects is the total factor productivity approach. With this approach, total factor productivity is calculated as a residual of the difference between change of output over time and the change of the input factors weighted by their cost shares. The change of factor productivity a is calculated from:

$$\dot{a} = \dot{q} - s_k^t \ \dot{k} - s_L^t \ \dot{l}$$

with

$$\dot{q} = \ln Q_t - \ln Q_{t-1}$$

$$s_k^t = (\frac{C_t K_t}{Y_t} + \frac{C_{t-1} K_{t-1}}{Y_{t-1}}) \ /2$$

$$s_L^t = (\frac{W_t L_t}{Y_t} + \frac{W_{t-1} L_{t-1}}{Y_{t-1}}) \ /2$$

$$Y_t = c_t K_t + W_t L_t$$

$$\dot{k} = \ln K_t - \ln K_{t-1}$$

$$\dot{l} = \ln L_t - \ln L_{t-1}.$$

$c_t K_t$ and $w_t L_t$ are the cost shares which can be calculated from the accounting data. This calculation can be based on a translog production function. The residual à can be used as the dependent variable in a regression. By using a codetermination dummy and a growth rate for the industry, one can determine whether a change in à can by explained out of codetermination in a pooled cross-section time series or a cross-section analysis.

The necessary data to perform such a study can be collected from the published accounting data of stock companies. These yearly published reports contain information on the capital structure, the number of employees, output and profit. Many stock companies are too small to be covered by the Codetermination Law of 1976. Hence, both a cross-section and a pooled time-series - cross-section study can be performed.[17] At the International Institute of Management, data from 350 companies over the period 1962-82 is collected. Of the companies eighty-eight are covered by the Codetermination Law of 1976.

4. Conclusion

Codetermination was instituted in Germany over thirty years ago, but, until now, no conclusive study has measured its impact on wages, productivity, or profitability. This is rather unsatisfactory given the controversial hypotheses on the effects of codetermination and the fact that the necessary data is available at least for stock companies. Studies on the perception of codetermination effects and the differences in the companies' acceptance of the Codetermination Law are certainly useful, but the research should not end here. There is a considerable need for an empirical test to determine whether codetermination reduces efficiency and distorts the market remuneration for capital and labour or improves communication and productivity, or whether it is simply too weak a law to have any effect at all. Any hypotheses of theorists on the impact of codetermination has not until now been empirically verified.

Footnotes:

* I would like to thank Jürgen Backhaus and Hans G. Nutzinger for helpful comments.

1 Only the steel and iron producing industry is covered by this law, not the manufacturing industry.

2 One problem of this study is the time period of data collecting. In this period some companies had already implemented the provisions of the Codetermination Law, but others had not. Aggregating the responses of companies with different institutional backgrounds is not without difficultes.

3 Cf. Witte (1980a), p. 12.

4 In 1948 the German currency was changed from the Reichsmark to the Deutsche Mark. Before that time foreign currencies had been the values people trusted in. Equalizing the Reichsmark- with Deutsche Mark-wages can be difficult.

5 Cf. Barthel and Dikau (1980).

6 See Eger and Weise (1987) and Furubotn (1987) in this volume. Arguments why codetermination might enhance efficiency are improvements in information gathering, greater social acceptability of decisions, an increase in employee motivation and the investment in specific human capital by which employees are risk bearers like the entrepreneurs and have therefore to participate in decisions.

7 Svejnar (1982b) estimates the production function under the restriction of constant returns to scale without changes in the results of the codetermination variables.

8 Conrad (1985) shows that the growth of total factor productivity is declining over time during the regarded period.

9 Cf. Furubotn and Pejovich (1970), Pejovich (1971), Furubotn (1980), Schlicht and von Weizsäcker (1977).

10 Cf. Michaelis and Picot (1987) for a discussion on this point.

11 Cf. Azariadis (1975), Baily (1974), Rosen (1985).

12 Cf. Modigliani and Miller (1958).

13 The iron-ore-mining industry is neglected.

14 In the meantime Benelli, Loderer and Lys (1987) here based on the same theory-performed an empirical test with firm level data. None of their hypotheses finds support.

15 The following is a description of a research project to be implemented at the Internal Institute of Management in collaboration with Felix FitzRoy.

16 The J-Tests of Davidson and MacKinnon (1981) and of Fisher and McAleer (1981) are frequently applied to test non-nested hypotheses.

[17] Cf. FitzRoy and Kraft (1986, 1987) on the effects of profit-sharing on productivity and profitability. Their work is based on unpublished data from medium-sized firms in the German metal industry.

References:

Alchian, A. A. (1984), " Specificity, Specialization, and Coalitions", *Zeitschrift für die gesamte Staatswissenschaft*, vol. 140, 34-49.

Azariadis,C. (1975),"Implicit Contracts and Underemployment Equilibria",*Journal of Political Economy*, vol. 83,1183-1202.

Baily, M.N. (1974),"Wages and Employment under Uncertain Demand", *Review of Economic Studies*, vol. 41,37-50.

Barthel, E.,and Dikau, J.(1980), *Mitbestimmung in der Wirtschaft*, Berlin: Colloquium Verlag.

Benelli,G.,Loderer, C.,and Lys, T. (1983),"Labor Participation in Private Business Policy-making Decisions:The German Experience with Codetermination", *Paper presented at the Interlaken Conference on Analysis and Ideology.*
---,(1987), "Labor Participation in Corporate Policy-making Decision: West Germany's Experience with Codetermination", *Journal of Business*, vol. 60, 553-557.

Conrad,K. (1985),"Theory and Measurement of Productivity and Cost Gaps in Manufacturing Industries in U.S., Japan and Germany", *Paper presented at the fourth International Karlsruhe Seminar on Measurement in Economics*, July 1985, and at the International Institute of Management, October 1985.

Davidson, R., and MacKinnon, J. (1981), "Several Tests for Model Specification in the Presence of Alternative Hypotheses",*Econometrica*, vol. 49,781-793.

Eger,Th., and Weise, P. (1987),"Worker Participation in a Perfect and an Imperfect World", this volume.

Fisher, G.R., and McAleer, M.(1981),"Alternative Procedures and Associated Test of Significance for non-nested Hypotheses", *Journal of Econometrics*, vol. 16,103-119.

FitzRoy, F.R., and Kraft, K. (1985),"Unionization, Wages and Efficiency: Theories and Evidence from the U.S. and West Germany", *Kyklos*, vol. 38,537-554.

FitzRoy, F.R., and Kraft, K. (1986), "Profitability and Profit-Sharing", *Journal of Industrial Economics*, vol. 35,13-30.

FitzRoy, F.R.,and Kraft, K. (1987),"Cooperation, Productivity and Profit-Sharing",*Quarterly Journal of Economics*,vol.102,23-35.

FitzRoy, F.R., and Mueller, D.C. (1984),"Cooperation and Conflict in Contractual Organization",*Quarterly Review of Economics and Business*, vol. 24,24-49.

Furubotn,E.G.(1980),"Tradable Claims and Self-Financed Investment in the Capitalist Labor-Managed Firm", *Zeitschrift für die gesamte Staatswissenschaft*, vol. 136,630-641.

Furubotn, E.G. (1987), "A General Model of Codetermination", this volume.

Furubotn, E.G., and Pejovich, S. (1970), "Property Rights and the Behaviour of the Firm in a Socialist State: The example of Yugoslavia", *Zeitschrift für Nationalökonomie*, vol. 30,431-454.

Gerum,E.,Richter, B., and Steinmann, H. (1981),"Unternehmenspolitik im mitbestimmten Konzern", *Die Betriebswirtschaft*, vol. 41, 345-360.

Hausman, J.A. (1978), "Specification Tests in Econometrics", *Econometrica*, vol. 46,1251- 1272.

Jürgensen,H. (1981),"Entwicklung der Mitbestimmung in der Bundesrepublik Deutschland", *Zeitschrift für Unternehmensgeschichte*, Beiheft vol. 9,74-91.

Kirsch,W.,and Scholl,W. (1983),"Was bringt die Mitbestimmung:Eine Gefährdung der Handlungsfähigkeit und/oder Nutzen für die Arbeitnehmer?", *Die Betriebswirtschaft*, vol. 43, 541-562.

Kmenta,J.(1967),"On Estimation of CES Production Function", *International Economic Review*, vol. 8, 180-189.

McCain,R. A.(1980),"A Theory of Codetermination", *Zeitschrift für Nationalökonomie*, vol. 40, 65-90.

Michaelis, E.,and Picot, A. (1987), "Zur ökonomischen Analyse von Mitarbeiterbeteiligungsrechten",in: *Mitarbeiterbeteiligung und Mitbestimmung im Unternehmen*, eds. F. FitzRoy and K. Kraft, Berlin: De Gruyter, 83-127.

Modigliani, F., and Miller, M. (1958),"The Cost of Capital, Corporation Finance, and the Theory of Investment", *American Economic Review*, vol. 48, 261-297.

Pejovich,S.(1971),"Towards a General Theory of Property Rights", *Zeitschrift für Nationalökonomie*, vol. 31, 141-155.

Rosen,S. (1985),"Implicit Contracts", *Journal of Economic Literature*, vol. 23,1144-1175.

Schlicht,E., and von Weizsäcker, C.C. (1977),"Risk Financing in Labour Managed Economies: The Commitment Problem", *Zeitschrift für die gesamte Staatswissenschaft*, Special Issue Profit-Sharing, 53-66.

Scholl,W. (1984), "Handlungsfähigkeit und Mitbestimmung",in: *Mitbestimmung: Theorie, Geschichte, Praxis*, eds. H. Diefenbacher and H.G. Nutzinger, Heidelberg: Forschungsstätte der Evangelischen Studiengemeinschaft, 229-246.

Steinmann,H.,Fees, W.,and Gerum, E. (1984),"Multinationale Unternehmen und Mitbestimmung", *Zeitschrift für Betriebswirtschaft* vol. 54,368-387.

Steinmann,H.,Fees, W.,and Gerum, E. (1987),"Trennung von Eigentum und Verfügungsgewalt und Mitbestimmung", in: *Mitarbeiterbeteiligung und Mitbestimmung im Unternehmen*, eds. F. FitzRoy and K. Kraft, Berlin: De Gruyter, 159-172.

Svejnar,J. (1981),"Relative Wage Effects of Unions, Dictatorship and Codetermination:Econometric Evidence from Germany", *Review of Economics and Statistics*, vol. 63, 188-197.

Svejnar, J.(1982a),"Employee Participation in Management, Bargaining Power and Wages", *European Economic Review*, vol. 18, 291-303.

Svejnar,J.(1982b),"Codetermination and Productivity: Empirical Evidence from the Federal Republic of Germany", in: Participatory and Self-Managed Firms, eds. D.C. Jones and J. Svejnar, Lexington, Mass.: Lexington Books, 199-212.

Weizsäcker, C.C. von (1984), "Was leistet die Property Rights Theorie für aktuelle wirtschaftspolitische Fragen ?", in: Ansprüche, Eigentums- und Verfügungsrechte, ed. M.Neumann, Berlin: Duncker und Humblot, 123-154.

Witte,E.(1980a),"Das Einflußpotential der Arbeitnehmer als Grundlage der Mitbestimmung",*Die Betriebswirtschaft*, vol. 40, 3-26.

Witte, E. (1980b), "Der Einfluß der Arbeitnehmer auf die Unternehmenspolitik", *Die Betriebswirtschaft*, vol. 40, 541- 559.

Witte,E.(1981), "Die Unabhängigkeit des Vorstandes im Einflußsystem der Unternehmung", *Zeitschrift für betriebswirtschaftliche Forschung*, vol. 33, 273-296.

Witte, E.(1982),"Das Einflußsystem der Unternehmung in den Jahren 1976 und 1981", *Zeitschrift für betriebswirtrschaftliche Forschung*, vol. 34, 416-434.

ABOUT THE AUTHORS

Backhaus, Jürgen, born 1950, Dr. rer. pol. et Lic. jur., Professor of Public Economics at the University of Limburg at Maastricht (Netherlands). Main fields: public finance, the economics of firms with labor participation, law and economics.

Bartölke, Klaus, born 1949, Dr. rer. pol., Professor of Business Administration at the University of Wuppertal (W. Germany). Main fields: Management, personnel, organization, industrial democray.

Eger, Thomas, born 1949, Dr. rer. pol., Assistant Professor, Department of Economics, University Kassel (W. Germany). Main fields: comparative economic systems, economic analysis of law.

FitzRoy, Felix, born 1938, Dr. rer. pol. Senior Research Fellow at the International Institut of Management, Science Center, Berlin (W. Germany). Main fields: industrial organization, economics of participation.

Furubotn, Eirik G., Ph. D. in economics, James L. West Professor, University of Texas at Arlington. Main fields: general eonomic theory, comparative economic systems, theory of the firm, property rights analysis.

Jones, Derek C., born 1946, Ph.D. in economics, Professor of Economics at Hamilton College, Clinton, N.Y. Main field of research: empirical analysis of participatory and labor managed firms.

Kappler, Ekkehard, born 1940, Dr. oec. publ., Professor of Business Administration, University of Witten-Herdecke (W. Germany). Main fields: management, organization, codetermination, economic methodology.

Kraft, Kornelius, born 1955, Dr. rer. pol., Assistant Professor, Department of Economics, University of Kassel (W. Germany). Main fields: labor economics, health economics, industrial economics.

McCain, Roger A., born 1942, Ph. D. in economics, Professor of Economics at Fordham University, New York City. Main fields: worker participation in management, rationality in macroeconomics, economics of the arts.

Monissen, Hans Georg, born 1937, Dr. rer. pol., Professor of Economics, University of Würzburg (W. Germany). Main fields: economic policy, macroeconomics.

Nutzinger, Hans G., born 1945, Dr. rer. pol., Professor of Economics, University of Kassel (W. Germany). Main fields: theory of the firm, codetermination, and environmental economics.

Rothschild, Kurt W., born 1914, Dr. jur., Emeritus Professor of Economics, University of Linz (Austria). Main fields: general economic theory, labor economics, economic forecasting, economic development, and international trade.

Samuels, Warren J., born 1933, Ph. D. in economics, Professor of Economics, Michigan State University, East Lansing, Michigan. Main fields: law and economics of property, genesis of modern economics.

Schlicht, Ekkehart, born 1945, Dr. rer. pol., Professor of Economic Theory, Darmstadt Institute of Technology (W. Germany). Main fields: labor economics, psychology and economics.

Stephen, Frank H., born 1946, Ph. D. in economics, Reader in Economics, University of Strathclyde (Scotland). Main fields: economics of participation, law and economics.

Thimm, Alfred L., born 1923, Ph. D. in economics, Professor of Economics, University of Vermont. Main fields: codetermination, dynamic planing models.

Weise, Peter, born 1941, Dr. rer. pol., Professor of Economics, University of Kassel (W. Germany). Main field: microeconomics.

Wenger, Ekkehard, born 1952, Dr. rer. pol., Professor of Business Economics, University of Würzburg (W. Germany). Main fields: organization, finance, and labor markets.

NAME INDEX

SUBJECT INDEX